Understanding Diversity

SECOND EDITION

Understanding

Diversity

An Introduction to Class, Race, Gender, Sexual Orientation, and Disability

Fred L. Pincus

LYNNE
RIENNER
PUBLISHERS

BOULDER
LONDON

Published in the United States of America in 2011 by
Lynne Rienner Publishers, Inc.
1800 30th Street, Boulder, Colorado 80301
www.rienner.com

and in the United Kingdom by
Lynne Rienner Publishers, Inc.
Gray's Inn House, 127 Clerkenwell Road, London EC1 5DB

Library of Congress Cataloging-in-Publication Data
Pincus, Fred L.
  Understanding diversity : an introduction to class, race, gender, sexual
orientation, and disability / Fred L. Pincus. — 2nd ed.
      p. cm.
  Includes bibliographical references and index.
  ISBN 978-1-58826-621-7 (pbk. : alk. paper)
  1. Cultural pluralism. 2. Cultural pluralism—United States.
3. Minorities—United States. 4. Prejudices—United States.
5. Discrimination—United States. 6. United States—Social conditions—
21st century. I. Title.
  HM1271.P56 2011
  305.0973—dc22

                                                                2011011386

British Cataloguing in Publication Data
A Cataloguing in Publication record for this book
is available from the British Library.

Printed and bound in the United States of America

       The paper used in this publication meets the requirements
  ∞   of the American National Standard for Permanence of
       Paper for Printed Library Materials Z39.48-1992.

10 9 8 7 6

Contents

Preface

Since the publication of the first edition of *Understanding Diversity*, a number of important events have occurred. Two stand out: the Great Recession that began in late 2007 and the election of the first black president of the United States in 2008. Both of these momentous events have had an impact on the contents of this book.

When I submitted the manuscript for the first edition in 2005, I never would have imagined that a black man would be elected president. This was true of most scholars and journalists who write about race relations. Barack Obama's victory showed the amazing progress that has been made since the 1960s, when most African American citizens in the southern United States finally won the right to vote. However, it does not mean that we are in a postracial society where race no longer matters. Racial oppression is still alive and well.

I was not, on the other hand, surprised by the deep recession that began in late 2007; after all, business cycles have always been a part of capitalism. Most of the proposed solutions to the recession have fallen heavily on the backs of working people. Class oppression remains a major issue in the United States.

Several other events are equally noteworthy. A woman, Hillary Rodham Clinton, came close to winning the US Democratic Party's nomination for president in 2008. That she was such a strong contender was also a first, although it does not mean that we now are living in a postgender society.

In the realm of sexual orientation, same-sex marriage is now legal in five states—Connecticut, Iowa, Massachusetts, New Hampshire, and Vermont—as well as in the District of Columbia. (Elsewhere, same-sex marriage is now legal in Argentina, Belgium, Canada, Iceland, the Netherlands, Norway, Portugal, South Africa, Spain, and Sweden.) In a similar vein, the repeal of the Don't Ask, Don't Tell law in December 2010 means that gay men and women soon will be able to serve openly in the military for the first time in US history.

An increasingly important topic in the area of diversity studies is disability. Thus, this edition includes an entirely new chapter that shows the prevalence in our society of people with disabilities; changes in our understanding of what it means to be disabled, both for the individuals directly affected and for society overall; and the progress that has been made in this arena since the passage of the Americans with Disabilities Act in 1990.

All of these events indicate both progress and continuing problems. How far have we come, and how much farther do we have to go? These are among the important questions that are addressed in this book.

This new edition reflects feedback from students that I received during the five years that I used the first edition in my classes; I am grateful for their input. I would also like to thank Charlie Cooper, Roz Benjamin Darling, Betty Robinson, and Christian Villenas for commenting on various chapters.

I dedicate this book to my wife, Natalie J. Sokoloff, who recently retired from a long career as an academic sociologist. She has taught me about intersectionality, and about life.

—*Fred L. Pincus*

1

Introduction

The first black president was elected in the United States in 2008, but in the same year, 4,700 hate crimes based on race and ethnicity were reported to the police. In 2010, three women justices sat on the US Supreme Court for the first time, but in the same year, women made only 76 cents for each dollar a man made. There were more than 400 billionaires in 2009, but unemployment was the highest that it has been in thirty years. Young and educated Americans continue to show more acceptance of gays and lesbians, but there is still great opposition to same-sex marriage. There are more federal laws than ever before to protect individuals with disabilities from discrimination in employment, but almost 20,000 employment discrimination claims were filed with the US Equal Employment Opportunity Commission (EEOC) in 2008 by people with disabilities.

These are some of the many contradictions when considering diversity in the United States in the twenty-first century. There is growing diversity along with continuing inequality. Is the glass half full, or half empty? Addressing these issues is the goal of this book.

In spite of all the talk about diversity, most of us grow up in a world that seems fairly homogeneous. Our neighbors and schoolmates are generally from the same race and social class as we are. Between 5 and 10 percent of the people in our neighborhoods are probably gay or lesbian, although many of us don't know who they are. Fifteen to 20 percent have a disability.

Upon entering college, students often feel assaulted by diversity, especially those who live in campus residence halls. Suddenly, roommates or those on the same floor can be of different races, religions, ethnicities, and economic backgrounds. Some are from different regions of the United States and even from different countries. The sounds and smells and visual images are often unfamiliar. Men and women may live on the same floor. A gay person may live a few doors down, or in the same suite. Sexual relations with the opposite sex (or with the same sex) are not supervised, and alcohol and drugs are everywhere.

Walking around the campus, it is not unusual to see tables and signs promoting the women's union, the black student union, the gay liberation organization, and international student organizations. You can take courses such as "Black History," "Women's Literature," and "Gay Cinema."

On the one hand, this campus diversity can be very exciting because there can be new and stimulating experiences every day. On the other hand, it can be very disconcerting. Are people who speak Spanish talking about you? Is that gay person down the hall checking you out? Do you feel embarrassed that someone of the opposite sex sees you in your nightclothes or without makeup? Why are those guys down the hall so loud, or so quiet? That music is awful; how can they like it? Are those people going to rob you? Maybe you're uncomfortable seeing that girl in the wheelchair every morning. It's not always easy to be around people who are different from you.

For better or worse, *diversity* has become one of the buzzwords of the early twenty-first century. Two-thirds of colleges and universities have some kind of diversity requirement in their curricula, and many have ethnic and women's studies programs. Two of the national college rating publications contain a diversity criteria or indicator. *U.S. News and World Report* has a mathematical index showing the likelihood of having interactions with someone of a different race on campus. *Princeton Review* asks a nonrandom sample of students about their perceptions of interactions across race or class and the degree of discrimination against homosexuals.

Increasing numbers of large corporations have diversity departments that include recruiters, trainers, and troubleshooters. The website *DiversityInc* rates corporations on various aspects of diversity. Politicians, including many conservatives, and the media often extol the history of immigration that has made the United States a pluralistic society characterized as a melting pot, a salad bowl, or a patchwork quilt.

There is another side to the diversity picture, however. Colleges and universities are accused of being too "politically correct" in their "pandering" to minority groups. Corporations are accused of hiring "unqualified" minorities and women in order to satisfy federal affirmative action guidelines. "Reverse discrimination" against white males is said to have replaced traditional discrimination in the eyes of many white Americans.

Many mainstream politicians and media commentators are concerned about how contemporary immigration is allegedly threatening the integrity of American culture and the English language.

Gay marriages and civil unions have become controversial issues in elections since 2004. Labor unions have been redefined as "special-interest" groups, and politicians who talk about growing economic inequality are often accused of fomenting class conflict, whereas corporations are thought to represent the interests of the entire country. Women have also been defined as a special-interest group, and pro-choice advocates have been redefined as "baby killers," in contrast to anti-abortionists and those who still believe that a woman's place is in the home, who are said to be "protectors of family values."

Even the term *liberal* has become controversial. In the 2008 presidential election, the only people using the L-word were conservative Republicans when they criticized Barack Obama as a "tax and spend liberal" who "panders to special interests." Democrats, in comparison, did everything they could to minimize the use of political labels. There is no doubt that the debate over diversity will continue during the foreseeable future.

Defining Diversity

What is diversity? According to Merriam-Webster Online (2004), **diversity** means *variety, multiformity, difference, or dissimilarity*. The opposite of diversity is uniformity. This can apply to people, cultures, plants, animals, and a number of other topics. From a social science perspective, this definition is not very helpful because it is much too broad.

There are at least four ways that social scientists use the concept of diversity. **Counting diversity** refers to *empirically enumerating differences within a given population*. In a given country (or state, city, school, workplace), we can count how many members of different races, ethnicities, religions, genders, and so on, there are. A particular country can be described as relatively *homogeneous* if most people are of the same race (religion, ethnicity, etc.) or relatively *heterogeneous* if there are many different races. Although this may seem uncontroversial, we will see how difficult it is to actually determine who is in what race.

Although counting diversity is important, it only tells part of the story. For example, the 2010 cabinet of President Obama and the 2007 cabinet of former President George W. Bush were demographically similar. In each case, two-thirds of the fifteen members were white and one-third were people of color. This is close to the national racial distribution. Obama's cabinet was 33 percent female, compared with Bush's 27 percent female, a minor difference. Women were heavily underrepresented in both cases. In spite of these race and gender similarities, however, the *policies* enacted by the two cabinets were often different because of the conservative philosophy of the Bush administration and the centrist liberal philosophy of the Obama administration. The race and gender of cabinet members don't necessarily influence how they will act.

Culture diversity refers to *the importance of understanding and appreciating the cultural differences between groups.* The focus here is on how rich and poor, whites and people of color, men and women, disabled and nondisabled, and homosexuals and heterosexuals have different experiences, worldviews, modes of communication, and behaviors as well as different values and belief systems. Those who use this definition tend to seek lower levels of prejudice, higher levels of tolerance, and more inclusion so that diversity can be celebrated. Usually, the assumption is that appropriate attitudinal changes can take place without large-scale structural changes in the economic and political systems.

Whites, for example, sometimes wonder why blacks can use the "N-word" while whites can't. *Nigger,* of course, is a derogatory term that whites have used for centuries as part of the systematic oppression of blacks. It is still viewed as objectionable by most blacks and whites. *Some* blacks, however, have begun to use *nigga* as a term of endearment and a sign of ingroup solidarity. So, a black saying "Hi, Nigga" to another black has a totally different meaning than if the same sentence came from a white. Not understanding these cultural differences can lead to difficult interracial interactions.

Good-for-business diversity refers to the argument that *businesses will be more profitable, and government agencies and not-for-profit corporations will be more efficient, with diverse labor forces.* Supporters of this definition would argue, for example, that a female car salesperson would be more effective than a man in selling cars to women customers. Along the same lines, a Hispanic police officer would do a better job than a white in policing the Hispanic community. Not having diverse employees, according to this view, is simply bad for business.

A good example of this good-for-business diversity is the occasional diversity supplement to the *New York Times Magazine*. The October 4, 2009, "special advertising supplement" (technically called an *advertorial)* features short articles about the Executive Leadership Council, a corporate-sponsored organization that trains people of color as executives. Eight different corporations are featured, including Target, the Kellogg Company, ING, and, of course, the *New York Times*. The ING ad states: "We fundamentally believe that diversity and inclusion is an important business strategy that enhances our performance, engages our employees and leads to better results" (A9).

Finally, **conflict diversity** refers to *understanding how different groups exist in a hierarchy of inequality in terms of power, privilege, and wealth*. Scholars who use this definition emphasize the way in which dominant groups oppress subordinate groups who seek liberation, freedom, institutional change, and/or revolution. According to this perspective, calls to celebrate diversity within a fundamentally unjust system are insufficient.

Sexual orientation, for example, would be viewed as a system of oppression of homosexuals by heterosexuals that is manifested through laws, organizational practices, the media, and individual behavior. Gay-bashing hate crimes would be seen as just one manifestation of a hierarchical structure that privileges heterosexuals. Laws prohibiting same-sex marriage would also be seen as an example of oppression.

Although these definitions are not always mutually exclusive, this book utilizes the conflict diversity definition described above. I will analyze the conflicts based on class, race, gender, sexual orientation, and disability in the United States.

The Study of Diversity

Studying group conflict within the population is nothing new. Sociologists and historians have been studying immigration and race relations for more than a century. W. E. B. DuBois and Robert Park conducted empirical studies in the early twentieth century, and other scholars debated whether the appropriate metaphor for American race and ethnic relations was the "melting pot" or the "salad bowl" or "anglo-conformity." Karl Marx and Max Weber wrote about class inequality in the nineteenth century. Both race relations and social **stratification** have for decades been recognized as legitimate sociological specializations. Although a few scholars had been studying male-female conflicts in the early twentieth century, the social scientific study of gender inequality exploded in the 1960s, soon to be followed by a dramatic growth in the study of homosexuality and disability.

Black/African American studies programs began to develop in the late 1960s, with Hispanic, Asian, and Native American studies emerging in the next few decades. Women's studies programs were first institutionalized in the 1970s, followed by gay and lesbian studies. The fields of working-class and disability studies are still in their infancy.

Most of these earlier approaches, however, tended to focus on only one group or category at a time. Race relations, for example, tended to focus on racial differences without considering class and gender. Stratification studies tended to ignore gender and race. Almost all academic programs ignored sexual orientation and disability.

Eventually, increasing numbers of scholars, especially women, grew to understand that it was necessary to go beyond single categories. Predominantly white socialist feminists began to use both class and gender in their analyses, and black feminists began to incorporate race, gender, and class. Multiculturalists, especially in the field of education, crossed the boundaries of race, religion, ethnicity, and nationality.

It wasn't until the late 1980s that social scientists began to systematically discuss race, class, gender, and sexual orientation *together.* The first edition of Paula Rothenberg's *Race, Class, and Gender in the United States* was published in 1988 under the title *Racism and Sexism: An Integrated Study.* Margaret L. Anderson and Patricia Hill Collins published the first edition of *Race, Class, and Gender* in 1992. The scholarly journal *Race, Gender, and Class* began publication in 1993 under the editorship of Jean Belkhir. Bonnie Thornton Dill and Maxine Baca Zinn's *Women of Color in US Society* was published in 1994. Even in specialty areas like criminal justice, Barbara Price and Natalie Sokoloff used a race-class-gender approach in the second edition of their anthology *The Criminal Justice System and Women* (1996).

Theoretically, there are a variety of ways to understand conflict diversity. Some scholars take a single-issue approach and tend to see one aspect of diversity as more fundamental than all others. Marxists tend to emphasize class, feminists tend to emphasize gender, critical race theorists tend to emphasize race, and so forth. It's not that these scholars ignore other aspects of diversity, but they view things through the lens of what they see as most fundamental.

Other scholars refuse to engage in debates about whether or not Hispanics are more oppressed than women or whether poor people are more oppressed than the disabled.

Intersectionality theorists, for example, assert the existence of parallel systems of oppression (race, disability, sexual orientation, etc.) that sometimes reinforce each other and sometimes are in contradiction with each other. Although intersectionality proponents agree that no aspect of diversity is most fundamental, they also argue that in different situations, different aspects of diversity are more important than others. In discussing rape, for example, gender may be the most important factor although poor women of color are the most vulnerable. In discussing the economic inequality that is endemic to capitalism, class may be the most important, although black and Hispanic men and women are overrepresented among the poor.

I had been teaching race and ethnic relations for twenty-seven years when I first became interested in the broader topic of diversity in 1996. I was never satisfied with the way I handled class and gender in my own teaching, and I totally ignored sexual orientation and disability. I also began to realize that most undergraduates left the university without any exposure to women's studies, black studies, or any other aspect of diversity. In 1999 I took over teaching a graduate course called "Constructing Race, Class, and Gender" when the person who designed the course left the university. I include sexual orientation even though it isn't in the title.

For several years I worked with an interdisciplinary committee to design an introductory undergraduate course that came to be called "Diversity and Pluralism: An Interdisciplinary Perspective." The course was originally team-taught by a pair of faculty who are "demographically different" from one another and are also from different departments. This book grew out of the "Diversity and Pluralism" course. Theoretically, this book is eclectic although it draws mainly from both Marxism and intersectional theory.

Levels of Analysis

Understanding conflict diversity is incredibly complex. After teaching about these issues for more than forty years, I have come to realize that there are no simple causes of, or solutions to, group conflict. In 1992 a jury acquitted the white police officers that were videotaped beating Rodney King, a black man. A four-day riot exploded in Los Angeles, resulting in 52 deaths, 8,000 injuries, 12,000 arrests, and $800 million in property damage. During the melee, a distraught Rodney King asked, "Why can't we just get along?" A simple question without a simple answer.

Like most social phenomena, it is necessary to look at group conflict from different levels of analysis. In the United States, we are used to *individualizing* group conflict and other social problems. It is also necessary to look at group conflict from the *structural* level by looking at the society in which the conflict took place.

We can illustrate these two levels of analysis using Hurricane Katrina, which devastated New Orleans in August 2005. The massive storm resulted in more than 1,800 deaths, 275,000 homes destroyed, and more than $100 billion in property damage.

At the individual level, why did some people remain in the city while others evacuated? Why did some engage in illegal behavior like taking food and appliances from stores? Are there personality differences, or attitudinal differences, or differences in the family structures of their homes? Why did some whites prevent blacks from crossing a bridge to safety? What lessons did people draw from Katrina and its aftermath? For example, in a 2005 survey by the Pew Research Center for People and the Press, only 32 percent of whites agreed that "this disaster shows that racial inequality remains a major problem in this country." Almost twice as many people of color (62 percent) agreed with the same statement. These are useful questions, but the individual-level analysis only tells part of the story.

It is also necessary to analyze Katrina from the structural level by looking at the larger society. Although the hurricane was a "natural" event (some would say "act of God"), it's also important to understand that the destruction of the wetlands that used to surround New Orleans made the city more vulnerable to floods. New Orleans has a long history of racism, so the actions of the whites on the bridge were not just individual quirks. The city's public transportation system wasn't adequate to provide escape routes for those without cars.

Why were Hispanic immigrants brought in for some of the cleanup and redevelopment projects rather than contacting blacks who had left the city? Is there really an attempt to change the racial distribution of the city by making it difficult for poor blacks to return to their neighborhoods? These questions address the nature of the entire society, not just the individuals who are involved in a particular event.

In order to understand both the individual and structural levels of analysis, we must look at group conflict in an interdisciplinary way. We can't be limited by any one discipline. For example, how can we explain the fact that among year-round full-time workers, women earn only 76 cents for each dollar that a man earns? At the psychological level, we may try to understand why an individual woman decides to enter a predominantly female profession such as teaching, which pays less than a predominantly male profession such as engineering. At the historical level, we can learn how and why teaching and clerical work changed from being predominantly male occupations to predominantly female ones. At the economic level, we can learn why clerical workers earn less than truck drivers even though they have comparable levels of skill. At the sociological level, we can learn how family structures and gender role socialization have a strong influence on the world of work. Using the tools of only one academic discipline will always be incomplete.

The need for an interdisciplinary and multilevel analysis puts a great burden on those of us who teach and write about diversity from a group conflict perspective. Most of us have been trained to look at social phenomena from only one discipline, so we must educate ourselves about intellectual approaches that we didn't learn in graduate school. It is often difficult to find faculty to teach diversity courses because of the intellectual challenges that these courses pose.

It also puts a great burden on students who are trying to understand the world in which they live. Many students enroll with the hope that they will find an answer to Rodney King's question, "Why can't we just get along?" What they find is that the answer is much more complicated than they ever imagined.

The Rest of the Book

This book is intended to be a companion to one of the many anthologies that address race, class, gender, sexual orientation, and disability.

The strength of anthologies is their breadth in providing descriptions and analyses of many different groups. They have articles on prejudice toward several different racial groups, not just blacks. There may be one article about discrimination against working-class white women and another about discrimination against middle-class Asian women. An article about the health problems of gay men could be contrasted with another about the process of going through a sex-change operation.

However, these same anthologies often do not provide a careful discussion of basic concepts or systematic comparisons between groups or up-to-date statistical data. This is what I will try to do in this short book.

Chapter 2 will introduce some of the basic analytical concepts that are used in the study of diversity. Students who are also using one of the anthologies will benefit from having these concepts clearly defined in a single chapter. However, because social scientists don't always agree on these important concepts, the definitions in this book may not always be the same as the definitions in your anthology. A listing of all the key terms used in the book can be found at the book's end.

Chapters 3, 4, 5, 6, and 7 will cover the issues of class, race, gender, sexual orientation, and disability, respectively. Each of these chapters will have a similar structure:

1. show how the concepts discussed in Chapter 2 apply and introduce new concepts;
2. present descriptive statistics about differences in wealth, income, unemployment, education, occupation, and so on;
3. discuss the research on prejudice and ideology;
4. discuss the research on discrimination and structure

Chapter 8 will address the issue of change and will emphasize the importance of collective social action. A list of activist organizations that students can join is provided.

Some of the material we will be dealing with may be unsettling. Students will no doubt agree with some things and strongly disagree with others. I encourage you to plunge in and keep an open mind. I invite you to question and challenge the issues discussed in this book. If you don't understand something, ask your instructor. If you disagree with something, ask your classmates what they think.

I also encourage you to disagree with your instructor and your classmates—in a respectful manner, of course. I hope your instructor has provided a safe and comfortable atmosphere in which to discuss some of these issues. Many of the students in my classes say that this was the first time they were able to discuss diversity issues with people different from themselves. I invited a lesbian speaker to one class toward the end of a semester to answer questions about sexual orientation; three students came out on that day. Another student told me that he was going to be absent for two weeks because he was going on a *hajj* (Islamic pilgrimage to Mecca). He conducted a wonderful question-and-answer session with the class when he got back.

I encourage you to read the newspapers and watch television news with a new, critical perspective. When you watch TV sit-coms, you will be able to see the gender stereotyping that goes on. On crime shows, what are the race and class of the criminals, and how do they compare with those of the police and the lawyers? How are gays, lesbians, and people with disabilities presented, if at all?

I promise that by the end of the book, you will have a much different understanding of diversity and group conflict than you do now. Perhaps you will begin to look at the world in a different way. That's how change begins.

2

Basic Concepts
of Diversity

When I enrolled in my first sociology class more than forty years
ago, the instructor said that we would be learning "soc-speak." By that,
he meant that we would be learning some of the terminology that sociologists use to communicate with each other. Some of my classmates
argued that sociology was nothing but using jargon to describe what
everyone already knows. Although this characterization of sociology is
overly harsh, it's certainly the case that professional jargon sometimes
makes it exceedingly difficult to understand what is being discussed.

All academic disciplines, including the study of diversity, have
their own jargons that make it easier to communicate. Some of the
concepts are shared by all members of a discipline and have common
definitions. Other concepts are quite contentious, and people argue
over their definitions. Sometimes there are also arguments about
whether the concepts are appropriate to use at all.

In this chapter I'd like to introduce you to some of the important
general concepts used in the study of diversity. In my former instructor's tradition, we can call this "diverspeak." I will concentrate on
concepts that will appear throughout the book. Some concepts, such
as racism and sexism, I will discuss in other chapters because they are
both contentious and somewhat narrower in scope. The concepts will
appear in **boldface** and the definitions in *italics*.

Master Status

Two of the most basic concepts in sociology are status and role.
Status refers to *a position that one holds or a category that one occupies*

in a society. Each individual holds many positions and belongs to many categories. For example, a particular person can be white, female, mother, sister, child, worker, neighbor, middle age, suburbanite, flute player, and so on. Each of these statuses has a culturally defined **role** that *specifies expected behavior that goes along with a specific status.* Teachers, for example, are supposed to help students learn certain content, treat students fairly, correct papers, issue grades, and so on. Students are supposed to attend class, study hard, and respect the teacher.

In a diverse society like ours, however, people don't always agree on the appropriate behavior that should be associated with a particular status. For example, some would say that "good" mothers are supposed to stay home and take care of children, whereas others would say that good mothers can have jobs outside of the home. More important, within a particular culture, "appropriate" roles might look different at different levels of society. From a boss's perspective, for example, workers trying to organize a union might be viewed as troublemakers and be fired. From a worker's perspective, in contrast, organizing a union might be one of the few ways of trying to improve their lives.

Although we all occupy many different statuses, some are culturally defined as more important than others. A **master status** is *one that has a profound effect on one's life, that dominates or overwhelms the other statuses one occupies* (Rosenblum and Travis 2003, 33). In our society, master statuses include race, class, gender, sexual orientation, and disability. Age can also be viewed as a master status, but it will not be discussed in any depth in this book. These master statuses have a much stronger impact on our lives than things like being a friend or a chess player.

Master statuses are culturally determined, not a matter of individual choice. I know people, for example, whose religion is the most important part of their self-identity. In our country, however, social scientists don't usually view religion as a master status because it usually does not determine how one is perceived and treated by the larger society. In the Middle East, in contrast, religion would be considered to be a master status given the political and cultural conflicts in that area.

Some religions, such as Islam, have been viewed with great suspicion in the United States, and the practice of Islam in the United States has the potential to rise to the level of master status. The controversy over building an Islamic community center near ground zero in New York City (one of the sites of the September 11, 2001, terrorist attacks) has shown that many Americans have limits to their belief in the freedom of religion. Although New York City authorities have given the go-ahead to the building, which would contain a small mosque, many Americans feel that this is an insult to those who died in the collapse of the World Trade Center towers on 9/11. This is not just a local story, for there is also opposition to the building of mosques in other parts of the country. A substantial portion of this opposition is due to anti-Islam prejudice.

Dominant and Subordinate Groups

Within each of the five master statuses that we will be discussing, some groups have more power and influence than others. A **dominant group** *is a social group that controls the political, economic, and cultural institutions in a society.* In contrast, a **subordinate group** *is a social group that lacks control of the political, economic, and cultural institutions in a society.*

In the area of race in the United States, for example, whites are the dominant group and people of color are the subordinate groups. Scholars of race relations have traditionally used the terms *majority group* and *minority group* to describe dominant and subordinate groups, respectively. People of color (nonwhites) in the United States are minority groups both numerically and in terms of power. However, if one were to apply this terminology to South Africa during apartheid, the white numerical minority would be called the majority group because it had power, and the black numerical majority would be called the minority group. Because power is more important than numbers in studying diversity, I will use the terms *dominant* and *subordinate*.

In terms of gender, men are the dominant group and women the subordinate group.

In terms of sexual orientation, heterosexuals are the dominant group. The subordinate group, however, is made up of a variety of groups that challenge traditional definitions of sexual orientation, including gays (male homosexuals), lesbians (female homosexuals), bisexuals (those who are sexually attracted to both males and females), and transgendered people (whose identity is inconsistent with their biological makeup). Collectively, this group is often referred to by the acronym **LGBT**.

Finally, people with disabilities are the subordinate group relative to the nondisabled dominant group. We will discuss labels like "nondisabled" and "able-bodied" in Chapter 7.

It is also possible to discuss dominant and subordinate *class* groups even though this is often not done by scholars who write about stratification. Although this will be discussed more in Chapter 3, I will call the wealthiest and most powerful 1 or 2 percent of the population the *dominant group.* The subordinate group consists of the large majority of the population who work for a living or who want to work and can't find decent jobs.

Social Construction

In discussing race and gender, most Americans assume that there is something biological that differentiates whites from other races and men from women. This view, called **essentialism**, means that *reality exists independently of our perception of it; that is, that there are real and important (essential) differences among categories of people* (Rosenblum and Travis 2003, 33). Essentialists would also argue that there are also biological differences between heterosexuals and LGBT people and between the disabled and nondisabled.

According to essentialists, then, racial groups can scientifically be differentiated by skin color, hair texture, facial shape, or other genetic characteristics. Men and women can be differentiated by primary and secondary sexual characteristics, hormones, body shape, and so on. The disabled have physical traits that differentiate them from everyone else. Finally, essentialists would argue that homosexuals have some differences in areas of the brain or some other genetic characteristic that predisposes them to be attracted to people of the same sex.

The **social constructionist** perspective argues, in contrast, that *reality cannot be separated from the way a culture makes sense of it—that meaning is "constructed" through social, political, legal, scientific, and other processes* (Rosenblum and Travis 2003, 33). This means that in the United States, there are socially and culturally defined reasons that people are assigned to being white, black, Asian, or Native American that may have nothing to do with biological categories. For example, although we say that skin color is the defining characteristic, some people who are culturally defined as "black" have lighter skins than some people who are culturally defined as "white." Should a person with an Asian mother and a black father be defined as either Asian or black, as opposed to being in a separate "mixed race" category? President Barack Obama, who had a black father and a white mother, is always described as either "black" or "biracial," but never "white."

Racial categories are not real in a biological sense, but they are real in a social or cultural sense: people who are defined as white are treated differently from people defined as black. We will discuss this in much more detail in Chapter 4.

Along the same lines, the distinction between male and female can be problematic among people with ambiguous sexual organs or who have both male and female sexual organs. What should we call someone who is genetically female but who has a penis? What should we call someone who was born genetically male but who has undergone a sex-change operation, or someone who is genetically female but dresses and acts like a man?

We usually try to fit people into one category or the other, but the decisions are often arbitrary (see Chapter 5). The controversy over the sex of South African runner Caster Semenya is illustrative. After Semenya had won many important races as a woman, people challenged her sexual identity. Semenya was forced to undergo a series of tests after which the International Amateur Athletic Federation finally ruled that she can continue to compete as a woman. The details of the test results were kept private. Here we have an athletic commission determining someone's sex.

Sexual orientation is also a problematic category to define. Most people would have no trouble saying that a woman who has sexual relations with other women throughout her life is a homosexual/lesbian. However, what do we call someone who has occasional homosexual relations but is in a long-term heterosexual relationship? How about someone who was in a homosexual relationship for one year of his or her life but was otherwise heterosexual? There are also people who are attracted to people of the same sex but who are celibate. Our culture tries to force people into one or the other category, but this has nothing to do with biology or with other essentialist criteria (see Chapter 6).

These same issues can also be raised in the area of disability. Not being able to see (being blind) is certainly a biological impairment. However, many people defined as "legally blind" still have some vision; that is, the cutoff point for being legally blind is culturally determined. Also, the presence or absence of accommodations for blindness makes the difference between whether a given individual can perform a task. Having the proper computer software that "speaks" the written text permits a blind person to use the computer. Should this person still be considered disabled? (See Chapter 7.)

The essentialist/constructionist distinction can also be applied to the category of class. Although most people, including social scientists, don't equate class with any biological reality, there is still the widespread belief that terms like *middle class* and *poor* actually refer to something essential or real. Social scientists often quantify the percentage of the population that is in various classes. The United States is often called "a middle-class society."

Constructionists argue that these class divisions are often arbitrary and are quite variable from one social scientist to another. Marxists, for example, argue that the majority of Americans are *working class*, with the poor being included as the lowest level of the working class. Others don't even use the term *working class* and say that there is a *lower middle class* that is separate from the lower class or poor. Some social scientists define the *upper class* as those in the top 10 percent of the income distribution, but they don't differentiate those who make $200 million per year from those who make $200,000. We will discuss the social construction of class in more detail in Chapter 3.

Sometimes the concept of social construction is easier to see if we look at other countries. Throughout Latin America, for example, class is seen as a more important concept than race even though lighter-skinned people are generally more economically privileged than darker-skinned people. Race is seen as a more continuous category rather than the "either-or" category that often exists in the United States. I've had many Latin American students who hadn't even thought much about race in their own countries until they took my course.

In Great Britain, a formal aristocracy based on family lineage still exists, though it has much less power than in the past. Eligibility for the House of Lords, one of the two houses of the parliament, is based on family background, though the House of Commons is responsible for most legislation. Although there are "high society" lists in some major cities in the United States, we do not have a formal aristocracy.

The important point to take away from this discussion is that the master statuses and their subcategories are all socially constructed in each society. There is nothing real about them in either an essential or a biological sense.

Oppression

Some concepts, such as oppression, are frequently used in an imprecise and rhetorical way without being carefully defined. Often, an oppressed group is thought of as being extremely poor and/or living in a ruthless authoritarian police state filled with random acts of violence. The lack of a clear definition is most unfortunate in the study of diversity because the concept of oppression is central to understanding group conflict. After reviewing definitions put forward by a variety of writers, I have settled on the following definition, adapted from Blauner (1972): **oppression** *is a dynamic process by which one segment of society achieves power and privilege through the control and exploitation of other groups, which are burdened and pushed down into the lower levels of the social order.*

Several important implications follow from this definition. First, because oppression involves power, only the dominant group can be the oppressors, and only the subordinate groups can be the oppressed. In the area of gender, for example, we can say that women are oppressed because they are pushed down by the legal system, the economic system, and/or the family structure. Many writers have observed that one of the difficulties that men face is the inability to express emotions to women and to other men. Although this is a *limitation* that may prevent men from achieving their full potential, it is not an example of oppression because men tend to control most of the dominant social institutions (Frye 1983). Similarly, whites are not oppressed by racism even though their prejudiced attitudes may prevent them from forming friendships with people of color.

The term **exploitation** means that *the dominant group uses the subordinate group for its own ends, including gaining economic profit and maintaining a higher position in the social hierarchy.* In the area of class oppression, for example, employers try to keep wages as low as possible so that their profits can be as high as possible. In the area of racial oppression, whites have used housing and educational segregation as a way of controlling the more desirable neighborhoods and schools. In the traditional male-controlled family, men often have their meals cooked, their houses cleaned, and their children taken care of through the unpaid labor of their spouses.

The oppression and exploitation of homosexuals and people with disabilities are more social and cultural than economic. Because only heterosexual romantic/sexual relations are widely accepted, homosexuals are at the bottom of the social hierarchy and are often shunned, harassed, and physically brutalized. Similarly, the disabled are relegated to the bottom because they can't conform to the dominant "able-bodied" norms of behavior. Rather than making profits from the labor of the disabled, society must pay for their care.

Privilege

In a society characterized by oppression, some groups have more advantages than others. **Privilege** means that *some groups have something of value that are denied to others simply because of the groups they belong to; these unearned advantages give some groups a head start in seeking a better life.* Understanding this concept may be difficult, especially for those who are privileged.

In some cases, privileges are quite subtle—at least to those who have them. Heterosexuals, for example, assume that it's okay for them to display a picture of their significant other on their desk at work or to hold hands in a public place. Gays and lesbians, in comparison, are often wary about displaying this type of public affection, often with good reason.

A white customer in a store can usually assume that those who work in the store believe that she is there to purchase a product. Black customers, however, are often viewed with suspicion and are followed or watched by the store staff because they are not assumed to be legitimate customers.

In both of these "subtle" examples, members of the dominant groups (i.e., heterosexual office workers and white store customers) are simply going about business as usual, as they should. The problem is that they usually don't realize that the very same behavior by members of subordinate groups (homosexual office workers and black customers) is viewed quite differently. Business as usual for subordinate groups is not the same as for dominant groups.

In other cases, privilege is not at all subtle. Upper-income families, for example, usually can afford to live in a safe neighborhood and to send their children to high-quality schools. The children benefit because of the family that they were lucky to be born into. Working-class and poor families have fewer options, and their children will live in less safe neighborhoods and attend lower-quality schools. Similarly, men have a chance to compete for a number of high-status, well-paying jobs where the expectation is that the job will probably go to a male. Women, even if they are qualified, have much less of a chance in this competition.

Everyone should have the same opportunity to live in a safe area, attend a high-quality school, enter a fair competition for a job, hold hands with a loved one, and be assumed to be honest. These should be rights of citizenship. The problem is that the dominant groups have much greater access to these privileges than do the subordinate groups.

The nondisabled have the privilege of being able to use public buildings that were designed for them—stairs, doors that must be pushed open, standard-size toilet stalls, signs with no raised letters, and so forth. Although most nondisabled people take these things for granted, public buildings look much different to the disabled. Accommodations such as ramps, wider toilets, and braille signs, which make buildings more accessible, have only been mandated since the passage of the Americans with Disabilities Act in 1990.

One of the most important privileges of the dominant group members is not having to know that they are privileged in the first place. They assume, incorrectly, that everyone else has access to the same privileges that they do. When I was teaching my teenage son to drive, for example, I recall reading an article about black parents who were teaching their sons to drive. One important lesson that the black teenagers learned was to keep their hands on the steering wheel if they were stopped by the police. This, hopefully, would reduce any accidental shootings by the police, who might think a black driver was reaching for a weapon. I never even dreamed of talking to my own white son about this. Not surprisingly, members of the subordinate groups can more easily recognize the existence of privilege than members of the dominant group.

When I discuss privilege and oppression in class, I often get two reactions from members of dominant groups. Some of the privileged feel guilt or discomfort in learning that they are privileged. They want to cast off their privilege in order to maintain their image of being a fair-minded person. Responding to these feelings, Allan Johnson (2001, 15) argues that privilege and oppression are "rooted in a legacy we all inherited, and while we're here, it belongs to us. It isn't our fault. It wasn't caused by something we did or didn't do. But now that it's ours, it's up to us to decide how we're going to deal with it before we collectively pass it along to the generations that will follow ours."

Other members of the privileged react with denial. A working-class white male student, for example, raises his hand and says, "I'm not privileged; I've had to fight for everything that I got." Often, this comment is followed by an angry but heartfelt story of someone from a poor family who really did have to struggle in life, including having to work and take out loans to pay for college. "And I had to do it without the benefits of affirmative action," he continues. Other white males (and some females) often nod in agreement, suggesting that the concept of race and gender privilege is a figment of my imagination.

My response usually is to say that the student's story is one that reflects *class* oppression, something we don't talk about very much in our society. The student lacks *class* privilege even though he still has race and gender privilege. We in the United States often attribute economic oppression only to race, because class remains largely invisible.

This illustrates another important point: people can be in the oppressor group with regard to one master status but in the oppressed group with regard to another. My student still has some of the privileges of being white and male, but he lacks the privileges of being wealthy or middle-income. Not all members of the oppressor group benefit in the same way, and not all members of the oppressed group are harmed in the same way. Sometimes this explanation neutralizes the students' anger somewhat, for they have gained a broader way to understand the complex reality of oppression and privilege.

One way to grasp the complexity of different kinds of privilege is shown in Table 2.1. Each category of privilege is trichotomized (i.e., separated into three parts). Those in the most privileged categories (i.e., capitalist, white, male, heterosexual, nondisabled) would receive 2 points for each privilege, for a total of 10 points. Those in the least privileged categories (working class, nonwhites and non-Asians, those whose sex is not clearly determined, bisexual/transgendered people, and the disabled) would receive 0 points. Others, with other combinations of privilege, would receive the appropriate score with points in between 0 and 10. Those with scores closer to 10 have more privilege than those with scores closer to 0.

Using the discourse of oppression and privilege is really quite subversive in the United States. We often like to think of ourselves as a middle-class society that is gradually breaking down barriers of race (Barack Obama) and gender (Hillary Clinton and Sarah Palin). The terms *postrace* and, less frequently, *postgender* have been used to describe this idealized view of the United States. Assimilation, inclusion,

Table 2.1 Rate Your Relative Privilege and Oppression by Diversity Category

Relative Privilege	Type of Diversity Category				
	Class	Race	Gender	Sexual Orientation	Disability Status
Most (2)	Capitalist	White	Male	Heterosexual	Nondisabled
Less (1)	Middle	Asian, Biracial	Female	Homosexual	Differently abled
Least (0)	Working	Black, Hispanic, Native American	Not clearly determined	Bisexual, Transgender	Disabled

Directions: For each type of diversity category, circle the term that best describes you. To determine your relative level of privilege, give yourself a 2 each time you are in the "most" category, a 1 when you are in the "less" category, and a 0 when you are in the "least" category. Then, add up your total points. If your score is 10, you have the highest possible privilege. If your score is 0, you have the lowest possible privilege. Other scores fall somewhere in between the two extremes.

and upward mobility are the preferred discourse, not oppression, exploitation, and privilege.

Culture, Attitudes, and Ideology

Diversity and group conflict also have important attitudinal components in terms of how different groups see one another. This is reflected in the culture as well as in how individuals think, feel, and believe. Privileged groups, being dominant groups in terms of power, usually have the ability to define nonprivileged groups in an "us" versus "them" type of way. When a subordinate group is defined as the **"other,"** it is *viewed as being unlike the dominant group in profoundly different, usually negative, ways.* Groups that are "othered" are often seen as inferior, dangerous, and/or immoral. This is more than simply being seen as different.

This "othering" process is not inevitable when different groups come into contact with one another. Theoretically, the dominant racial group could view other groups as interesting curiosities rather than evil competitors. Men could view women as having different dispositions rather than as a weaker group to be dominated. *Different* does not have to mean inferior or threatening.

Groups defined as the "other" are usually stigmatized in a variety of ways. **Stigma** is an *attribute for which someone is considered bad, unworthy, or deeply discredited because of the category that he or she belongs to.* Being a homosexual or a person with a disability is often viewed by many as grounds for social ostracism, no matter what else that person might have accomplished. In Nazi Germany, in fact, homosexuals were required to wear pink triangles to differentiate them from the rest of the population, just as Jews were required to wear yellow stars. In the present era, being on welfare is seen as a stigma.

Othering and stigmatization are both social processes that influence how given individuals may think. The same is true for **stereotypes**, which are *cultural beliefs about a particular group that are usually highly exaggerated and distorted, even though they may have a grain of truth.* Stereotypes are passed down from one generation to the next, often through the mass media.

Gay males, for example, are supposed to act feminine ("swishy"), and lesbians are thought to look masculine ("butch"). These images are often promoted by comedians, television, and the movies even though only a minority of gays and lesbians fit this stereotype. Most homosexuals are indistinguishable from heterosexual men and women.

According to another stereotype, blacks in our society are supposed to be naturally talented at basketball and football. Even though blacks are highly overrepresented in the National Basketball Association and the National Football League (this is the grain of truth), it's safe to say that most blacks, like most whites, have only average ability in these two sports.

These athletic stereotypes were brought home to me when I was coaching my son's peewee league basketball team some years ago. Two black boys were among the dozen children that were assigned to the team, and I was thrilled for two reasons: I was happy the team was integrated, and I hoped that the black boys would raise the level of skill of the team. The first child did not disappoint me; he was a mini Michael Jordan. The second child, whom I'll call James, was a tall, broad-shouldered child who looked like the perfect center. The first time the ball was passed to him, James fumbled it, picked it up, fumbled it again, picked it up a third time, tucked it under his arm, and ran with it like a football player. He had no conception of dribbling, he couldn't jump, and he knew absolutely nothing about basketball. So much for the natural talent stereotype.

Hillary Clinton's unsuccessful presidential campaign in 2008 brought up a number of gender stereotypes. On the one hand, she was criticized for not being feminine enough—pant suits, forceful speaking, an aura of being aloof. On the other hand, the one time she confirmed the stereotype by shedding a tear during a speech, critics said this was proof that she was too emotional to be president.

In addition to being inaccurate, stereotypes often portray the group in question in negative ways. The black basketball image stereotype is part of a more general stereotype that blacks can only excel physically, not intellectually. It also goes along with the "dumb athlete" stereotype. Dumb blonde jokes portray women as stupid. In addition, the swishy/butch homosexual images are often objects of derision.

In this whole process of othering, stigmatization, and stereotyping, the negative attitudes are part of a social process whereby the dominant group oppresses the subordinate group. The negative attitudes, in this view, act as justification for the political and economic oppression. In other words, the oppression causes the negative attitudes, not the other way around. The implication here is that it would be impossible to eliminate the negative attitudes until the oppression is eliminated.

Traditional social psychologists, however, often don't use this approach. Instead, they focus on the concept of **prejudice**, which generally refers to *negative attitudes toward a specific group of people.* This refers to what people think, feel, and believe. Although most of the research on prejudice has taken place in the context of studying race and ethnic relations, the concept can also be applied to gender, sexual orientation, disability, and class. Although some prejudice clearly incorporates cultural stereotypes, there are a variety of other interpersonal dynamics that may be involved as causal factors.

The nature of prejudice can change over time, both in content and intensity. Some social scientists, for example, have argued that antiblack prejudice on the part of whites has dropped dramatically in the years since the 1950s. They present evidence that white Americans are less supportive of segregation, are less likely to stereotype blacks, and are less likely to accept biological explanations of black inferiority. Others counter that although this traditional prejudice has declined, it has been replaced by a new form of "color-blind" prejudice that is still quite intense. We will return to this argument in Chapter 4.

Although othering, stigmatization, and stereotyping tend to come from the dominant group against the subordinate group, prejudice can also be multidirectional. For example, Hispanics' antiwhite attitudes or women's antimale attitudes are just as prejudiced as the anti-Hispanic attitudes held by whites or the antifemale attitudes held by males. Whether one is worse than another is a more complex question. Dominant-group pejorative terms used against subordinate groups (e.g., nigger, welfare cheat) are much stronger and more demeaning than the other way around (e.g., honky, rich snob). Tim Wise (2002) suggests that this is because dominant groups have the power to reinforce these pejorative terms with negative behavior whereas subordinate groups don't. As we will see in subsequent chapters, dominant-group prejudice toward subordinate groups tends to be much stronger than any prejudice that exists in the other direction.

The negative attitudes about a particular group can also exist as part of an **ideology**, which is *a body of ideas reflecting the social needs and aspirations of an individual group, class, or culture.* There are several different bodies of ideas, for example, to explain why some people are successful in our society while others are not. One view is that successful people worked hard to get to where they are. According to this view, individual effort can overcome barriers caused by adverse family circumstances or race/gender discrimination. A corollary of this view is the belief that most of those who are not successful didn't work hard enough.

A very different explanation of success, which we might call the "oppressive society" perspective, is that those born into privileged positions are the most likely to be successful because they control the dominant social institutions. A corollary of this view is that less privileged people are usually held back by an unjust society, no matter how hard they work.

Along the same lines, there are different views of the type of equality that should be guaranteed to each citizen. According to the equal opportunity perspective, all citizens should have the same right to compete in the marketplace by selling their labor, investing their money, getting an education, and so on. Presumably, policies that prevent individuals from competing because of their race or gender would be inconsistent with this equal opportunity perspective. However, there is no guarantee of equal results. Suppose a corporation hired ten wealthy white males because they were viewed as the best candidates—that is, they beat out everyone else in a fair and competitive race. This would still be consistent with the equal opportunity perspective. According to this view, the United States is (or should be) a **meritocracy** where *the most skilled people have the better jobs and the least skilled people have the lowest-paying jobs, regardless of race, gender, age, and other factors.*

An alternative perspective on equality could be called the "group rights" perspective. According to this view, dominant groups have unfair advantages in what might appear to be a fair race. For example, although subordinate group members have an abstract right to invest their money, most don't even have enough to live on, much less invest. A few subordinate group individuals might be successful, but most will be left behind. The solution, according to this perspective, is for the subordinate group to collectively demand that the structure of the race be changed and/or that its members be given the chance to compensate for their lack of privilege.

Ideologies tend to reflect the interests of certain groups in society. The "hard work" and "equal opportunity" perspectives tend to support the positions of the dominant groups because they justify their dominance. In contrast, the "oppressive society" and "group rights" perspectives tend to be critical of the dominant groups and supportive of the right of subordinate groups to fight against oppression as groups, not just as individuals. The goal would be to substantially reduce or eliminate the social and economic differences between different groups.

Within any given culture, *some ideologies are so influential that they dominate all other ideologies.* These dominant perspectives are called **hegemonic ideologies** and are widely held by members of both dominant and subordinate groups. Hegemonic ideologies are often invoked by those in power who are trying to enact social policies. In our society, the "hard work" and "equal opportunity" perspectives are the hegemonic views of success and equality. Describing the United States as an oppressive society or invoking the idea of "group rights" is often viewed as un-American by politicians and business leaders. As you may have already guessed, this book is an attempt to counter hegemonic ideology.

Discrimination

Whereas prejudice refers to what people of one group think, feel, and believe about members of other groups, **discrimination** *refers to actions* *that deny equal treatment to persons perceived to be members of some social category or group.* To simplify things, prejudice is what people think, and discrimination is what people do. The following are all examples of discrimination: not renting an apartment to a welfare recipient who can pay the rent, not hiring a homosexual who has the necessary qualifications, not permitting a woman to join a social club when a comparable man would be admitted, not providing access ramps for people in wheelchairs, and not admitting a well-qualified Native American to a school.

Although the concept of discrimination seems straightforward, it is actually very complex. There are different levels of discrimination; an individual landlord refusing to rent to a Hispanic is not the same as a large bank that refuses to grant mortgages to houses in Hispanic communities. The direction of the discrimination is also important. Is the dominant group discriminating against the subordinate group, or is it the other way around? Finally, there is the question of motivation or intentionality; if a particular policy is gender-blind in intent but negatively impacts women more than men, is this discrimination?

There are three different types of discrimination. **Individual discrimination** *refers to the behavior of individual members of one group or category that is intended to have a differential and/or harmful effect on members of another group or category.* Examples of this type of discrimination include attacking a gay person, not allowing a poor person in the corner store, refusing to rent your basement apartment to a black, and not hiring a qualified woman to supervise male workers. These are all actions taken by individuals on their own that are intended to have a differential and/or harmful effect on members of subordinate groups.

Individual discrimination can be multidirectional. In addition to dominant-group individual discrimination against the subordinate group, subordinate groups can practice individual discrimination against dominant groups or against other subordinate groups if they have the power to do so. A Native American can attack a white person or a black person. A gay landlord can refuse to rent an apartment to heterosexuals. A deaf person may refuse to associate with hearing people. A female employer can refuse to hire a male worker.

A poor person, however, couldn't prevent a rich person from entering his or her store because the poor person probably wouldn't own a store. This is an example of not having the resources to practice a particular type of discrimination. However, the poor person could yell at a rich person or attack that person. All of these examples are actions by one individual in one group against one individual in another group.

Much discrimination, however, involves more than just individuals. **Institutional discrimination** *refers to the policies of dominant group institutions, and the behavior of individuals who implement these policies and control these institutions, that are intended to have a differential and/or harmful effect on subordinate groups.* Laws that separated blacks and whites in the South from the late 1870s through the 1950s are an excellent example of institutional discrimination. Another example would be the Catholic Church and Orthodox Judaism not permitting women to become priests and rabbis. The military's "Don't Ask, Don't Tell" policy, repealed in 2010, which prevented homosexuals from being publicly "out," is another example. A final example is the multinational corporation that refuses to provide accommodations for the disabled.

In all these cases, these policies are enacted by large, dominant group institutions and are intended to have a differential and/or harmful impact on subordinate groups. In most cases, institutional discrimination is the dominant group acting against the subordinate group. Usually, the subordinate group doesn't have the power or resources to practice institutional discrimination against the dominant group, although it is still theoretically possible. For example, if Hispanics controlled a local government and refused to hire non-Hispanics as workers, this would be an example of institutional discrimination.

What about institutional discrimination based on class? Clearly, the wealthy act in a variety of ways that are intended to have a differential and/or harmful impact on working people and the poor. Employers try to keep wages low to increase profits. They will abandon one city or even the entire country for another with a cheaper labor force. They don't want to be burdened by health and safety laws that protect workers. Walmart and many other corporations try to prevent workers from unionizing.

There's no question that these things happen all the time, but there is a question about whether the label *institutional discrimination* is appropriate to describe these actions. The basis of the capitalist economic system is for employers to do everything they can to increase their profits, including keeping their labor and production costs as low as possible. Workers often bear the brunt of these policies because they have less power than the employers. However, to describe these practices as "institutional discrimination" would suggest that the capitalist system itself favors employers over employees—another subversive idea. We will return to this issue in Chapter 3.

The third type of discrimination, **structural discrimination**, *refers to policies of dominant group institutions, and the behavior of the individuals who implement these policies and control these institutions, that do not intend to harm people because of their group membership but that have a differential and/or harmful effect on subordinate groups.* The policy *impact* is more important than the intent in this kind of discrimination.

Bank mortgage policies, based on family income and assets, tend to disadvantage non-Asian people of color because of their lower incomes. Tests of physical strength that are based solely on upper body strength disadvantage women, who excel more in lower-body strength exercises. Providing fringe benefits only to married partners would disadvantage gay couples, who can't get married in most states. Having a management retreat at a nineteenth-century inn that is not handicapped accessible disadvantages those with disabilities. Providing federal income tax cuts only to those with incomes disadvantage poor people who have such low incomes that they don't pay any income taxes, although they still pay more regressive sales taxes. All of these policies don't intend to disadvantage subordinate groups, but they do.

The role of structural discrimination can be seen in the transformation of the job of baggage screeners at US airports since September 11, 2001 (Alonso-Zaldivar and Oldham 2002). Prior to the September 11 terrorist attacks in New York and Washington, the majority of those who screened baggage were minorities, many of whom were not US citizens. Their average salary was only $11,000 per year, and they were employed by private companies.

Since September 11, Congress passed legislation raising the salary to $23,000–$35,000 per year and requiring baggage screeners to be federal employees. They also must be US citizens, have a ninth-grade reading capacity, and must pass a battery of employment tests. Consequently, the racial composition of baggage handlers has changed dramatically. In September 2002 the majority of baggage handlers were white. This dramatic turnabout was caused by the new requirements that Congress deemed necessary to be an effective baggage handler, yet they had a negative impact on people of color. One can't help wonder what Congress was thinking by making citizenship a requirement of baggage handlers while 31,000 noncitizens have been issued guns and are on active duty in the armed forces.

Some diversity scholars, along with public opinion, restrict the concept of discrimination to intentional actions and policies—individual and institutional. I believe that it is also useful to characterize unintentional actions and policies as structural discrimination to highlight their negative impact. Good people implementing bad policies can be just as harmful as those who intentionally discriminate.

Many diversity scholars put unintentional discrimination in the "institutional discrimination" category along with intentional discrimination. I prefer to keep institutional and structural discrimination conceptually separate because this emphasizes the negative impact of unintentional discrimination. Perhaps capitalism itself is an example of structural discrimination.

Unfortunately, scholars do not always agree on the definitions of prejudice, discrimination, and other important concepts. For example, it is common for scholars to speak of individual and institutional racism, sexism, and heterosexism rather than discrimination. Other scholars use racism, sexism, and heterosexism to describe prejudiced attitudes rather than discriminatory behavior. Still other scholars use these same terms to refer to a combination of prejudice and discrimination. The lack of consensus about these important concepts can cause a great deal of confusion and misunderstanding. As we proceed through the book, I will try to carefully define these terms in their relevant chapters.

Politics and Political Labels

It is impossible to discuss the issue of diversity without also discussing politics. Most Americans restrict the concept of politics to elections and what goes on in government. The only way people can participate in politics, according to this view, is to vote and to write letters to members of the legislature. Although electoral politics is certainly important, this definition is too restrictive. I prefer to define **politics** as *any collective action that is intended to support, influence, or change social policy or social structures.*

With this broader definition, we can think of a whole range of activities that are political. Fighting for a women's or gay studies program on college campuses is political. International protests against the wars in Iraq and Afghanistan are political. Residents' trying to prevent Walmart from opening a store in their community is political. Organizing a new trade union is political. Boycotting a business that doesn't hire enough people of color is political. Demanding sign-language interpreters for deaf students is political. Armed struggle, including terrorism, is also political, although it is often immoral and counterproductive.

Of course, the goals of political actions can be quite different. Anti-abortion (sometimes called pro-life) demonstrations have different goals than pro-choice demonstrations. Pro–affirmative action and anti–affirmative action demonstrations also have different goals. Sometimes there are even political differences within movements, like those that oppose the World Trade Organization and the International Monetary Fund.

This brings us to the often-used but not-well-defined labels of *conservative, liberal,* and *radical.* Most readers have heard these terms many times but are not sure what they mean. This is complicated by the lack of consensus in our society over these labels. In the following paragraphs, I will not provide crisp definitions as I have done throughout this chapter. Instead, I will try to outline some of the themes that people who use these labels share and try to avoid caricaturing those perspectives with which I disagree.

Conservatives

People who call themselves *conservative* are procapitalist and believe that the market economy, free of regulation, will result in the greatest good for the greatest number of people. Economic conservatives also believe in a limited federal government so that businesses can compete with each other to make more profits and create jobs, thereby strengthening the economy. Therefore, conservatives generally oppose strong federal regulations (e.g., civil rights, the environment, health, and safety) and favor low taxes. They generally oppose more federal spending for schools, job training, and housing although they favor spending on the military. They tend to subscribe to the "hard work" and "equal opportunity" ideologies mentioned earlier and argue that most poor people are poor because of weak families and a lack of motivation, in part caused by an overly generous welfare system.

Social conservatives, while agreeing with much of the above, spend most of their energy promoting and protecting what they see

as traditional family values. They favor male-dominated nuclear families and are strongly opposed to abortion and gay rights. They are
also concerned with bringing prayer and creationism back into
schools, and they object to the concept of a separation between church
and state. Many social conservatives identify themselves as evangeli-
cal Christian fundamentalists who believe in a literal interpretation of
the New Testament.

Economic and social conservatives don't always agree on important issues. Some economic conservatives, such as former California
governor Arnold Schwarzenegger and former New York mayor Rudy
Giuliani, argue that abortion and gay rights are private matters that
the federal government should not be involved with, just as it shouldn't
be involved in the economy.

President George W. Bush combined some aspects of each strand
of conservatism. Consistent with economic conservatives, he argued
for reducing the role of the federal government and slashed taxes on
corporations and the wealthy, arguing that this will create more jobs.
This is the Bush version of trickle-down economics. Even so, he devi-
ated from economic conservatives by creating huge budget deficits and
by ordering local schools to participate in an expensive testing program
through the No Child Left Behind Act. Most economic conservatives
would prefer that the federal government *reduce* its role in education.
Bush is also a born-again Christian whose attitudes reflect the social
conservative views of opposition to abortion and gay marriage.

Ironically, Bush's biggest deviation from traditional conservatism
came at the end of his term in 2008 when he pushed through the Targeted Asset Relief Program (TARP) to bail out the banks and insurance companies that were deemed "too big to fail." Even the former
president noted this contradiction in a September 24, 2008, address
to the nation:

> I'm a strong believer in free enterprise, so my natural instinct is to
> oppose government intervention. I believe companies that make
> bad decisions should be allowed to go out of business. Under nor-
> mal circumstances, I would have followed this course. But these are
> not normal circumstances. The market is not functioning properly.
> There has been a widespread loss of confidence, and major sectors
> of America's financial system are at risk of shutting down. The gov-
> ernment's top economic experts warn that, without immediate
> action by Congress, America could slip into a financial panic and a
> distressing scenario would unfold.

Many members of President Bush's own party strongly disagreed with him on the TARP issue. In the 2010 midterm election, Tea Party conservatives disagreed with the Republican Party establishment.

Liberals

Liberals are also strongly procapitalist, but they have less faith in an unregulated market economy. They believe that an unrestrained free market can generate serious problems (e.g., the 2008–2010 recession, global warming, the massive oil spill in the Gulf of Mexico, etc.) and that the federal government must provide adequate regulations so that capitalism doesn't self-destruct (e.g., TARP and the various stimulus packages of the Obama administration). They also argue that the federal government has an important role to play in the field of job training and education.

Liberals tend to be more tolerant than conservatives when it comes to issues of civil rights, women's rights, gay rights, unions, programs for the poor, and so on. They tend to argue that poverty is caused by a lack of opportunity. The goal of liberals is to have a fairer, more efficient form of capitalism.

I can't emphasize strongly enough that liberals are *not* socialists, because they still favor a privately owned economy—which is the essence of capitalism. Liberals simply want the government to be more involved in regulation and in helping those who are poor and unemployed through no fault of their own. Most European countries, including those in Scandinavia, are capitalist in that more than 90 percent of the economy is privately owned. They simply have a more generous welfare state than the United States.

Like conservatives, there is a range of views among liberals. Mainstream liberals, sometimes called *progressives* (e.g., the late senators Edward Kennedy and Paul Wellstone and Representative Dennis Kucinich), tend to argue for somewhat more regulation and government spending to help the poor. In contrast, more centrist liberals, such as former President Bill Clinton and President Barack Obama, tend to fall somewhere in between mainstream liberals and economic conservatives. It was Clinton, for example, who signed the welfare reform act in 1996 that restricted recipients to only five years of welfare payments over the course of their lifetimes.

During the health care reform debate in 2009, President Obama didn't permit any discussion of a single-payer system and caved in on giving people the opportunity to select a public plan as one choice among a variety of private plans.

Radicals

Most discussions of political labels are restricted to discussing liberals and conservatives. The Pew Research Center for the People and the Press, for example, has an interesting website wherein you can answer a series of questions and be placed in one of nine different political categories (http://typology.people-press.org). However, there is no category to the left of liberal.

Unlike conservatives and liberals, radicals are anticapitalist in that they see competition, private ownership of the means of production, and profit seeking as major causes of economic inequality and social injustice. Some radicals are socialists and want to see government ownership of the economy, economic and social planning, and genuine democratic civil institutions. Unfortunately, there are no current models of advanced industrialized societies that they can point to. Other radicals want more of a "mixed economy" that would combine government ownership with a market economy and a more generous welfare state that would include some form of national health care, low-cost childcare, more extensive maternity/paternity leave, and so on. Still other radicals are anarchists who reject large bureaucratic structures and want small, localized, collectively run institutions. All three varieties of radicals would hold the "oppressive society" and "group rights" ideologies described earlier and believe that capitalism must be replaced with a more equitable form of economic organization.

A Note on Other Political Terminology

If all this isn't confusing enough, many radicals use the term *neoliberal* to criticize conservatives and liberals. In the nineteenth century, the term *economic liberalism* referred to the belief in small government, business competition, low taxes, and low trade tariffs. In today's world, according to radicals, neoliberals extend this analysis to a more globalized economic system. Neoliberals argue that global capitalism and free trade benefit both rich and poor countries. Within individual countries, neoliberals want limited government, low taxes, and maximum competition in order to maximize profits. In other words, neoliberalism is actually a form of what I have called economic conservatism. However, some centrist liberals can also be described as neoliberals.

Radicals are critical of neoliberalism. Although neoliberals argue that their policies will benefit everyone, radicals say that only rich countries will benefit while poor countries will be hurt. More important, radicals argue that the business classes of both poor and rich countries will benefit more than the working classes (Navarro 2007).

Another confusing terminology is describing political tendencies in terms of *left* and *right*. The term *right* generally refers to conservatives, but the *left* can refer either to liberals or radicals. When conservatives use the term, *left* refers to liberals; radicals are either off the political map or are conflated with liberals. When radicals use the term, they call themselves "the left" and refer to Barack Obama as a "neoliberal" or "conservative liberal." I will try to avoid using the left-right terminology throughout this book because it is so imprecise. Hopefully, this brief discussion of political tendencies has caused more enlightenment than confusion.

* * *

Congratulations. You have made it through this introduction to diverspeak. In the rest of the book, I will be using these and other concepts to discuss race, class, gender, sexual orientation, and disability. For your convenience, I have included all the concepts in a list at the back of the book so that you can consult them when necessary. Let us begin.

3

Class

In most diversity anthologies, the section on class comes after the chapters on race and gender. I decided to discuss class *before* discussing the other issues because most Americans aren't used to thinking in class terms. As I will demonstrate, class provides the context in which conflict over race, gender, sexual orientation, and disability exists. This is especially relevant in light of the Great Recession that began in late 2007.

When discussing economic inequality with my students, I find that they are more comfortable and familiar with discussing racial and gender differences than with discussing class differences. Although both race and gender are intimately connected with class, I shall not emphasize these connections in this chapter (they will be discussed extensively in Chapters 4 and 5). By focusing more narrowly on class, my goal is to help students think in class terms, perhaps for the first time.

Terminology

Unfortunately, due to the lack of consensus among social scientists about the nature of class, it is impossible to provide a definition with which everyone will agree. Dennis Gilbert (2008, 11), for example, defines class as "groups of families more or less equal in rank and differentiated from other families above and below them with regard to characteristics such as occupation, income, wealth and prestige." Although this definition has some value, disagreements over the meaning of "rank" and "differentiated" make this and other definitions of limited use. There is also disagreement about whether the American stratification system is a continuous one (i.e., there aren't clear distinctions between one class and another) or whether there are discrete classes.

In thinking about class, one of two economic indicators are often used. **Income** *is the amount of money that a family earns from wages and salaries, interest, dividends, rent, gifts, transfer payments (e.g., unemployment insurance and welfare payments), and capital gains (profits from the sale of assets).* Generally, income refers to the money that a family has coming in during a certain period of time.

Wealth, in contrast, *refers to the assets that people own.* In addition to assets like a house, car, and other personal property, wealth includes stocks, bonds, mutual funds, trust funds, business equity, and real estate. Usually, wealth is expressed as *net worth*, which is the value of what you own less the value of what you owe.

Using the income criteria, one can imagine a vertical line whereby families with the lowest incomes are at the bottom and those with the highest incomes are at the top. The US Census Bureau routinely divides this income distribution into five quintiles (or fifths), each of which has the same number of families. Social scientists can then attach labels to these quintiles so that the lowest might be called the "lower class" or "poor." The highest might be called the "upper-middle class," and the middle three would be "the middle class." Both these divisions and the labels are arbitrary.

The problem is that social scientists don't agree on how many classes there are or what they should be called. In the above example, there are three different classes—upper-middle, middle, and lower. However, there could just as easily have been five; e.g., lower class, working class, lower-middle class, upper-middle class, and upper class. Or the distribution could have been separated into ten deciles (or tenths), each of which could have been given a label. In each case, there is no hard-and-fast distinction between one class and another, except that some have higher incomes than others. Usually the main distinction is between the poor and everyone else, the latter of whom are referred to as the middle class.

Using this continuous distribution approach minimizes the effect of those with very high incomes. For example, in 2009, the top 5 percent of households had incomes of $180,000 and higher. If we call this the upper-middle class, it means that a family making $180,000 is in the same class as the family of the chief executive officer of a large corporation who makes millions. I will discuss this further in the next section.

Sometimes the occupational category is the key measure of social class, with professionals and managers being the upper-middle class and unskilled blue-collar and service workers being the lower class. Education can also be used as a measure of class, where people with advanced degrees make up the upper-middle class and high-school dropouts make up the lower class. Finally, prestige (i.e., perceived social status) is sometimes used to measure class.

A variation of this theme is to create a measure of socioeconomic status (SES) by combining measures of income, occupation, and education into a single index. The simplest way to proceed is to take each of these three variables and dichotomize them, that is, split them into two. For income, those who earn more than the median income would get a score of 1, and those who earn less would get a 0. For occupation, white-collar workers would get a 1 and manual workers would get a 0. For education, those who have more than a high school education would get a 1, and those with a high school education or less would get a 0.

Using this method, everyone who is in the labor force will get a score from 0 to 3. For example, a college-educated corporate executive who earns more than the median income would get a score of 3. A high-school dropout who works as a janitor and earns less than the median income would get a score of 0. Because we have four levels of SES, we can attach labels to each level. The corporate executive at level 3 might be called "upper-middle class" while the janitor at level 0 might be called "lower class." Although this is more sophisticated than using income alone, we are still left with a continuous distribution of SES scores with arbitrary labels attached to them.

Occasionally, analysts will use a continuous distribution approach with wealth as the main criterion. For example, Dinesh D'Souza (1999), the well-known conservative writer, has developed a six-class model that is based on a combination of wealth and income—super-rich, rich, upper-middle, middle, lower-middle, and poor. Readers may note that in D'Souza's scheme, there is no working class; he has defined it out of existence.

A dramatically different approach to class is provided by neo-Marxists, who use the concepts of wealth and power to differentiate between classes. Economist Michael Zweig (2000), for example, argues that a small group of people (1 or 2 percent of the adult population) own the means of production and have a lot of decision-making power in society. They are called the employer class, or the capitalist class. The majority of the population (62 percent) own very little and have scant decision-making power. This heterogeneous working class includes both blue-collar and white-collar workers and various levels of skill. The poor, according to Zweig, are considered to be the lowest level of the working class. The remaining 36 percent of the population is the middle class, which includes small business owners, freelance artists and writers, upper-level managers who are not wealthy, and highly paid athletes and entertainers.

In this neo-Marxist view, the capitalist class and the working class are in political and economic conflict with each other, with the middle class caught in between them. Because the capitalist class makes its profits from the labor of the working class, the capitalists are always trying to push labor costs lower while the workers are trying to gain more power to increase their incomes and control over the work process. Class is not just a descriptive category, as it is in the stratification perspective, but has important political ramifications.

Although other neo-Marxists agree with the concept of class conflict between the working class and capitalist class, they don't always agree on the number of classes that exist. Erik Olin Wright (1997), for example, has a twelve-class model where he describes different subdivisions within the working and middle classes.

Dennis Gilbert (2008), who is not a Marxist, agrees that there is a small capitalist class at the top of the class structure, but he divides the rest of the population into five additional classes—upper-middle, middle, working, working poor, and lower. For Gilbert, the *source of income* is the key to who is in what class, and the main division is between the top two classes (capitalist and upper-middle) and the other four classes.

Given these divergent and sometimes imprecise views, can we say class is a socially constructed concept? Is the social definition of class more important than its material essence? On the one hand, there certainly are different cultural definitions of class in terms of how many classes there are and what labels should be used. On the other hand, there appears to be something real about class because we can measure income, wealth, and other important variables and we can see that some members of a population have a lot more of these things than other members. It's also clear that people at the higher class levels have more power than those at the lower class levels. The disagreements are about how class works and how it should be measured, not about whether it exists. There appears to be some essence of class even though there is no unity about what it is.

Another important concept is **social mobility**, which refers to *individuals moving up or down in terms of their class level.* The belief in upward mobility is an important part of American mythology, which is encapsulated in the "log cabin to White House" journey of Abraham Lincoln. We will examine the extent of upward mobility in the next section.

Sociologists talk about two types of mobility. **Intergenerational mobility** *refers to a child's class position relative to the child's parents.* Both Barack Obama and Bill Clinton came from modest backgrounds and were upwardly mobile relative to their parents. George W. Bush, in contrast, was born into a wealthy and powerful family, so he was not socially mobile.

Intragenerational mobility *refers to the degree to which a young worker who enters the labor force can improve his or her class position within a single lifetime.* This is the "stock clerk to CEO" version of upward mobility. Bill Gates was upwardly mobile in the intragenerational sense because he founded Microsoft as a small company and eventually became the richest man in the United States.

Some diversity writers characterize the economic inequality associated with capitalism as a form of *classism,* another one of those ill-defined concepts. Some writers see classism as a system of oppression that stigmatizes poor and working-class people and their cultures (Cyrus 2000, 6). Other writers define classism as prejudice and discrimination based on socioeconomic level or class (Blumenfeld and Raymond 2000, 25). In this view, class oppression is equivalent to racism, sexism, and heterosexism in terms of importance. We will return to this issue later in the chapter.

Descriptive Statistics

Because there is no consensus on the definition of class, it is difficult to say who is in what class and how many people are in what class. However, it is not at all difficult to describe the degree of economic inequality that exists in the United States. The federal government collects a great deal of economic data, and I will use some of it here.

The distribution of income in 2009 is presented in Table 3.1. On the top half of the table, all households are separated into quintiles, or five categories, with the same number of households in each. Twenty percent, or one-fifth, of households earn between $0 and $20,453 annually. If we look at the combined income of these 23.5 million households and compare it with the combined income of all 117 million households in the country, we see that the poorest 20 percent of households have only 3.4 percent of the total income.

There are also 23.5 million households that earn more than $100,001, and they make up the richest 20 percent of all households. Their share of the total household income is a whopping 50.3 percent. Remember, there are the same number of households in the poorest and richest quintiles, but their shares of the total household income are dramatically different. The median household income, where half the households earn more and half the households earn less, was $49,777 in 2009.

Table 3.1 Distribution of Income of All Households, by Quintile, and Income of Highest Paid Chief Executive Officers, 2009

Income Quintile	Income Range	Percentage of Total Income
Poorest 20 percent	0–$20,453	3.4
Fourth 20 percent	$20,454–$38,550	8.6
Middle 20 percent	$38,551–$61,801	14.6
Second 20 percent	$61,802–$100,000	23.2
Top 20 percent	$100,001+	50.3
Top 5 percent	$180,001+	21.7

Rank of Highest Paid CEOs	Individual Income
400th	$2,170,000
300th	$2,700,000
200th	$5,820,000
100th	$10,200,000
1st (highest paid)	$141,360,000

Sources: US Census Bureau 2009; Forbes 2010.

Note: The annual incomes of the poorest 20 percent of all households ranged from $0 to $20,453. The combined incomes of these 23.4 million households account for only 3.4 percent of the total income of all 117.5 million households combined. The median income of all households in the country was $49,777. Individual income of the CEOs is the total compensation they received from their companies. The individual CEO who was 400th on the list received $2.17 million in compensation in 2009.

The table also shows that the top 5 percent of households, earning above $180,000 annually, account for 21.7 percent of the total income. Now, $180,000 is not a bad income, but it pales in comparison with some of the incomes of people in the top 1 percent of households. *Forbes*, the business magazine promoted as "the capitalist's tool," collects information each year on the incomes of chief executive officers (CEOs) of the nation's 500 largest corporations. This includes the total compensation from their companies but does not include other income they may have earned or the incomes of other family members. The average income of these CEOs in 2009 was $8 million—a 30 percent *cut* from 2008 due to the recession!

The five-hundredth best-paid CEO (Steve Jobs, Apple Computers) earned nothing from his company. Don't worry: his income over the previous five years was $661 million. The highest-paid CEO was H. Lawrence Culp Jr. (Danaher), who made $141,360,000. Not bad for a recession year.

If we were to construct a graph of income inequality with each inch representing $100,000 of income, someone with the median household income would be about a half-inch above the floor. The beginning of the top 5 percent income bracket would be two inches off the floor. The average salary of the top 500 CEOs would be seven feet above the floor. H. Lawrence Culp Jr.'s income would be 118 feet above the floor, on the ninth or tenth floor of an average building.

This extraordinarily high level of income inequality is much greater than in Europe. According to World Bank data from the mid-1990s, the bottom income quintile in European industrialized countries accounted for 7–10 percent of the aggregate income, a much higher figure than in the United States. The top income quintiles in Europe accounted for 34–45 percent of the aggregate income, a much lower figure than in the United States (Hurst 2004; Kerbo 2009).

In addition, the CEOs in other industrialized countries earned substantially less than did American CEOs. Between 2003 and 2005, for example, Swiss CEOs earned a little more than one-third of the income of their American counterparts. German CEOs earned less than one-fourth, and French, British, and Dutch CEOs earned less than one-fifth of what their American counterparts earned (Kerbo 2009).

Just stating that income inequality exists is not sufficient. Another question is whether the degree of income inequality is growing, shrinking, or staying the same. Fortunately, the federal statistics allow us to examine this question. We have just discussed the share of aggregate household income that each quintile accounted for in 2009. These same data for other years are shown in Table 3.2.

As the table illustrates, the lowest quintile had a slightly *lower* proportion of the aggregate income in 2009 (3.4 percent) than in 1970 (4.1 percent). This means that the poor were worse off relative to everyone else in 2009 than they were in 1970. Looking at the households in the top 20 percent and the top 5 percent, the reverse is true. These better-off households have a *higher* proportion of the aggregate income in 2009 than they did in 1970. This means that the higher-income households are earning even higher incomes now than in the past while the lower-income households are losing ground. To put it another way, income inequality is getting worse. Incorporating the effect of taxes doesn't change this trend (Browning 2003).

The gap between the salaries of CEOs and average workers has been growing rapidly. According to Sara Anderson and her colleagues (2008), CEOs made 42 times the salary of the average worker in 1980. By 2008, the CEOs on the Standard and Poor's 500 list made 344 times more than the average worker. Using a slightly different methodology, the Economic Policy Institute estimates that the CEO/worker income gap increased from 24 times the salary in 1967 to 300 times in 2000 (Mishel, Bernstein, and Allegretto 2005). Whichever data you prefer, economic inequality is increasing at an alarming rate.

As bad as income inequality is, wealth inequality is even worse. Table 3.3 shows the distribution of net worth in 1991 and 2004. Almost 16 percent of households had a zero or negative net worth in 2004;

Table 3.2 Share of Aggregate Household Income Received by Different Income Groups, 1970–2009

Year	Lowest 20 Percent of Households	Highest 20 Percent of Households	Top 5 Percent of Households
2009	3.4	50.3	21.7
2000	3.6	49.8	22.1
1990	3.8	46.6	18.5
1980	4.2	44.1	16.5
1970	4.1	43.3	16.6

Source: US Census Bureau 2009.
Note: In 2009, the poorest 20 percent of households received only 3.4 percent of the aggregate income while the top 5 percent of households received 21.7 percent of the aggregate income.

Table 3.3 Distribution of Wealth (net worth) of All US Households in 1991 and 2004 and Net Worth of the Richest People in the United States in 2010

All US Households	Percentage Distribution	
Net Worth	1991	2004
0 or negative	12.6	15.6
$1–$4,999	14.2	9.1
$5,000–$9,999	6.5	4.1
$10,000–$24,999	11.2	6.3
$25,000–$49,999	12.2	7.4
$50,000–$99,999	15.1	11.6
$100,000–$249,999	17.6	19.6
$250,000–$499,999	7.0	13.4
$500,000+	3.5	12.8

Richest 400 People in the United States

Net Worth, 2010	Rank of Person
$1 billion	400th (16-way tie)
$1.4 billion	290th (10-way tie)
$2 billion	182nd (18-way tie)
$3.2 billion	98th (3-way tie)
$45 billion	2nd (Warren Buffett)
$54 billion	Richest (Bill Gates)

Sources: US Census Bureau 1995, 2003b; Armstrong and Newcomb 2004; Forbes 2010.
Note: In 2004, 9.1 percent of all households had a net worth between $1 and $4,999. The median net worth was $79,800 in 2004 and $38,500 in 1991. In 2010, the poorest of the richest individuals had a net worth of $1 billion.

that is, they owed more than they owned. At the other end of the spectrum, 12.8 percent of households had a net worth of $500,000 or more. The median net worth was about $82,000 in 2004.

When comparing the 2004 data with the 1991 data, it is clear that wealth inequality has gotten worse. The percentage of households with zero or negative net worth increased from 12.6 percent in 1991 to 15.6 percent in 2004. The number of households with a net worth of $500,000 or more also increased, from 3.5 percent in 1991 to 12.8 percent in 2004.

As we saw with income inequality, these data understate the true degree of wealth inequality. *Forbes* (2010) magazine also collects data on the 400 richest Americans. The poorest people on the Forbes 400 list in 2009 (a sixteen-way tie) each have a net worth of $1 billion. The net worth of the wealthiest person in the country, Bill Gates, is $54 *billion*. If we were to make a wealth graph that began on the first floor of a building wherein each inch would represent $100,000 of net worth, the median family net worth would be less than one inch above the floor. The sixteen people with a $1 billion net worth would be 833 feet above the floor—about the height of a 75-story building. Bill Gates's net worth, in comparison, would be 45,000 *feet* from the bottom, above the cruising level of most jet airliners!

The federal government also collects data on poverty. The measure of poverty goes back to the 1960s, when it was assumed that families spend about one-third of their income on food. The US Department of Agriculture publishes an emergency food budget each year for different-sized families; the larger the family, the larger the food budget. The government takes this figure and multiplies it by three; the product becomes the official poverty threshold.

A family's before-tax money income includes wages, salaries, cash transfer payments like welfare, social security, and unemployment insurance. Capital gains and losses and the value of in-kind government services (e.g., food stamps, Medicaid, subsidized housing) are not included. This income is then compared with the poverty threshold. For a family of four, including two children, the poverty threshold was $21,756 in 2009. This means that if the family income was less than $21,756, those four people would be counted as among the poor. A three-person family with two children, in contrast, would have a poverty threshold of $17,285, and a family of five would have a poverty threshold of $26,245. Using these calculations, 43.6 million people were counted as poor in 2009. This accounted for 14.3 percent of the US population. The 2007 pre-recession poverty rate was "only" 12.5 percent.

Most poor adults work for at least part of the year. According to Yates (2005), almost one-quarter of all workers had such low hourly wages that they would still be poor even if they had worked year-round and full-time in 2003.

Some have argued that this measure is too generous and that it *overestimates* the number of poor people. Most important, many conservatives argue that the value of noncash in-kind government services (e.g., food stamps, subsidized housing and health care, etc.) should be *included as income*. They would also deduct income and payroll taxes and include the value of capital gains (of which the poor have virtually nothing). Keeping the same threshold levels, this revised measure eliminates more than eight million people from the poverty count. These people have the same low incomes that they had by the previous measure; they are just not counted as poor anymore.

After looking at these numbers, we can return briefly to our discussions of class. The data show the limitations of the mainstream approach that doesn't deal with wealth and that stops at the highest quintile or decile of the income distribution. Someone with $500,000 in wealth just can't be in the same class as someone with billions. The Marxist approach, with its emphasis on wealth, can easily incorporate these figures by saying that these very wealthy people with high incomes are members of the capitalist class.

Finally, we will look at some numbers about social mobility, or the extent to which people move up and down the stratification system. In order to understand how a person's class origin affects his or her life, we look at intergenerational mobility by comparing the current family wealth quintile of adult children with the past wealth quintile of their parents when the children were growing up (Table 3.4). Thirty-six percent of the children who grew up in the poorest wealth quintile found themselves in the poorest wealth quintile as

Table 3.4 Adult Children in Each Wealth Quintile Compared to Their Parents' Wealth Quintile (as a percentage)

Parental Wealth Quintile	Adult Children's Wealth Quintile					
	Poorest	Second	Middle	Fourth	Richest	Total
Poorest	36	29	16	12	7	100
Second	26	24	24	15	12	100
Middle	16	21	25	24	15	100
Fourth	15	13	20	26	26	100
Richest	11	16	14	24	36	100

Source: Haskins 2008.
Note: As the table indicates, 36 percent of children who grew up in the poorest quintile were in the same quintile as adults. Seven percent of children who grew up in the poorest quintile moved up to the richest quintile as adults.

adults (not mobile). Only 11 percent of the children who grew up in the richest wealth quintile found themselves in the poorest wealth quintile as adults (downwardly mobile).

In contrast, 7 percent of the children who grew up in the poorest wealth quintile found themselves in the richest wealth quintile as adults (upwardly mobile). Thirty-six percent of the children who grew up in the richest wealth quintile found themselves in the richest wealth quintile as adults (not mobile).

Although Table 3.4 shows that there is both upward and downward mobility in terms of wealth, children are most likely to end up in the same or adjacent wealth quintile as adults as when they were children. Parents' financial position has an important influence on the financial destination of their children.

The *Economist* (2004), a mainstream British magazine, reviewed several studies and concluded that social mobility in the United States is declining:

> A growing body of evidence suggests that the meritocratic ideal is in trouble in America. Income inequality is growing to levels not seen since the Gilded Age, around the 1880s. But social mobility is not increasing at anything like the same pace; would-be Horatio Algers are finding it no easier to climb from rags to riches, while the children of the privileged have a greater chance of staying at the top of the social heap. The United States risks calcifying into a European-style class-based society.

Though some upward mobility can be attributed to the superior work ethics of individual men and women, a lot of mobility is due to structural changes in the labor force. The number of people employed in farming has been declining for decades, so many of the children of farmers have to find nonfarm jobs. Also, white-collar occupations have been increasing faster than manual occupations, so that some of the children of lower manual workers are automatically pushed up in the occupational hierarchy.

These data show that while there is upward and downward mobility of children in terms of wealth, the best chance of being wealthy is being born into a wealthy family. In addition, most of the mobility consists of small steps between adjacent strata rather than big jumps from the bottom to the top. These findings are consistent with previous studies of social mobility. In addition, mobility rates in the United States are about the same as they are in other industrialized countries (Kerbo 2009; Beeghley 2005).

There is also a certain amount of mobility among the wealthy. A group called United for a Fair Economy (UFFE) analyzed the family origins of those people on the 1997 Forbes 400 list of the richest people in America. UFFE used a baseball analogy of starting in the batters' box and ending up on home plate. It found that 43 percent of the Forbes 400 started out on home plate; that is, they inherited enough wealth—at least $475 million in 1997—to be on the list without doing anything (e.g., J. Paul Getty Jr. and David Rockefeller). Seven percent were born on third base—they inherited at least $50 million, so they had to work to increase their wealth in order to get on the list (e.g., Kenneth Feld and Walter Annenberg). Six percent were born on second base by inheriting a small company and/or wealth of more than $1 million (e.g., Donald Tyson and Frank Purdue). Fourteen percent began on first base by being born into a prominent family but didn't inherit more than $1 million (e.g., Bill Gates). That left 30 percent who began in the batters' box, meaning that their families didn't have great wealth (e.g., H. Ross Perot and John Werner Kluge). However, even most of those who began in the batters' box did not come from poor or working-class families. If you want to be rich, your best chance is to be born into a rich family.

Most Americans believe that the key to upward mobility is through higher education. It's certainly true that the more education a person has, the higher his or her income. However, children from higher-income families tend to get more education than those from lower-income families. Table 3.5 shows that whereas 54 percent of

Table 3.5 Distribution of Bachelor's Degree Recipients in 1988 and 2008 by Family Income Quartile (as percentage of all recipients)

Family Income Quartile	1988	2008
Lowest	8	9
Second	14	12
Third	27	25
Highest	51	54
Total	100	100

Source: Chronicle of Higher Education 2010.
Note: As this table indicates, in 2008, 9 percent of children from families in the lowest income quartile and 54 percent of the children from families in the highest income quartile had received a bachelor's degree.

the bachelor's degrees awarded in 2008 went to children from high-income families, only 9 percent went to children from low-income families. What is even more distressing is that the distribution has not changed much since 1988. To the degree that a college degree is important for upward mobility, higher education is reproducing inequality.

Attitudes and Ideology

Most mainstream commentators would argue that the United States is a middle-class society, implying that most Americans are middle class. As we saw in the previous section, however, there is no agreement on how class should be measured. In addition, the way Americans identify their class position is highly dependent on how the question is asked. Table 3.6 shows examples of class identification from three different national studies with three different lists of class options. What's clear from these three measures is that few Americans identify themselves as being in the upper or lower classes. Also, when given the option, a substantial proportion (34–46 percent) see themselves as being in the working class. Everett Ladd and Karlyn Bowman (1998) review the literature and show how this has been true since at least the 1940s. Pew does not give people the option of saying whether they are in the working class or not.

Table 3.6 Distribution of Social Class Identification in Three Different Studies

*New York Times/*CBS News Poll (2005)		Pew Research Center(2008a)		National OpinionResearch Center(2006)	
Category	Percent	Category	Percent	Category	Percent
Upper	2	Upper	2	Upper	2.8
Upper-middle	10	Upper-middle	19		
Middle	40	Middle	53	Middle	46.2
Working	34	Lower-middle	19	Working	45.6
Lower	13	Lower	6	Lower	4.7
Total	100		100		100

Note: According to the 2006 National Opinion Research Center poll, nearly 46 percent of the respondents believed they were in the working class.

Another aspect of the middle-class society ethos is the connection between hard work and economic success. Ladd and Bowman show that this has been an enduring belief among most Americans. In a 1952 survey, for example, respondents were asked the following: "Some people say there's not much opportunity in America today; that the average man doesn't have much chance to really get ahead. Others say there's plenty of opportunity, and anyone who works hard can go as far as he wants. How do you feel about this?" (quoted in Ladd and Bowman 1998, 54). Eighty-seven percent said that there was opportunity if people worked hard, and 8 percent said that there was only little opportunity.

Unfortunately, the question was asked differently in different years. The *New York Times*/CBS News poll (2005) asked how important various qualities are for "getting ahead in life." Eighty-seven percent said that hard work was "essential" or "very important" for getting ahead. Having a good education was almost as important, at 85 percent. This was followed by having natural ability (71 percent), knowing the right people (48 percent), and coming from a wealthy family (44 percent).

A Pew (2008) survey changed the question again by asking why rich people were rich. This time, more people (46 percent) said that the rich knew the right people or were born into it than said it was due to hard work, ambition, or education (42 percent). Although it is not possible to compare all these surveys because the questions are different, a substantial proportion of Americans clearly still believe strongly in the work ethic.

The Great Recession might be causing Americans to question this faith in hard work. According to a 2010 ABC/Yahoo News Poll, 42 percent of Americans said that the American dream of working hard to get ahead used to be true but is no longer. Half of Americans said that the dream was still true. The high proportion who questioned the American dream alarmed many pundits, who felt that some of the cultural glue that has held the country together may be unraveling.

The flip side of the work-success question concerns explanations for poverty. The following question was put to national samples between 1964 and 1997: "In your opinion, which is more often to blame if a person is poor—lack of effort on his own part, or circumstances beyond his control?" (Ladd and Bowman 1998, 52). In 1964, two-thirds of the population thought that lack of effort was either partially or completely the cause of poverty (Ladd and Bowman 1998). This is sometimes called the "blame the victim" explanation of poverty because the cause is located within poor individuals. By 1997 slightly more than half of the respondents still felt that lack of effort was a partial or complete explanation of poverty, a substantial decline from 1964.

The blame-the-victim explanation of poverty is one of the enduring beliefs in American culture and social science. In the 1960s, anthropologist Oscar Lewis coined the phrase "culture of poverty." This term has gone through a variety of changes, with one of the more recent simply referring to *the cultural explanation of poverty* (Harrison 1992; Small, Harding, and Lamont 2010). The argument put forward by conservative scholars is that some substantial proportion of poor people have cultural values, passed on from one generation to the next, that cause them to be noncompetitive in the modern labor force. The components of this culture are said to be living in the present rather than planning for the future and have feelings of powerlessness, broken families, confused gender roles, a proclivity for deviant behavior, and a dependence on welfare.

According to this view, then, poverty is caused by the attitudes of poor people themselves, not by circumstances beyond their control, such as economic recession, racial and gender discrimination, globalization, or the actions of the capitalist class. The solution is to change their culture, not to provide more opportunities. The assumption is that substantial opportunities are there for the taking.

I can't help wondering if the skyrocketing unemployment rates caused by the Great Recession (from 4.6 percent in 2007 to 9.6 percent in 2010) will cause people to modify these beliefs. Clearly, the thrust of this book is inconsistent with the culture of poverty analysis. Cultural differences cannot explain the growing income and wealth inequality that we discussed earlier.

Americans are certainly aware of the inequality that exists in the United States, although they seem to have ambivalent attitudes about it. The polls show that while they admire people who got rich through hard work (89 percent) and think that the country benefits from having a class of rich people (62 percent), they don't think it's likely that they will become rich (61 percent). They also think that the rich don't pay their fair share of taxes (72 percent) and that the tax system is unfair to working people (74 percent). In addition, 76 percent agreed with the statement "The rich are getting richer and the poor are getting poorer" (Ladd and Bowman 1998).

In spite of these beliefs about the unfairness of economic inequality, Ladd and Bowman (1998) provide data showing that Americans disagree on whether and how the government should respond to income inequality. Using a seven-point scale, respondents were asked to use a score of 1 to indicate their belief that the government should reduce income differences by raising taxes on the wealthy and giving income assistance to the poor. A score of 7 would indicate that the government should not concern itself with income inequality.

When the question was first asked in 1973, almost half (48 percent) said that the government should try to reduce inequality, and less than one-quarter (22 percent) said that it shouldn't. The remaining 27 percent were in between.

By 1996, however, things had changed dramatically. Only 28 percent said that the government should decrease inequality, a substantial drop from 1973. Twenty percent said that the government shouldn't decrease inequality, a small drop from 1973. Half were now in the middle, a sharp rise from 1973. During the conservative 1990s, there was considerably less enthusiasm for government action to reduce inequality.

Not surprisingly, people from different income levels had different attitudes about government action. In 1996, low-income people were much more supportive of government action than were high-income people. From the 1970s to the 1990s, low-income support for government action remained stable, but high-income support dropped.

In 2010, Americans also were divided on how government benefits for poor people actually affect the poor. Thirty-eight percent said these programs "encourage them to remain poor" while 47 percent said these programs "help them until they begin to stand on their own" (*New York Times*/CBS News 2010).

The results of these national surveys do not show an American population that is united over the theme of middle-class America. What they do show is a population with differing viewpoints on the importance of hard work and the role of government, depending on where respondents are in the system of inequality.

Discrimination and Capitalism

Since the 1970s, capitalism has not been kind to working people. Although there have been a variety of corporate scandals in the first years of the twenty-first century that have hurt working people in a variety of ways, it is the legal workings of capitalism that are the larger problem.

In the previous chapter I introduced the concept of discrimination and defined it as *actions that deny equal treatment to persons perceived to be members of some social category or group*. As we will see in the following chapters, I will show how the dominant groups (i.e., whites, men, and heterosexuals) still practice intentional discrimination in terms of race, gender, and sexual orientation in a variety of ways (e.g., employment, housing, education, etc.). Sometimes this discrimination is at the individual level, and sometimes it is institutional. Sometimes it is illegal, and sometimes it isn't.

Even so, the concept of discrimination doesn't adequately describe the nature of class domination. The capitalist class has power over other classes and can live in neighborhoods and go to restaurants that working-class people can't, but this usually doesn't involve unequal treatment due to membership in a certain category, and there is usually nothing illegal about it. A secretary can't buy a home in Beverly Hills because he or she can't afford it. A restaurant can refuse service to people who can't pay its prices. Most families can't afford private schools, so they send their kids to public schools. A factory owner has the legal right to hire and fire workers and to boss them around. A wealthy political candidate can legally outspend a middle-class opponent by using millions of his or her own personal fortune to win an election. These and other policies, which are certainly unfair, are built into the capitalist system. The concept of discrimination doesn't capture the essence of this type of unfairness. Exploitation, where *the dominant group uses the subordinate group for its own ends*, seems closer to the truth.

Increasingly, capitalism has become a global economic system. Private corporations and their national governments have always tried to look outside their borders for raw materials, new markets, and cheap labor. This goes back to the seventeenth and eighteenth centuries, when European countries established colonies around the world.

With the development of rapid transportation, more sophisticated production techniques, and the information technology explosion, globalization has taken a great leap forward. Huge multinational corporations operate around the world, and their country of origin has become less important. Corporations move their operations to areas of the world that offer cheaper labor costs, lower taxes, and fewer environmental regulations. Countries compete with one another in what some have called *the race to the bottom* (Zweig 2000).

Globalization causes real problems for working people in the United States and other industrialized countries due to their relatively high wages compared with workers in the developing world. It's often cheaper for American companies to have their products assembled in Third World countries and ship them to the United States than to pay American workers to do the work. It's impossible for American workers to compete with workers in China or El Salvador who make only a few dollars per day. According to some estimates, the United States lost as many as *1 million jobs* between 2000 and 2004.

This has resulted in a phenomenon known as "displaced workers." According to the US Bureau of Labor Statistics (BLS) (2010), displaced workers are "persons 20 years of age and older who lost or left jobs because their plant or company closed or moved, there was insufficient work for them to do, or their position or shift was abolished." Between January 2007 and December 2009, the BLS estimates that as many as 15.4 million workers were displaced. This was more than double the number displaced in the previous three-year period, mostly due to the effects of the Great Recession.

The BLS then surveyed displaced workers who had been with their employer at least three years prior to displacement. At the time of the survey in January 2010, only 49 percent of these workers had found new jobs. In a previous survey in January 2008, 67 percent of displaced workers had found new jobs. Of those who were reemployed in the 2010 survey, 45 percent were earning at least as much as they had been paid at their former job. In the 2008 survey, 55 percent earned at least as much as the job they lost.

When most of us think of displaced workers, we probably think of factory workers in the steel, auto, rubber, or textile industries. But one-quarter were professional and managerial workers, and another quarter were sales and office workers.

Increasing numbers of American corporations "outsource" some of their work to companies in Ireland, India, and other low-wage countries. In India, the average manufacturing wage in 2005 was only 91 cents per hour. This is only 3 percent of the comparable labor cost in the United States (Sincavage, Haub, and Sharma 2010). Jobs in aircraft, engineering, investment banking, and pharmaceuticals have also gone to India. IBM has reduced its American labor force by 31,000 and increased its Indian workers from 0 to 51,000 ("Outsourcing Is Breaking Out of the Back Office" 2007).

Legal work is also being outsourced. In 2005, forty American law firms had subsidiaries in India. By 2009 that number had grown to 140.

Indian lawyers cannot advise American clients, but they can do much of the routine work that junior lawyers do. The billing cost is one-tenth to one-third of the cost of American lawyers (Timmons 2010).

The relentless search for lower labor costs to increase profits is costing working people good jobs. Americans often blame Indian or Chinese workers for "taking their jobs," but it is the profit-oriented corporations that are truly to blame.

Globalization is also a contributing factor to the decline of labor unions in the United States. In 1955 more than one-third of the labor force belonged to a union. In 2009 that figure had plummeted to 12.5 percent (US Bureau of Labor Statistics 2010). This is much lower than other countries in the industrialized world. More than one-fourth of Japanese workers and 42 percent of workers in England are unionized (Zweig 2000; Kerbo 2009). The decline in the American manufacturing industries, many of which were unionized, is one reason for the drop in union membership. Now, government workers, including teachers, are much more likely to be unionized (37 percent) than workers in the private sector (7 percent).

Without unions, working people cannot negotiate effectively with employers for wages, benefits, and working conditions. According to Michael Yates (2005), unionized workers earn 15 percent more than nonunion workers after controlling for factors such as education, work experience, and age. The decline in unionization has contributed to the growth in income inequality. However, even unionized workers have had a difficult time holding on to hard-fought gains.

Another structural issue is the types of jobs that are available in the United States. According to popular knowledge, high-skilled, high-paying jobs are displacing lower-skilled, low-paying jobs because of high-tech industries. The reality, as we shall see, is considerably more complex.

Every two or three years, the Bureau of Labor Statistics revs up its computers and does a ten-year projection of which jobs will grow and which won't. The most recent projections are for the period 2008–2018 (Lacey and Wright 2009). Table 3.7 shows the occupations that are expected to produce the most new jobs by 2018. Registered nurses top the list and are expected to add 581,500 new jobs by 2018. This is certainly consistent with the popular view that more and more jobs require education beyond high school, an associate degree in this case. However, the next six occupations on the list require

Table 3.7 Occupations Projected to Add the Most New Jobs, 2008–2018

Occupational Category	Employment in 2008 (thousands)	New Jobs by 2018 (thousands)	Percent Change	Income Quartile[a]	Qualifications/ Training
Registered nurses	2,619	582	22	1	Associate degree
Home health aides	922	461	50	4	Short-term OJT[b]
Customer service representatives	2,252	400	18	3	Moderate-term OJT
Food preparation and serving workers, including fast food	2,702	394	15	4	Short-term OJT
Personal and home care aides	817	376	46	4	Short-term OJT
Retail salespersons	4,489	375	8	4	Short-term OJT
Office clerks, general	3,024	359	12	3	Short-term OJT
Accountants and auditors	1,291	279	22	1	Bachelor's degree
Nursing aides, orderlies, attendants	1,470	276	19	3	Postsecondary vocational degree
Postsecondary teachers	1,699	257	15	1	Doctoral degree

Source: Lacey and Wright 2009.
Notes: a. Quartiles by median wage in 2008 dollars: 1 ($51,540 or more), 2 ($32,390–$51,530), 3 ($21,590–$32,380), 4 (under $21,590).
   b. On-the-job training.
As the table indicates, 2,619,000 registered nurses were employed in 2008. An additional 582,000 registered nurses were expected to be employed by 2018, a 22 percent increase.

only modest skills—home health aides, customer service, food preparation and service, personal and home care aides, retail sales, and office clerks. In fact, seven of the ten occupations that are expected to add the most new jobs by 2018 are in the lower two income quartiles, and six only require on-the-job training! Only two of the jobs require a bachelor's degree or more.

Where are the high-tech computer jobs that everyone has been talking about since the 1980s? How do we reconcile this list with the belief that most jobs these days require high levels of education? Well, let's consider another list.

Table 3.8 lists the ten *fastest-growing* jobs. Here we find seven occupations that require at least a bachelor's degree. Biomedical engineers are supposed to increase by 72 percent, and systems and data communication analysts are projected to increase by 53 percent. All seven of these college-level jobs are in the top two income quartiles. But even this list has three occupations that are in the bottom two income quartiles—home health aides, personal and home care aides, and skin care specialists.

For those who find this all confusing, let me explain. Table 3.7 identifies *large* occupations that are growing at *modest* rates. There

Table 3.8 Fastest Growing Occupations, 2008–2018

Occupational Category	Employment in 2008 (thousands)	New Jobs by 2018 (thousands)	Percent Change	Income Quartile[a]	Qualifications/ Training
Biomedical engineers	16	12	72	1	Bachelor's degree
Network systems and data communications analysts	292	156	53	1	Bachelor's degree
Home health aides	922	461	50	4	Short-term OJT[b]
Personal and home care aides	817	376	46	4	Short-term OJT
Financial examiners	27	11	41	1	Bachelor's degree
Medical scientists	109	44	40	1	Doctoral degree
Physicians assistants	75	29	39	1	Master's degree
Skin care specialists	39	15	38	3	Postsecondary vocational degree
Biochemists and biophysicists	23	9	37	1	Doctoral degree
Athletic trainers	16	6	37	3	Bachelor's degree

Source: Lacey and Wright 2009.

Notes: a. Quartiles by median wage in 2008 dollars: 1 ($51,540 or more), 2 ($32,390–$51,530), 3 ($21,590–$32,380), 4 (under $21,590).

b. On-the-job training.

As the table indicates, 16,000 biomedical engineers were employed in 2008. An additional 12,000 biomedical engineers were expected to be employed by 2018, a 72 percent increase.

were 2.6 million registered nurses employed in 2008; this number is expected to grow by 581,500 by 2018, resulting in a growth rate of 22 percent. Only 16,000 people were employed as biomedical engineers in 2008, the top job on the fastest-growing list of Table 3.8. This relatively small occupation is projected to expand by 72 percent, an increase in 11,600 jobs. The other six college-level occupations are also relatively small in number.

What does this mean? For the next decade or two, there will still be more openings for home health aides, customer service representatives, and fast food workers than for biomedical engineers, systems analysts, and financial examiners. A college degree in the right major increases one's chances of getting one of the better-paying jobs, but there are more college graduates than college-level jobs. This means that the job structure provides opportunities for upward mobility for some college graduates but also restricts these opportunities for others.

Another barrier to upward mobility is what some have called the Walmart Revolution (*Fortune* 2010). The statistics are astonishing. In 2009 Walmart's 8,500 stores had sales of $408 billion, making it the world's largest company based on sales. Ranked number one on the Fortune 500, it had higher sales than Ford (#8), J. P. Morgan Chase (#9), and Hewlett Packard (#10) combined. Walmart has higher sales than the gross domestic products of most of the world's countries. In addition, Walmart had over $14 billion in profits in 2009 and employed 2.1 million people in the United States and other countries.

The secret to Walmart's success is high volume and low labor costs, which result in low prices. Most Walmart employees work part-time with no benefits. The average wage is $11.75 an hour, below the average for retail sales workers reported by the Bureau of Labor Statistics and lower than workers at Target and Kmart. The average full-time worker at Walmart earns about $21,000 per year, which is below the poverty level for a family of four (according to www. wakeupwalmart.com). Needless to say, Walmart is aggressively antiunion. Early in the twentieth century, Henry Ford tried to keep wages low, but he understood that he had to pay his assembly-line workers sufficient wages that they could buy the cars they produced. Walmart doesn't even pay enough for a family head to provide enough food for his or her family. This is an example of economic exploitation.

Walmart has such power that it suppresses wages in the communities where it has stores. Smaller chains find it difficult to compete with Walmart, and local businesses find it almost impossible. Walmart also drives hard bargains with the manufacturers of the products it sells. By insisting on the lowest possible prices, Walmart is practically forcing manufacturers to move to China, where labor costs are extremely low. This, of course, means fewer jobs for Americans. To the extent that Walmart becomes the business model of the future, working people are going to be in trouble.

* * *

I hope that readers now feel more familiar with the current nature of class in the United States. Although we are a class-based society, we don't usually talk about class. As I stated at the beginning of this chapter, I have purposely stayed away from looking at how race, gender, and sexual orientation are intertwined with class. I made this decision because I wanted to emphasize class inequalities without getting sidetracked into a discussion of race and gender inequality. In Chapter 4, however, I will discuss race and try to show how class is integral to understanding racial conflict. I also hope to show how race is integral to understanding class conflict.

4

Race

Racial conflict and inequality is still one of the major issues facing the United States in the twenty-first century. In 1903 W. E. B. DuBois (1990, 3) wrote, "The problem of the 20th Century is the problem of the color line." This is still true in the twenty-first century.

When DuBois wrote those words, white supremacy over blacks was the main issue. In the twenty-first century, however, this bipolar model is no longer adequate. US Census Bureau (2004a) figures show that the Hispanic population has surpassed the black population and that the Asian population is growing rapidly. US Census Bureau projections suggest that sometime in the 2050s, non-Hispanic whites may cease to be the numerical majority. Most social science research has not caught up to these changing demographics and is still stuck in the bipolar model.

The nature of racial conflict has also changed over the past century. When DuBois wrote his treatise on race, there was legal segregation in the South and in many other parts of the country, and there was virtually no black political representation at the state and federal levels. Today, we have a black president, black and Hispanic Supreme Court justices, and a growing black and Hispanic middle class. Some people have argued that we are in a "postrace" society where race no longer matters.

Readers may wonder why it is necessary to talk about "non-Hispanic whites" rather than just "whites." Are there also non-Hispanic blacks or Asians? What about the mixed-race population? Before answering these and other questions, it is necessary to define some basic terms.

Terminology

Although many of us assume that we know what race means, it's really not so simple. Before proceeding, try writing out a definition and you'll find out what I mean. For the purposes of this book, a **racial group** *is a social group that is socially defined as having certain biological characteristics that set them apart from other groups, often in invidious ways.* The key aspect of this definition is that race is defined socially, not biologically.

Many people don't realize that most biologists and geneticists argue that race is not a biologically meaningful term. Of course, there are observable, biological differences between some groups of people in terms of skin color, hair texture, facial shapes, and so on. However, when one examines the genetic makeup of people from different races, there is more genetic variation within a given race than between races. In other words, the genes for skin color and for a few other observable characteristics may be different, but nearly everything else is the same.

It's also impossible to tell where one race stops and another begins. Speaking in the excellent video *Race: The Power of an Illusion* (2003), evolutionary biologist Joseph Graves Jr. puts it this way:

> If we were to only look at people in the tropics and people in Norway, we would come to the conclusion that there is a group of people who have light skin and a group of people who have dark skin. But, if we were to walk from the tropics to Norway, what we would see is a continuous change in skin tones. At no point during that trip would we be able to say, "Oh, this is the place in which we go from the dark race to the light race."

Although race is not a valid biological concept, it is still a powerful cultural concept, especially in the United States. We *think* race is important, and we *treat* people in different ways according to the race we think they belong to. In other words, we have socially constructed racial categories even though they have no biological significance. Consequently, our approaches to race are often illogical and inconsistent.

In trying to determine who is black, Americans have generally used the "one drop" rule. People are considered black if they have any black ancestors, regardless of the color of their skin. In the past, this has been encoded into law. In more recent years, it's simply part of the culture. Some light-skinned people with black ancestors can be "mistaken" for being white if no one knows the history of their family. This phenomenon of **passing** *refers to a subordinate group member who does not reveal the stigmatized status that he or she occupies.* If the secret is revealed, the person previously defined as white, for example, becomes redefined as black.

Contrast this with how Native Americans are defined through their "blood quantum." If you have a Native American mother and a white father, you are considered to be "half Indian." If one of your grandparents was a Native American and the other three were not, you are one-fourth Indian. Individual tribes can define the blood quantum level that is necessary to be a member of the tribe. This can range from being half Indian to being one-fourth Indian to simply self-identifying as Indian. In contradistinction to the one-drop rule for blacks, Native Americans have to prove that they are "Indian enough" to be a member of the tribe. The federal government requires that people be at least one-fourth Indian to qualify for programs sponsored by the Bureau of Indian Affairs.

The census data on race that I mentioned earlier are totally unscientific because they are based on people's self-identification. That is, individuals are asked to check one of the boxes in the question on race—white, black, Asian, Pacific Islander, Native American, or "Some Other Race." However, none of the boxes say "Hispanic" because the census defines being Hispanic as an ethnicity, not as a race. Respondents first are asked whether they are Hispanic and then are asked to indicate their race. This means that Hispanics can be of any race.

An **ethnic group** is defined as *a social group that has certain cultural characteristics that set them off from other groups and whose members see themselves as having a common past.* Language and culture, according to the census, are what set Hispanics off from other groups. Arab Americans would also be an ethnic group for the same reason.

This race-versus-ethnicity issue becomes both interesting and problematic in trying to answer a simple question like "What percentage of the population is white?" The top half of Table 4.1 presents the data using the five standard racial categories plus a mixed-race category. Out of the 308 million Americans in 2010, 224 million were white, which accounts for 72.4 percent of the population. Reading down the columns, we can see that 12.6 percent of the population was black, 4.8 percent was Asian, 0.9 percent was Native American, 0.2 percent was Pacific Islanders, 6.2 percent was some other race, and

**Table 4.1 Two Views of the Race/Ethnic Distribution of the
US Population, 2010**

Racial Group Plus Hispanics	Number (millions)	Percent Distribution
Whites	223.6	72.4
Blacks	38.9	12.6
American Indians/Alaska Natives	2.9	0.9
Asian	14.7	4.8
Native Hawaiian/Pacific Islanders	0.5	0.2
Some other race	19.1	6.2
Two or more races	9.0	2.9
Hispanic[a]	50.5	16.3
Total	359.2	116.3

Race/Ethnic Group		
Non-Hispanics		
Whites	196.8	63.8
Blacks	37.7	12.2
American Indians/Alaska Natives	2.2	0.7
Asian	14.5	4.7
Native Hawaiian/Pacific Islanders	0.5	0.1
Some other race	0.6	0.2
Two or more races	6.0	1.9
Hispanic[a]	50.5	16.4
Total	308.8	100.0

Source: US Census Bureau 2011.

Note: a. Hispanics can be of any race.

2.9 percent was mixed race. In addition, 16.4 percent of the population was Hispanic. If all these numbers are added together, they come out to 116.3 percent, and the total population comes to 359.2 million! What's going on here? The problem is that because Hispanics can be of any race, they are counted twice. A white Hispanic would be counted once as a white and once as a Hispanic. The categories are not mutually exclusive.

A second way to answer the question can be found in the bottom half of Table 4.1, which separates Hispanics and non-Hispanics. In this case, there are 196.8 million non-Hispanic whites, accounting for 63.8 percent of the population. The white category thus lost 26.8 million people who were placed in the Hispanic category. The black category also fell by 1.2 million. The total non-Hispanic population is 258.3 million, or 83.6 percent of the population. The Hispanic number (50.5 million, or 16.4 percent) is the same in both halves of the table. Most Hispanics are white, although others are from different races. This time, the total adds up to 308.8 million and 100 percent. The categories in the lower half of Table 4.1 are mutually exclusive in that everyone is only counted once.

So, are whites 72.4 percent of the population, or 63.8 percent of the population? Actually, both are correct. If ethnicity is ignored and all those who check the white box are counted, whites are 72.4 percent of the population. If only whites who are not also Hispanics are counted, non-Hispanic whites are 63.8 percent of the population. Sometimes federal officials use one number, and sometimes they use the other.

I will use the "non-Hispanic white" category when the data are available because it makes it easier to see the advantages that non-Hispanic whites have in terms of income, occupation, and education. The gaps between non-Hispanic whites and people of color are usually larger than the gaps between all whites and people of color.

But wait, there's more. Remember the "some other race" category? In the 2010 census, 39 percent of Hispanics checked this box because they didn't think they fit into any of the standard race categories. In fact, most people who check "some other race" are Hispanic. This really upset census officials. Because some government agencies use the Modified Age/Race and Sex File (MARS), which doesn't include the "other" category, census officials must reassign those who select "some other race" to one of the standard categories. This creates many errors as well as a lot of extra work. In order to "encourage" Hispanics to select one of the standard racial categories, census officials considered eliminating the "some other race" category for the 2010 census. This, in turn, provoked the following comment from Carlos Chardon, chair of the Census Bureau's Hispanic Advisory Committee: "We don't fit into the categories that the Anglos want us to fit in. The census is trying to create a reality that doesn't exist" (Swarns 2004, A18). In the 2010 census, people still were able to check the "some other race" option.

Prior to the 2000 census, there was a big controversy over how to deal with mixed-race people. For example, professional golfer Tiger Woods is usually described as black even though he is half Asian. After the conservative southern senator Strom Thurmond died in 2003, a dark-skinned woman revealed that she was his daughter. In his youth, Thurmond fathered a daughter by having a relationship with one of his black servants. The daughter, however, is always described as black even though she is half white. The same is true for President Obama.

In previous years, a person who is half Asian and half Native American had to select only one box. Some biracial people argued for a separate "mixed race" category on the 2000 census because those from more than one racial background share a variety of similar issues. The final decision, however, was to allow people to check more than one box. In fact, 1.5 million Americans made that choice. The issue of allowing a mixed-race box versus a multiple-race one had absolutely nothing to do with biology.

In addition to language and national origin, an ethnic group can be characterized by religion, especially if it is not the dominant religion. The 7.5 million Muslims in the United States can be referred to as an ethnic group. It is important not to equate being Muslim with being Arab. The Arabic language and culture are very prevalent in North Africa and the Middle East, although Iran and Turkey are not Arab countries. The dominant language in Iran is Farsi, and the dominant language in Turkey is Turkish. However, these two countries are Muslim countries in terms of their dominant religion.

There are about 1.6 billion Muslims in the world, most of whom are not Arabs. There are over 358 million Arabs in the world, most of whom are Muslim. To make matters even more confusing, half of the 3.5 million Arab Americans are Christian. On top of that, the census defines people from North Africa as white!

Jewish Americans are also an ethnic group, although there are important cultural differences among them. Ashkenazi Jews originally came from central and eastern Europe whereas Sephardic Jews came from Spain and Northern Africa. The vernacular language for Ashkenazi Jews was Yiddish, and the vernacular for Sephardic Jews was Ladino. There are also differences in rituals and holiday celebrations.

Most Jews say they are religious and belong to one of the four major denominations—orthodox, conservative, reform, and reconstructionist. However, there are also many people who define themselves as Jews culturally but who are not religious. In fact, 80 percent of Jews in Israel are secular. In the United States, there are two national secular Jewish organizations—the Congress of Secular Jewish Organizations and the Society for Humanist Judaism (Seid 2001).

Technically, Protestants and Catholics are also ethnic groups by virtue of their religions, but they are not usually referred to this way because Christianity is the dominant religion in the United States. Ethnicity usually refers to groups that are culturally different from the dominant group or groups.

Now we get to the really big concept—racism. Believe it or not, there is no commonly accepted definition of this widely used term. Some social scientists use the term synonymously with *prejudice* in terms of one person having a negative attitude about someone from another group. Others see racism as the same thing as *discrimination* (i.e., differential treatment). In an often-cited article, Bob Blauner (1992) argues that there are at least four additional uses of the term.

The most useful definition of **racism** is *a system of oppression based on race*. According to this view, racism involves the power of one group to oppress another group. Racism, then, is systemic; it doesn't just exist in the minds of individuals. Joe Feagin (2000, 6), for example, states, "Systemic racism includes the complex array of antiblack practices, the unjustly gained political-economic power of whites, the continuing economic and other resource inequalities along racial lines, and the white racist ideologies and attitudes created to maintain and rationalize white privilege and power."

Although this definition of racism may seem straightforward, it has some important and controversial implications. Because racism involves power and oppression, it follows that only the dominant group can be racist. In the United States, this means that only whites can be racist. People of color cannot be racist because they don't have the power. Many whites strenuously object to this argument and say, "I know plenty of people of color who hate whites." True enough, there are people of color who are *prejudiced*. However, people of color are not *racist* because they lack the collective power to oppress whites as a group.

Others have argued that "all whites are racist." If what is meant by this statement is that all whites are prejudiced, this is certainly not the case, as we will discuss shortly. If what is meant is that all whites discriminate against people of color, this is also not the case. Many whites don't have the power to discriminate. If, however, what is meant is that all whites participate in an oppressive system that benefits them, this comes closer to the truth. One group of whites who are committed to fighting against white racism goes so far as to describe themselves as "antiracist racists" rather than "nonracists." They agree with the argument that all whites are racist in that they participate in a racist system, but they see themselves as trying to fight for a more equal world (O'Brien 2001). We will discuss these issues in the rest of this chapter.

Finally, there is the issue of what terminology to use when referring to different race and ethnic groups. Once again, there is no scientific answer here. The issue of "labels" is a contentious one that changes over time. It also involves how groups are labeled by outsiders versus how groups refer to themselves. In attempts to politically mobilize, subordinate groups often adopt new labels.

At various times in American history, it was considered appropriate by both blacks and whites to call blacks "colored" or "Negro." The National Association for the Advancement of Colored People (NAACP) was founded as an integrated antiracist organization in 1909. Martin Luther King Jr. used *Negro* in most of his speeches. Blacks in general do not like these terms today. In the 1960s, the term *black* replaced *Negro*. That was followed by *Afro-American* and *African American*. A 2007 poll of black Americans showed that 13 percent preferred "black," 24 percent preferred "African American," and 61 percent said that either term was acceptable (Newport 2007).

Some blacks from Africa and the Caribbean prefer to call themselves Nigerian, Kenyan, Haitian, or Jamaican. In addition to reflecting their country of origin, these labels can be an attempt to shield themselves from the racism experienced by American-born blacks. African and Caribbean blacks sometimes cultivate their distinctive accents in order to make themselves more attractive to potential employers who may discriminate against American-born blacks. Although this strategy may have some short-term positive impact, the American-born children of immigrants usually lose their accents and are seen as black.

What about pejorative terms such as *nigger*, *chink*, and *spic*? On the one hand, *nigger* has been such a powerful negative term throughout American history that many whites and blacks can't even say it out loud. Instead, they talk about "the n-word." On the other hand, some blacks use the term *nigga* to refer approvingly to each other but would consider it offensive if whites used the same term. This is an example of a subordinate group taking a term of approbation and turning it on its head. Although this may be confusing to whites, the safest thing is to stay away from *nigger* and *nigga*, as well as any other pejorative racial terms (Akom 2000).

The term *Hispanic* was adopted by Congress in the 1970s to categorize a diverse set of people who share a common language.

Previously, this population usually referred to themselves by their country of origin; for example, Cuban, Guatemalan, or Colombian. *Latino*, a term preferred by some political activists, also refers to Spanish-heritage populations. In a 1995 study (Infoplease 2004), 58 percent of those surveyed preferred "Hispanic," 12 percent preferred "Spanish origin," and 12 percent preferred "Latino." In a 2000 study of registered voters, 65 percent chose "Hispanic" and 30 percent chose "Latino" (Granados 2000). In the southwestern United States, Mexican Americans sometimes refer to themselves as "Chicano."

The terms *Native American* and *American Indian* are both used to describe people who are descendants of indigenous people. In the same 1995 study, half preferred "American Indian," and 37 percent preferred "Native American."

Prior to the 1960s, most people from Asia and the Pacific Islands referred to themselves by their or their ancestors' country of origin. During the 1960s, however, Asian student activists started promoting the term *Asian* as a way of unifying people for political purposes (Espiritu 1992). The 1995 study discussed earlier did not mention Asians. It did, however, ask what whites like to be called. Sixty-two percent said "white," and 17 percent said "Caucasian."

This issue of labeling may seem trivial and arbitrary to members of dominant groups, but it's not. Often, when a subordinate group is beginning to mobilize to fight oppression, the ability to label itself is part of the process. When the Black Power movement split off from the civil rights movement in the 1960s, for example, activists insisted on being called "black" rather than "Negro."

Descriptive Statistics

Virtually all the data collected by the federal government show substantial economic inequalities between whites and people of color. People are counted as unemployed if they don't have a job and are actively looking for work. Being in the labor force means that you are working or you are looking for work. Discouraged workers are not counted because they are viewed as having dropped out of the labor force. The unemployment rate is calculated as follows:

$$\frac{\text{no. looking for work}}{\text{no. working} + \text{no. looking for work}} = \% \text{ unemployed}$$

Table 4.2 shows that unemployment rates in 2009 were substantially higher for blacks and Hispanics (14.8 percent and 12.1 percent, respectively) than for whites and Asians (8.5 percent and 7.3 percent, respectively). This same trend is true for both males and females. The black unemployment rate is 1.7 times as high as the white rate, a somewhat lower black/white gap than has existed in the past. The irony is that although the black unemployment rate is skyrocketing, the gap with whites might be diminishing somewhat.

One common explanation for the difference between whites and Asians, on the one hand, and blacks and Hispanics, on the other hand, looks to education. Because low education leads to high unemployment and because blacks and Hispanics have lower levels of education than whites and Asians, the argument goes, it's not unreasonable to expect that there should be differences in unemployment. An extension of this argument is that at the same level of education, unemployment rates for whites, blacks, Asians, and Hispanics should be the same.

Table 4.3 allows us to examine this argument. By reading across the first four rows, it is clear that for each racial group, unemployment rates tend to decline as education increases. This is consistent with the argument that educational differences can explain racial differences in unemployment.

However, by reading down each column, it is also clear that at all but two levels of education, whites are less likely to be unemployed than people of color. At the bachelor's degree and above level, for example,

Table 4.2 Unemployment Rates for Sixteen-Year-Olds and Older in 2009 by Race, Spanish Origin, and Gender (percentage)

Race/Spanish Origin	Male	Female	Total
White	9.4	7.3	8.5
Black	17.5	12.4	14.8
Asian	7.4	6.6	7.3
Hispanic	12.5	11.5	12.1
Black/white	1.9	1.7	1.7
Asian/white	0.8	0.9	0.9
Hispanic/white	1.3	1.6	1.4

Source: www.bls.gov/cps.
Note: As the table indicates, 9.4 percent of white males were unemployed in 2009. The black male unemployment rate was 1.9 times higher than the white male rate.

Table 4.3 Unemployment Rates of Twenty-Five-Year-Olds and Older in 2009 by Race, Spanish Origin, and Education (percentage)

Race/Spanish Origin	Didn't Finish High School	High School Graduate	Some College, No Degree	Associate Degree	Bachelor's Degree or Higher
White	13.9	9.0	7.9	6.2	4.2
Black	21.3	14.0	12.1	10.3	7.3
Asian	8.4	7.5	8.9	7.5	5.6
Hispanic	13.7	10.4	9.6	8.5	5.7
Unemployment ratio					
Black/white	1.5	1.6	1.5	1.7	1.7
Asian/white	0.6	0.8	1.1	1.2	1.3
Hispanic/white	1.0	1.2	1.2	1.4	1.4

Source: www.bls.gov/cpshome.
Note: As the table indicates, 21.3 percent of blacks who didn't finish high school were unemployed; among those who didn't finish high school, the black unemployment rate was 1.5 times higher than the white rate.

blacks are 1.7 times as likely to be unemployed as whites. Hispanics and even Asians at this level are more likely to be unemployed than whites. At best, educational differences can only explain part of the racial differences in unemployment.

There are also important racial differences in the kinds of jobs people have. Table 4.4 looks at the distribution of different occupational categories in the United States. The best-paying and most skilled jobs are in the management and professional categories. Whereas 38 percent of whites and 49 percent of Asians are in these two categories, only 29 percent of blacks and 19 percent of Hispanics are managers or professionals. In the lower-paid, lower-skilled service category, in contrast, we find only 16 percent of white workers and 17 percent of Asians, compared to 25 percent of black workers and 26 percent of Hispanics. Clearly, Asians and whites are much more likely to have higher-paying jobs than are blacks and Hispanics.

Given these data, it is not unreasonable to expect that incomes for blacks and Hispanics would be substantially lower than incomes for whites and Asians. The first column of Table 4.5 looks at the median incomes for all families. As predicted, black and Hispanic families earned less than 60 percent of the income of white families in 2009.

Table 4.4 Employed Persons in 2009 by Occupation, Race, and Spanish Origin (percentage)

Occupational Category	White	Black	Hispanic	Asian
Management, business	16.2	10.1	8.4	15.9
Professional	21.8	19.1	11.1	33.0
Sales	11.4	10.0	9.5	11.3
Administrative support, office	12.8	15.3	11.8	9.9
Construction, extraction	5.8	3.0	10.8	1.5
Installation, maintenance, repair	3.7	2.8	3.7	2.3
Production	5.4	5.9	8.5	5.6
Transportation	5.7	8.5	8.5	3.3
Service	16.5	25.2	25.8	17.0
Farming, forestry, fishing	0.7	0.3	1.9	0.2
Total	100	100	100	100

Source: US Bureau of Labor Statistics 2010.
Note: The table indicates, e.g., that 33 percent of Asian workers were professionals but only 11.1 percent of Hispanics were professionals.

Table 4.5 Median Income of Families and Income Ratio in 2009 by Race/Ethnicity and Family Type

Race/Ethnicity	All Families	Married Couples	Male Head	Female Head
White, non-Hispanic	$67,341	$76,103	$45,803	$34,320
Black	38,409	61,360	32,415	24,963
Asian	75,027	82,958	52,483	49,966
Hispanic	39,370	47,728	37,216	24,827
Income ratio				
Black/white	0.58	0.81	0.71	0.73
Asian/white	1.14	1.09	1.15	1.09
Hispanic/white	0.59	0.63	0.81	0.72

Source: US Census Bureau 2010b.
Note: As the table indicates, white families had a median income of $67,341, and black families had a median income of $38,409; therefore, the median income of black families was 58 percent of the median income of white families.

Unfortunately, the black/white family income gap has been fairly stable since 1959.

Asian families, in comparison, make slightly *more* than white families. However, it is important to understand the great variation among

Asian families. According to the 2000 census, Japanese and Asian Indian families had median incomes of almost $71,000. Hmong and
Cambodian families had median incomes of only $32,384 and $35,621,
respectively (Watanabe and Wride 2004).

In trying to explain these income differences, many analysts point
to differences in family structure. The percentage of female-headed
families (i.e., a female adult plus children with no male living regularly in the home) is much higher among blacks than whites. In 2009,
for example, 33.7 percent of blacks were living in families headed by
women, compared to 21.1 percent of Hispanics, 12 percent of whites,
and 9.7 percent of Asians (US Census Bureau 2010a). Female-headed
families have much lower incomes than either male-headed families
(where there is no woman regularly living in the home) or married-
couple families where either one or both of the adults work.

The data in columns two, three, and four in Table 4.5 control for
type of family. Reading across the rows, married-couple families in
each race/ethnic group earn more than male-headed families, who, in
turn, earn more than female-headed families. Reading down the
columns, the black/white family income gap for married couples declines relative to all families, although it is still substantial. Black married couples earn 81 percent of the income of white married couples,
compared to the 58 percent figure for all families. The Asian/white
and Hispanic/white income gaps are not heavily impacted by comparing all families with married-couple families. Presumably, differences in the occupational distributions and the unemployment rates
contribute to these family income differences. It is also important to
note that Asian families earn more than white families in each family
type, in part because Asian families tend to have more workers.

These same group differences can also be seen by looking at the
incomes of year-round full-time workers in 2009. Table 4.6 shows
that the white median incomes are higher than the incomes of blacks
and Hispanics but lower than the incomes of Asians. Among men,
Hispanics in 2009 made only 60 percent of the income of whites.
Black males made 75 percent of the income of whites. Asians, in contrast, made 111 percent of the income of whites. A similar pattern
occurs with racial differences in the incomes of women, though the
racial gap for women was smaller than the racial gap for men. Asian
women actually had higher incomes in 2003 than white women.

Table 4.6 also shows the gender gaps in income within a given
race. The female-to-male income gap was highest among whites (0.77)
and was lowest among Hispanics (0.88), with blacks and Asians falling
in the middle. In other words, among non-Hispanic whites, women

Table 4.6 Median Income and Income Ratio of Year-Round Full-Time Workers, Aged Fifteen and Older, in 2009, by Race/Ethnicity and Sex

Race/Ethnicity	Male	Female	Male/Female Income Ratio
White, non-Hispanic	$52,469	$40,265	0.77
Black	39,362	32,470	0.82
Asian	53,428	44,627	0.83
Hispanic	31,638	27,883	0.88
All Workers	49,164	37,234	0.76
Income ratio			
Black/white	0.75	0.81	
Asian/white	1.11	1.11	
Hispanic/white	0.60	0.69	

Source: US Census Bureau 2010b.
Note: As the table indicates, the median income for white non-Hispanic females was $40,265, which is 77 percent of the income of white men. Black women made 81 percent of the income of white women.

earn only 77 cents for each dollar a man earns; but Hispanic women earn 88 cents for each dollar that a Hispanic male earns. We will discuss gender differences in more detail in the following chapter.

We can also look at the trends in racial income gaps over time, as illustrated in Table 4.7. Looking at the income ratio for blacks relative to whites, we can see that the income gap between black and white men closed slightly from 1967 to 2000, although it seems to be getting larger again. In contrast, the income gap between Hispanic and white men actually steadily increased between the early 1970s and 2009. The gap between Asian and white men has reversed, so that Asian men are now earning more than white men.

Looking at women, the black/white income gap declined substantially between 1967 and 1980 but then began to increase once again. The Hispanic/white gap for women, like that for men, has grown since the early 1970s. Asian women, however, continue to earn slightly more than white women. The income trends for black and Hispanic women are not encouraging.

There are also differences in poverty rates. In 2009, 9.4 percent of non-Hispanic whites were poor, compared with 25.8 percent of blacks, 25.3 percent of Hispanics, and 12.5 percent of Asians. In spite of these important differences in poverty rates, there were more poor

Table 4.7 Median Income and Income Ratio of Year-Round Full-Time Workers, 1967-2009, by Race/Ethnicity and Gender

Year	Median Income				Income Ratios		
	Non-Hispanic White	Black	Hispanic	Asian	Black/ White	Hispanic/ White	Asian/ White
Males							
1967	$7,396	$4,777	—	—	0.65	—	—
1970	9,223	6,368	8,885[a]	—	0.69	0.73[a]	—
1980	19,157	13,547	13,558	—	0.71	0.71	—
1990	28,881	21,114	19,136	26,765	0.73	0.66	0.93
2000	38,637	30,101	23,778	40,556	0.78	0.62	1.05
2009	52,469	39,362	31,638	53,428	0.75	0.60	1.11
Females							
1967	4,279	3,194	—	—	0.75	—	—
1970	5,412	4,447	5,925[a]	—	0.82	0.84[a]	—
1980	11,277	10,672	9,679	—	0.95	0.86	—
1990	20,048	18,040	15,672	21,324	0.90	0.78	1.06
2000	28,243	25,089	20,659	30,475	0.89	0.73	1.08
2009	40,265	32,470	27,883	44,627	0.81	0.69	1.11

Source: US Census Bureau 2010b.
Notes: a. Based on 1974 data.
As the table indicates, in 2009, the black male median income ($39,362) was 75% of the white male median income ($52,469).

non-Hispanic whites (18.5 million) than poor blacks (9.9 million) or poor Hispanics (12.4 million). The reason for this apparent contradiction is that non-Hispanic whites make up such a large percentage of the total population. Even though their rate of poverty is relatively low, the absolute number of poor non-Hispanic whites is very large (www.census.gov/hhes/www/poverty/poverty04/table3.pdf).

Racial differences in wealth are even more unequal than the differences in income. Table 4.8 shows that in 2007, white households had a median net worth of $170,400, compared to only $21,000 for Hispanics and $17,100 for blacks. This means that Hispanics' net worth is only 12 percent that of whites and that blacks' net worth is only 10 percent that of whites. In 2004, Asian net worth ($107,690) was higher than that of whites in the same year.

Comparing wealth differences over time is often problematic because methodologies are not always the same. However, using government figures for 1984 and 2007, there are virtually no changes

Table 4.8 Median Net Worth of Households in 1984 and 2007 by Race/Ethnicity

Race/Ethnicity	1984		2007	
	Net Worth	Wealth Ratio[a]	Net Worth	Wealth Ratio[a]
White	$38,915	—	$170,400	—
Black	3,342	0.09	17,100	0.10
Hispanic	4,871	0.13	21,000	0.12
Asian	—	—	107,690[b]	—

Sources: Shapiro, Meschede, and Sullivan 2010.

Notes: a. Black or Hispanic wealth relative to white wealth. In 2007, for example, the median black wealth was only 10 percent of the median white wealth.

b. 2004 data.

in the wealth ratios. Although everyone had more wealth in 2007, the relative differences between the groups stayed about the same.

There are also major differences in educational attainment by race and ethnicity. Table 4.9 shows that more than half of Asians had a bachelor's degree or higher in 2009. Only one-third of non-Hispanic whites, one-fifth of blacks, and one-seventh of Hispanics had bachelor's degrees or higher. At the other end of the spectrum, 38 percent of Hispanics did not finish high school, compared with 16 percent of blacks, 12 percent of Asians, and 8 percent of non-Hispanic whites.

Once again, there are great variations among different Asian groups. According to the 2000 census, 63.9 percent of Asian Indians had bachelor's degrees or higher. However, less than 10 percent of Cambodians, Hmongs, and Laotians had bachelor's degrees or higher (Watanabe and Wride 2004).

It is also important to look at trends in educational attainment. Data from the Department of Education show that the black/white gap in education has declined substantially since the 1940s. The Hispanic/white gap, in comparison, has increased slightly since 1980. The Department of Education doesn't track these data for Asians.

Some of the racial gap in income can probably be explained by differences in education. What would happen if we control for education and then look at racial differences in income? These data are presented in Table 4.10. Reading down the columns, we see that for

Table 4.9 Educational Attainment of the US Population Twenty-Five Years Old and Older in 2009 by Race/Ethnicity (percentage)

Highest Level of Education Reached	Race/Ethnicity			
	Non-Hispanic White	Black	Hispanic	Asian
Eighth grade or less	2.5	4.3	22.1	6.9
Some high school	5.8	11.7	16.0	4.9
High school graduate	31.5	35.4	29.3	19.4
Some college	17.6	20.3	13.3	9.8
Associate degree	9.7	9.0	6.1	6.6
Bachelor's degree	21.0	12.7	9.6	31.6
Master's degree	8.6	5.3	2.5	13.7
PhD	1.5	0.6	0.4	3.8
Professional degree	1.8	0.7	0.7	3.1
Total	100	100	100	100

Source: Chronicle of Higher Education 2010.
Note: As the table indicates, 6.9 percent of Asians and 22.1 percent of Hispanics didn't go beyond the eighth grade.

each race/ethnic group, a higher level of education results in higher incomes. This is true for both males and females.

Reading across the rows, it is possible to compare each race/ethnic group at the same level of education. Among males, non-Hispanic whites have higher incomes than men of color at the same educational level in all cases but two. For men with bachelor's degrees but no advanced degrees, for example, blacks made 78 percent the income of whites, Asians made 91 percent the income of whites, and Hispanics made 85 percent the income of whites. Asians with master's or first professional degrees have higher incomes than whites.

The data for women are similar. After controlling for education, white women had higher incomes than women of color in all cases but two. Once again, Asian women are shown to be the closest to having income parity with white women and in two cases even exceed the income of white women. It is also important to note that after controlling for education, women in each race/ethnic group earn lower incomes than comparable men. We will return to this issue in the next chapter.

Table 4.10 Median Income of Year-Round Full-Time Workers in 2009 by Race/Ethnicity, Sex, and Education

Education/Sex	Median Income by Sex and Race/Ethnicity				Income Ratios (comparison with white non-Hispanics)		
	White, Non-Hispanic	Black	Asian	Hispanic	Black/White Non-Hispanics	Asian/White Non-Hispanics	Hispanics/White Non-Hispanics
Males							
Some high school	$32,560	$26,524	$23,737	$25,096	0.81	0.73	0.77
High school graduate	41,714	32,325	32,291	31,668	0.77	0.77	0.76
Some college	50,360	40,138	42,129	41,274	0.80	0.84	0.82
Associate degree	51,460	41,797	46,074	42,348	0.81	0.90	0.82
Bachelor's degree	66,065	51,504	60,044	55,867	0.78	0.91	0.85
Master's degree	80,362	61,101	89,472	72,180	0.76	1.11	0.90
PhD	101,050	—	98,530	—	—	0.98	—
First professional degree	123,792	—	150,125	—	—	1.21	—
Females							
Some high school	21,917	22,298	—	20,038	1.01	—	0.91
High school graduate	30,539	26,843	27,266	25,768	0.88	0.89	0.84
Some college	35,432	31,724	35,002	31,566	0.90	0.99	0.89
Associate degree	39,784	31,936	38,089	31,794	0.80	0.98	0.80
Bachelor's degree	46,863	46,224	51,089	44,085	0.99	1.09	0.94
Master's degree	61,034	55,875	72,415	55,187	0.91	1.18	0.90
PhD	76,551	—	—	—	—	—	—
First professional degree	86,620	—	—	—	—	—	—

Source: US Census Bureau 2010b.

These data show continuing inequalities between whites and non-Asian people of color. In spite of some dramatic closing of the gap in educational attainment and some minor improvements in the income gap, economic inequality remains substantial. Asians have exceeded whites in educational attainment and have come the closest to having parity with whites in terms of income. There is still a lot of work to be done.

Attitudes and Ideology

There has been a long tradition in the fields of sociology and social psychology of studying racial prejudice. Until very recently, most of the studies addressed the issue of white prejudice toward blacks. Because this is part of a single chapter in a small book, I will focus on the black-white issue.

Traditional Prejudice

Most social scientists recognize that prejudice today is not the same as it was one hundred years ago or even fifty years ago. The *traditional prejudice* of the past focused on beliefs of black biological inferiority and the support of formal racial separation/segregation. Typical measures of traditional prejudice might have asked respondents to agree or disagree with the following statements:

"There should be laws against racial intermarriage."
"Blacks and whites should not attend the same schools."
"As a race, blacks are less intelligent than whites."

Most of us would acknowledge that agreeing with these statements would indicate that the respondent was prejudiced.

Most studies have shown that whereas a majority of whites would have agreed with these statements in the 1960s, only a small percentage still agreed with them after the 1960s. For example, in 1958 marriage between blacks and whites was disapproved of by 94 percent of whites; only 4 percent approved. In 2007, only 19 percent disapproved, and 75 percent approved (Carroll 2007). The same trend has been shown with many studies of racial stereotypes.

There are several different interpretations of these findings. On the one hand, it's possible that traditional prejudice among the white population has, indeed, declined dramatically. Members of white supremacist groups like the Ku Klux Klan and neo-Nazis, of course, would be the exception. On the other hand, it's possible that whites still believe these things but won't say so to an interviewer because it is no longer the socially desirable response. Although social desirability is an important factor, I think that most whites in the twenty-first century tend to see traditional prejudice as outdated and abhorrent.

New Prejudice

Many whites hold other negative and/or distorted attitudes toward blacks and other people of color. Consider these results from a 2009 national survey of white adults by the Pew Research Center (2010, 41–42). Respondents were asked to explain why "black people can't get ahead." Seventy percent said that blacks "were mostly responsible for their own condition," and only 15 percent said that it was due to racial discrimination. This is a classic "blame the victim" response. In the same study, 54 percent of whites said "Our country has made the necessary changes needed to give blacks equal rights with whites," but only 35 percent said the country "needs to continue making changes."

Many social scientists argue that since the 1970s, a new form of antiblack prejudice has replaced the traditional form. This *new prejudice* (often referred to as *new racism*) goes under a variety of different labels—symbolic racism, modern racism, aversive racism, laissez-faire racism, color-blind racism, and social dominance orientation (Jones 1997; Feagin 2010). Although there are some differences between them, the discussions of the new prejudice have certain factors in common:

1. A rejection of traditional prejudice and seeing oneself as non-prejudiced.
2. A rejection of legal discrimination.
3. The belief that racial discrimination is a thing of the past.
4. The belief that black culture causes black inequality.
5. A negative attitude toward blacks based on fear, resentment, and/or ambivalence, which is usually expressed indirectly.

Measures of the new prejudice might include the following statements:

"Blacks are getting too demanding in their push for equal rights."
"Discrimination against blacks is no longer a problem."
"Over the past few years, the government and the news media
have shown more respect to blacks than they deserve."
"Blacks would be more successful if they worked harder."

Agreement with these questions would indicate prejudice, and disagreement would indicate nonprejudice. Using these questions, a
substantial proportion of whites would score high on measures of the
new prejudice. Several studies have shown that those scoring high on
new prejudice also tend to oppose government programs intended to
promote racial equality, such as busing to achieve school integration,
affirmative action in hiring, and vigorous enforcement of civil rights
laws. Social scientists who believe this to be a valid concept argue that
the new prejudice is neither better nor worse than traditional prejudice; it's just different.

Some social scientists, especially conservatives, reject the idea
that there is a new prejudice. Traditional prejudice is the only valid
type of prejudice, according to conservatives, and that has diminished
(Sneiderman and Carmines 1997). They also see the new prejudice
concept as a misguided liberal attempt to equate conservative ideology with antiblack attitudes (Roth 1994). According to this argument,
it is possible to oppose policies like affirmative action for philosophical and political reasons without being prejudiced.

Implicit Prejudice

Still other social scientists argue that due to the growing social norms
against being prejudiced, many whites are not even aware that they
hold prejudiced beliefs. *Implicit prejudice* refers to prejudiced beliefs
that are unconscious and, therefore, not measurable by traditional in-
terviews or questionnaires. Several measures, using electronics and
computers, have been developed to measure these unconscious beliefs;
though they are too complicated to be discussed here, readers can go
to www.implicit.harvard.edu on the Internet and take the Implicit Association Test themselves.

Regardless of the type of prejudice we are discussing, most social
scientists would agree that prejudice involves a set of negative attitudes held by individuals. People learn these attitudes from their
families, their peer groups, the media, the schools, and other social

institutions. Social psychologists have also argued that racial prejudice serves certain personality functions among white individuals. Given this approach, these negative attitudes would predispose people to discriminate against and/or to reject policies that might benefit the black community. Because the prejudiced attitudes are an important cause of the discriminatory behavior and policies, according to this view, if one could change the individual attitudes, it would be easier to change social policies.

Racist Ideology

Eduardo Bonilla-Silva (2003, 2) takes a somewhat different approach by arguing that negative racial views are part of a **racial ideology** that is used to explain and justify racial oppression. This ideology, which he calls *color-blind racism*, consists of four frames (i.e., "set paths for interpreting information.") The *minimalism frame* (racism is no longer important) and the *cultural racism frame* (cultural explanations of inequality, like blaming the victim) are consistent with the various approaches to the new prejudice discussed above. He also discusses the *naturalization frame*, which is the belief that "birds of a feather flock together" because of common interests and values. Finally, he discusses the *abstract liberalism frame* that makes use of the themes of equal opportunity, individualism, and free choice. This last frame, according to Bonilla-Silva, ignores the reality that all races do not have the same access to equal opportunity and free choice. This ideology

> explains contemporary racial inequality as the outcome of nonracial dynamics. Whereas Jim Crow racism [in the South before the 1960s] explained blacks' social standing as the result of their biological and moral inferiority, color-blind racism avoids such facile arguments. Instead, whites rationalize minorities' contemporary status as the product of market dynamics, naturally occurring phenomena, and blacks' imputed cultural limitations. For instance, whites can attribute Latinos' high poverty rate to a relaxed work ethic ("the Hispanics are *mañana, mañana, mañana*—tomorrow, tomorrow, tomorrow") or residential segregation as the result of natural tendencies among groups ("Do a cat and a dog mix?").

In other words, Bonilla-Silva argues that color-blind racial ideology is not the *cause* of racial inequality but the *result* or justification of inequality (also see Feagin 2010).

Although scholars continue to debate the strengths and weakness of these various approaches toward understanding negative attitudes toward people of color, I think that the "new prejudice" and "racist ideology" approaches will emerge to be the most fruitful. The new prejudice is more consistent with twenty-first century realities than traditional prejudice. Color-blind racist ideology is part of the structure of the current century's racial oppression.

Discrimination

In spite of what many white Americans might think, discrimination is not a thing of the past. Previously, I defined discrimination as actions that deny equal treatment to persons believed to be members of some racial category or group. As I have shown in the previous section, most white Americans no longer see racial discrimination as a serious problem. They typically point to the demise of legal segregation in the South and the passage of numerous civil rights legislations at the federal, state, and local levels.

Although it is certainly true that substantial progress has been made in the past half-century, racial discrimination is still alive and well. At the individual level, discrimination refers to the behavior of members of one racial group or category that is intended to have a differential and/or harmful effect on members of another racial group or category. These discriminatory actions can range from racial slurs and graffiti, to not being hired or being unfairly fired, to not being able to rent an apartment or secure a home mortgage, to being physically assaulted. It is difficult to quantify these individual-level actions.

Studies of college campuses, for example, suggest that as many as one in four students of color experiences an ethnoviolent act on campus in a given academic year (Ehrlich 1999). **Ethnoviolence** refers to *acts motivated by prejudice intending to do physical or psychological harm because of group membership.* Most ethnoviolent acts involve name-calling and graffiti, though a small percentage involve physical violence. With more than four million students of color in the nation's colleges and universities, as many as one million college students may be victimized on campus in any given year. The Southern Poverty Law Center (2004) puts this estimate at more than 500,000 annually.

These actions are almost certainly more common in public spaces off campus (Feagin 1991). According to Federal Bureau of Investigation

(2009) statistics, 3,992 race-based hate crimes were reported to the police in 2008. Of this number, 2,876 were antiblack, 716 were anti-white, 137 were anti-Asian, and 54 were anti–Native American. In addition, 894 hate crimes were based on ethnicity or national origin, with 561 being anti-Hispanic. Finally, 1,519 hate crimes were based on religion—1,013 against Jews and 105 against Muslims.

Most social scientists would agree that these figures represent a small fraction of the hate crimes committed that year, because most victims don't report them to the police and because local police are inconsistent about reporting to the FBI. The Southern Poverty Law Center (2004), for example, estimates that the true number of hate crimes is fifteen times higher than the official reports.

Similarly, it is impossible to determine the true number of cases of employment discrimination experienced by people of color. In the four-year period of 2006–2009, more than 250,000 complaints alleging race discrimination in employment were filed with the federal Equal Employment Opportunity Commission (EEOC 2010f). Hundreds of thousands more were filed at the state level. The overwhelming majority of these cases were filed by persons of color.

Proving that you have been victimized by employment discrimination is extremely difficult, either at the EEOC level or in a court of law. My own research suggests that the EEOC rules in favor of the complainant in race discrimination cases in only 12 percent of the cases (Pincus 2003). Of the 111,000 complaints that were resolved between 2006 and 2009, the EEOC ruled in favor of the complainant in only 22,000 cases—about 19 percent of the total resolutions. This means that four-fifths of the discrimination complaints were unsuccessful.

Two additional studies, however, suggest that employment discrimination is much more widespread. Devah Pager (2003) sent out fictitious résumés that listed the applicant's race to employers in and around Milwaukee, Wisconsin. Half were from blacks and half from whites. Within each racial group, half had criminal records and the other half did not. Other than race and criminal record, the résumés were comparable. The main variable was whether the fictitious applicant would be invited for an interview. To no one's surprise, whites with no criminal record were most likely to be called in, and blacks with a record were least likely. The most shocking finding, however, was that whereas 17 percent of the whites *with* criminal records were called for an interview, only 14 percent of the blacks *without* a record were called for an interview. In this study, race was a more important factor than having a criminal record.

In a second study, Sendhil Mullainathan and Marianne Bertrand sent 5,000 résumés in response to employment ads in Boston and Chicago (Glenn 2003; Associated Press 2003). Each employer received four résumés. Half of the résumés showed weak employment histories and job skills, and the other half showed strong employment histories and skills. In addition, half of the résumés had stereotypical black names like Lakisha and Jamal, while the other half had more white-sounding names like Emily or John. Each résumé had a phone number with a voice-mail message by someone of the appropriate race and gender.

Once again, race was a factor in who got a callback. The white-sounding names got a callback once for every ten résumés sent out; the black-sounding names got one callback for every fifteen résumés. The Kristens and Carries got callbacks 13 percent of the time whereas the Keishas and Tamikas got callbacks less than 4 percent of the time.

Having a strong résumé helped whites more than blacks. Among the white-sounding names, having a strong résumé increased the likelihood of getting a callback by 30 percent compared to the weak résumés. For the black-sounding names, having a strong résumé increased the callback likelihood by only 9 percent.

These two recent studies are consistent with the findings of older studies that actually sent matched pairs of students (white and black, or white and Hispanic) to apply in person for a job. In these studies, discrimination occurred about 20 percent of the time (Bendick, Jackson, and Reinoso 1994). All these data clearly show that employment discrimination is still an issue.

Discrimination is not just practiced at the individual level by small employers and managers. Institutional discrimination remains in place as well. Here are several documented cases from 2010.

- Congress approved a $1.4 billion settlement in December 2009 to settle claims that Native American lands were illegally sold to non-Indian individuals in the late nineteenth and early twentieth centuries (Southhall 2010).
- The US Senate approved $4.55 billion in November 2010 to settle claims that black farmers were discriminated against by the Departments of Agriculture and the Interior (Southhall 2010).

- A federal court ruled against the New York City fire department for using a test the department knew was biased against black applicants. Only 3.4 percent of New York City firefighters are black, compared to the 25.6 percent black population in the entire city (Baker 2010).
- The US Supreme Court ruled against the Chicago fire department for using an exam that had a disparate impact on black applicants. The 1995 exam had an arbitrary cut-off score of 89 even though studies showed that applicants scoring in the 70s and 80s were capable of succeeding as firefighters (Savage 2010).
- The EEOC ruled in favor of an Arab school principal in New York City who was forced to resign. Debbie Almontaser, a Muslim of Yemeni descent, was the founding principal of the Khalil Gibran International Academy in Brooklyn. The public school emphasized Arab culture and language. A local newspaper tried to link Almontaser to a private group selling T-shirts with "Intifada NYC" on the front. This unfounded claim caused an upsurge of anti-Arab sentiment in New York, and the EEOC ruled that the Board of Education gave in to this outside political pressure (Medina 2010).

The year 2010 also provided examples of individual discrimination cases that ended in out-of-court settlements. Typically, the employer agreed to pay a fine and change its procedures without admitting any wrongdoing.

- The town of Green Brook paid $35,000 to settle a suit brought by a Hispanic worker who claimed he was subjected to racial harassment by his supervisor, including offensive slurs, jokes, and remarks. When the employee complained, the town then retaliated against him (US Department of Justice 2010).
- The Vanguard Group, which runs a variety of mutual funds, paid $300,000 to settle a suit by a black employee who claimed she was not hired because of her race. The employee was told that she was not hired because she lacked a financial planning certificate, but the company ended up hiring a white male who also lacked a certificate (McCullough 2010).
- Conmed Linvatec, a medical device company, fired an employee because of his race. The employee was reinstated and paid $250,000 in compensation. The company also agreed to provide

training for all managers who will interact with the employee (EEOC 2010b).

- Landwin Management, which runs the San Gabriel Hilton Hotel in California, agreed to pay $500,000 to settle a suit where Latino workers claimed to have been fired and replaced by less qualified Asian employees. The hotel is located in a pre-dominantly Asian area and caters to Asian tourists. This was a case of "national origin" discrimination (California Employment Lawyers Blog 2010).
- Spencer Reed Group, a firm that provides administrative and staffing services to employers, agreed to pay $125,000 to a white woman who claimed that she was discriminated against due to her race and age. Compared with her younger black colleagues, the employee was subjected to harsh discipline, denied training, and given harsher workloads (Kansas City InfoZine 2010).

Readers may wonder why there is so much talk about fines in these race discrimination cases and no talk of jail sentences. That's because employment discrimination is a violation of civil law, not criminal law. An employer can't go to jail for refusing to hire or promote someone because of his or her race.

An example of structural discrimination occurred in the Baltimore City Fire Department (BCFD). In winter 2004, the BCFD admitted an all-white class to its fire academy. This was the first time since the department integrated in 1953 that the class was composed only of whites. Although the population of Baltimore is 65 percent black, the BCFD is only 25 percent black (Fields 2004a, 2004b). As an explanation, officials said that relatively few blacks took the test, even fewer passed the test, and most of those who did were disqualified because of criminal records and failed drug tests.

Several factors about the test, however, favored white applicants. First, the test was not offered frequently or at regular intervals; the department's policy is to offer the test every eighteen months to three years. To make matters worse, the test was not advertised due to the lack of an advertising budget, so news of the test was based largely on word of mouth. Finally, the content of the test was based on prior firefighting knowledge rather than general aptitude. Hence, the entire structure of the test favored whites because they were more likely to belong to the in-group and more likely to have participated in rural and suburban volunteer firefighting companies. This could also explain why in spite of a BCFD policy of hiring Baltimore residents, only five out of the thirty recruits lived in the city. This is an example of structural discrimination because even if there was no intention to discriminate against blacks, the test had that effect.

A few days after the city's main newspaper ran a front-page story about the all-white class, embarrassed city officials announced immediate changes. The test would be offered monthly and advertised widely throughout Baltimore. This would increase the number of blacks who take the test. The BCFD appointed a recruitment committee to oversee diversity efforts. Applicants who had completed a certified emergency medical technician program could be admitted without taking the exam. Finally, BCFD officials would see whether a different kind of exam would be more appropriate. As a result, subsequent classes have been more diverse.

* * *

Although many readers might not believe that racial discrimination and prejudice still occur in the twenty-first century, the empirical data show that they do. Civil rights laws have not eliminated discrimination, although they have made it easier to prosecute. In sum, people of color still lack the equality of opportunity in the United States.

5

Gender

The conflicts between men and women are different from the class and race conflicts that we discussed in previous chapters. People of different classes and races often live very separate lives and often don't have direct interactions with one another—and if they do have contact, it is often in very impersonal ways. Men and women live together in families and have intimate contacts with one another. Most children know both male and female peers as well as adult relatives. In spite of this more personal contact, gender conflict has some of the same structural issues as do race and class conflict.

In recent years, several well-publicized articles have argued that gender conflict is no longer a major issue. The cover story of the October 2009 issue of *Time* magazine was "The State of the American Woman." The subhead of the lead articles states: "What unites men and women matters more than what divides them as old gender battles fade away" (Gibbs 2009, 25). The July/August 2010 issue of *The Atlantic* featured an article with the provocative title "The End of Men." Author Hanna Rosin (2010) asks: "What if modern postindustrial society is better suited to women?" If these articles are correct, perhaps chapters like this are no longer relevant. We shall see.

Terminology

Although people, including social scientists, often use the terms *sex* and *gender* interchangeably, they are really quite different. **Sex** *refers to the physical and biological differences between the categories of male and* *female.* This includes hormones, reproductive apparatus, body shape, and other physiological characteristics. **Gender** *refers to the behavior that is culturally defined as appropriate and inappropriate for males and females.* Gender, therefore, is totally socially constructed whereas sex has *some* basis in physical reality.

Although this distinction seems simple enough, the reality is considerably more complex. The ability to bear and breastfeed a child, for example, is clearly related to sex differences. Most women can do it and men can't. But what of the fact that in most societies, including our own, women tend to do most of the childcare work, both at home and in the paid labor force? Most social scientists would argue that this has to do with gender, not with sex. Physically, men can care for children and feed them out of bottles, either with formula or with expressed breast milk. Culturally, however, this is often defined as women's work.

Of course, sex (that is, physiological) differences are not always clearly defined. A small minority of the population is **intersexed** *in that they have physical attributes of both males and females.* At birth, it is sometimes difficult to tell if a baby is male or female because the genitalia are ambiguous. For years, pediatricians have suggested that surgery be performed on babies so that they can be assigned to one sex or the other. Is someone with both a penis and a vagina a male, or female? What happens when hormones may be inconsistent with chromosomes? In our society, we think we have to know which of the two sexes this individual *really* belongs to. The character of Pat on *Saturday Night Live* is continually frustrating to audiences because of her/his sexual ambiguity.

Anne Fausto-Sterling (1993, 2000) has done some fascinating writing on this topic. In a well-known 1993 article she argued that there are really five sexes, not just two. "True hermaphrodites," who have one testis and one ovary, she called *herms.* Female pseudohermaphrodites, who have ovaries and some aspect of male genitalia but who do not have testis, are called *ferms.* Male pseudohermaphrodites, who have testis and some aspects of female genitalia but who don't have ovaries, she calls *merms.* Rather than trying to force the herms, ferms, and merms into the categories of male and female, Fausto-Sterling argues to leave them separate. In a subsequent article, Fausto-Sterling (2000) rejects her own five-sexes argument and says that sex should not be seen as a simple continuum: "Sex and gender are best conceptualized as points in a multidimensional space. . . .

The medical and scientific communities have yet to adopt a language that is capable of describing such diversity" (107).

Transgendered people, for example, *feel that their gender identity doesn't match their physiological body*. These are physiological men who feel female, or physiological women who feel like men. One of my female students, who identifies as a lesbian, has a female partner who is transgendered. Although the partner always dressed in male-like clothing, at one point the partner decided to live as a male by taking a male name and insisting that everyone use the masculine pronoun to refer to her/him. After a few months, the partner returned to the female name. Eventually, she began the complex transition process that will end in her becoming a female-to-male transsexual.

When transgendered people take hormones, begin to live as the opposite sex, and have sex-change operations, they are **transsexuals**. This raises some really mind-blowing questions. Is a male-to-female transsexual a woman or a man? Should one refer to a transsexual as a he or as a she? Which bathroom should s/he use? If a female-to-male transsexual has sexual relations with the man s/he used to be married to, is this a heterosexual, or homosexual, relationship? As I wrote earlier, the male/female dichotomy is not as simple as it seems (Boylan 2003).

Gender is even more fluid than sex. First, gender varies from culture to culture. Men, for example, tend to be much more emotionally and physically expressive in many Hispanic cultures than in the United States. Gender also varies in a single culture over time; for instance, men in our country are much more involved with their children now than they were fifty years ago. Gender also varies within a culture: working mothers have always been more prevalent among working-class and black women than among middle-class and white women. Gender is also situational. Men hugging each other on the athletic field is not viewed in the same light as that action on a street corner.

Some cultures have more than two genders. In many Native American cultures, the *berdache* is a biological male who assumes the feminine gender. S/he dresses and acts like a woman and is a highly respected member of the community who is seen as having special spiritual powers. Young men have to participate in a special ceremony to assume the berdache status.

In traditional Albanian culture, a woman can become a "sworn virgin" and assume the role of a man. This would occur when the males in the extended family have died or been killed, leaving no one to assume property ownership and to care for the rest of the women. The sworn virgin dresses and acts like a man and is recognized as such by the rest of the community, in part, due to the sacrifice that she has made (Bilefsky 2008).

As Michael Kimmel writes,

> [Our gender] identities are a fluid assemblage of the meanings and behaviors that we construct from the values, images, and prescriptions we find in the world around us. Our gender identities are both voluntary—we choose to become who we are—and coerced—we are pressured, forced, sanctioned, and often physically beaten into submission to some rules. We neither make up the rules as we go along nor do we glide perfectly and effortlessly into preassigned roles. (2004, 194)

Understanding gender relations involves more than just culture. It also involves power and hierarchy. Most social scientists who write about gender would define **patriarchy** *as a hierarchical system that promotes male supremacy.* This refers to a set of institutions that are organized in a way that benefits the majority of men over the majority of women in the economy, the political system, the family, and so on. Of course, not all men benefit from patriarchy in the same way, and not all women are hurt in the same way. In fact, a small group of wealthy white men are at the top of the patriarchy, and they have power over all women and most men.

Many men reject the concept of patriarchy by saying that they don't *feel* powerful. Working-class and poor men have little power due to their *class* position, and men of color have little power due to their *race*. However, most of these men, along with white middle-class men, do exert power over women in their families and communities. Domestic violence and rape are usually male-initiated behavior in all communities. The concept of patriarchy is not an all-or-nothing concept. Different men benefit in different ways.

Finally, we come to the concept of sexism. Like the concept of racism, discussed in the previous chapter, the term *sexism* has been used in a variety of ways since the 1960s. Some see sexism as an ideological support for patriarchy. This refers to a set of cultural beliefs and personal attitudes that support male control of major social institutions. According to this view, believing that men should be the head of the house or that women should not supervise men on the job would be considered sexist. Later in the chapter I will discuss the way social psychologists measure sexist beliefs.

Though others agree, they would extend *sexism* to include both attitudes and behaviors that hurt women. According to this argument, those who refuse to hire women as managers or those who commit violence against women are exhibiting sexist behavior. It's not just the attitudes that are the problem, it's also the behavior.

Still others use *sexism* synonymously with patriarchy to describe a gender-based system of oppression that would include ideology and attitudes as well as behavior and institutional organization. In this case laws and religious practices that discriminate against women would be considered sexist. The important point here is that all the writers agree that there is a system that oppresses women and that part of that system consists of ideology and attitudes. The disagreement is over what labels to use.

In this book, I will use the more inclusive use of **sexism** as *a system of oppression based on gender.* This would include prejudice and discrimination toward women as well as ideologies and policies that keep women as second-class citizens. Because only women are oppressed because of their gender, only men and male-dominated institutions can be sexist according to this definition. Women, of course, can be prejudiced toward men and, in some limited cases, have the power to discriminate against men. As much as we may dislike these activities, they are not sexist because they are not part of an oppressive system. Marilyn Frye (1983) argued that though men can (and should) be unhappy because they can't express their feelings, this is not the same as being oppressed.

Finally, we come to the concept of *feminism*, which is often associated with what has come to be known as the women's liberation movement. Although most young women believe in things like equal pay for equal work, the need for more women in traditionally male jobs, and the need for men and women to share in childcare and housework, they would not describe themselves as feminist. What does feminism mean, and why is it so threatening?

More than twenty years ago, bell hooks wrote, "A central problem within feminist discourse has been our inability to either arrive at a consensus of opinion about what feminism is or accept definition(s) that could serve as points of unification" (hooks 2000, 238). This statement is still true today because there are a variety of different types of feminism. Barbara Price and Natalie Sokoloff (2004, 2–3), for example, describe five approaches to feminism:

- *Liberal feminism*, the most mainstream of the perspectives, stresses the importance of equality of women with men within the existing political and economic structures in society. From this perspective, the most common cause of gender inequality is identified as cultural attitudes with regard to gender role socialization. . . .
- *Radical feminism* identifies male dominance and control as the cause of gender inequality and argues that these must be eliminated from all social institutions. Men's control of women's sexuality and the norm of heterosexuality are identified as the core of women's oppression. . . .
- *Marxist feminism* views women's oppression as a function of class relations in a capitalist society. . . . Women are twice burdened in this analysis; they are oppressed economically in low-wage jobs in the labor market and they are oppressed by their unpaid family responsibilities centered around reproductive labor (childbearing, childcare and housework). . . .
- *Socialist feminists* combine the Marxist and radical feminist perspectives and identify as the causes of gender inequality and women's oppression both patriarchy and capitalism in public as well as private spheres of life. . . .
- *Women of color feminists* . . . introduce the concept of "intersectionalities" to understand the interlocking sites of oppression; they examine how the categories of race, class, gender and sexuality in intersecting systems of domination rely on each other to function. (also see Lorber 1998)

These diverse viewpoints can be frustrating for those who want a short answer to the apparently simple question, What do feminists believe? Fortunately, Margaret Anderson (2003, 9) tries to identify some of the issues that are common to all forms of feminism:

Feminism begins with the premise that women's and men's positions in society are the result of social, not natural or biological factors. . . . Feminists generally see social institutions and social attitudes as the basis for women's position in society. Because in sexist societies these institutions have created structured inequities between women and men, feminists believe in transforming institutions to generate liberating social changes on behalf of women; thus, feminism takes women's interests and perspectives seriously, believing that women are not inferior to men. Feminism is a way of both thinking and acting; in fact, the union of action and thought is central to feminist programs for social change. Although feminists do not believe that women should be like men, they do believe that women's experiences, concerns and ideas are as valuable as those of men and should be treated with equal seriousness and respect. As a result, feminism makes women's interests central in movement for social change.

This view of feminism is quite different from the popular stereotype of bra-burning, man-hating lesbians that many people wrongly associate with feminism. Although many lesbians are feminists, the overwhelming number of feminists are not lesbians. Although some feminists hate men, most do not. The bra-burning stereotype stems from a 1968 protest of the Miss America pageant in Atlantic City, New Jersey. Some of the 200 protesters threw bras and high heels into a "freedom trash can" to oppose the sexual objectification of women; they never burned them (Albert and Albert 1984).

Sarah Palin, the former governor of Alaska and former Republican vice presidential candidate, complicated matters when she declared herself to be a conservative feminist. In her famous 2008 interview with Katie Couric, Palin said,

I am a feminist who believes in equal rights and I believe that women certainly today have every opportunity that a man has to succeed, and to do it all anyway. And I'm very thankful that I've been brought up in a family where gender hasn't been an issue. You know, I've been expected to do everything growing up that boys have been doing. (Jezebel 2008)

Many feminists, however, would say that Palin's lack of concern with patriarchy and her opposition to abortion and homosexuality would disqualify her from assuming the feminist label.

So, what is the "true" definition of feminism? My own inclination is to go with Anderson's general comments cited above and to read about the different types of feminism in Ollenberger and Moore (1998), Lorber (1998), or Renzetti and Curran (1999). For those who absolutely need a formal definition, here's a short, snappy one provided by bell hooks (2000, 240): **feminism** is *"a movement to end sexist oppression."*

Descriptive Statistics

In discussing gender in the United States, it is important to understand that the majority of women work in the paid labor force. I use the phrase "work in the paid labor force" to underscore the importance of work that women perform in the home as housewives and mothers; they just don't get paid for it.

According to the most recent data in Table 5.1, 59.2 percent of women twenty years old or older worked in the paid labor force in 2009, compared to 74.8 percent of similarly aged men. More than three-quarters of married women with children ages six to seventeen work in the paid labor force. Even 58 percent of married women with children three years old or younger work in the paid labor force. The stay-at-home housewife/mom is becoming a thing of the past.

There has been a sea change in the labor force participation rates of women since the 1950s. Table 5.1 shows that in 1948, only 31.8 percent of all women worked in the paid labor force. In other words, the labor force participation rate for women has almost doubled since 1948. This increasing labor force participation rate applies to single women, married women, and women with young children.

In comparison, men are *less* likely to be in the labor force now than in 1948. Although men have always been more likely than women to work in the paid labor force, the gap has been steadily declining.

These same trends are true when whites, blacks, and Hispanics are compared. The labor force participation rates of white, black, and Hispanic women have increased dramatically since 1970, when data

Table 5.1 **Labor Force Participation Rates (in percentage) of Persons Twenty Years Old and Older, 1948–2009, by Race/Ethnicity and Sex**

Year	Total Population		Whites		Blacks		Hispanics	
	Male	Female	Male	Female	Male	Female	Male	Female
1948	88.6	31.8	—	—	—	—	—	—
1960	86.6	37.6	—	—	—	—	—	—
1970	82.6	43.3	82.8	42.2	78.4[a]	51.6[a]	85.9[a]	41.3[a]
1980	79.4	51.3	79.8	50.6	75.1	55.6	84.9	48.5
1990	78.2	58.0	78.5	57.6	75.0	60.6	84.7	54.8
2000	76.7	60.6	77.1	59.9	72.8	65.4	85.3	59.3
2009	74.8	59.2	75.3	60.4	69.6	63.4	83.2	59.2

Source: US Bureau of Labor Statistics 2010.
Notes: a. 1973 data.
As the table indicates, in 2009, 74.8 percent of males and 59.2 percent of females were in the labor force.

gathering for these groups began. The rates for white and black men have declined. Hispanic men, who have the highest participation rates of any of the race/gender groups, have been employed at a stable rate.

Men and women also have different types of jobs. Table 5.2 shows the gender composition of the labor force at different skill levels. At low-skilled jobs, truck drivers and grounds maintenance workers are more than 75 percent male whereas nurse's aides and home health workers are more than 75 percent female. At high-skill levels, CEOs, computer software engineers, and construction managers are more than 75 percent male whereas elementary and middle school teachers, registered nurses, and social workers are more than 75 percent female. This *differential distribution of men and women in the labor force* is called **occupational sex segregation**.

These data clearly show that occupational sex segregation is alive and well in the twenty-first century. Even more sobering is the fact

Table 5.2 The Three Largest Occupations for Each Broad Skill Level and Type of Gender Composition, 2009

	Gender Composition of Occupation		
Skill Level of Job	Male-Dominated (25 percent or less female)	Mixed (25.1 percent–74.9 percent female)	Female-Dominated (75 percent or more female)
Low-skilled	Truck drivers and driver/sales workers; grounds maintenance workers	Janitors and building cleaners	Nursing, psychiatric, and home health aides; personal and home care aides
Medium-skilled	Construction laborers; security guards and gaming security officers	First-line retail supervisors and managers; managers, all others	Secretaries and administrative assistants; bookkeeping, accounting, and auditing clerks
High-skilled	Chief executives; computer software engineers; construction managers	Accountants and auditors; secondary school teachers; financial managers	Elementary and middle school teachers; registered nurses; social workers

Source: Hegewisch et al. 2010.

that these data are *improvements* over what existed in the past. One common way to measure occupational sex segregation is through the Index of Dissimilarity, which ranges between 100 and 0. An index value of 100 means that all jobs are either totally male or totally female. A value of 0 means that all jobs have equal numbers of males and females. Ariane Hegewisch and her colleagues (2010) show that the Index of Dissimilarity declined from about 68 in 1970 to 50 in 2002, a substantial decline in segregation. The 2009 figure was 51, which shows that previous progress had all but ceased. There is still a long way to go.

The area of education has also shown substantial changes. As Table 5.3 illustrates, in 1940 only about one-fourth of the population twenty-five years of age or older had graduated from high school, and less than 5 percent had graduated from college. In that same year, women were somewhat more likely than men to graduate from high school but less likely than men to graduate from college.

By 2009, things had changed dramatically. Eighty-six percent of the population had graduated from high school, and 30 percent had graduated from college. High school graduation rates for men and women have been equal since 1970. More important, the male/female

Table 5.3 Percentage of Males and Females Twenty-Five Years and Older Who Completed High School and College, 1940–2009

	Completed Four Years of High School or More			Completed Four Years of College or More		
Year	Males (%)	Females (%)	M/F Ratio[a]	Males (%)	Females (%)	M/F Ratio[a]
1940	22.7	26.3	0.86	5.5	3.8	1.45
1950	32.6	36.0	0.90	7.3	5.2	1.40
1960	39.5	42.5	0.93	9.7	5.8	1.67
1970	55.0	55.4	0.99	14.1	8.2	1.72
1980	69.2	68.1	1.02	20.9	13.6	1.54
1990	77.7	77.5	1.00	24.4	18.4	1.33
2000	84.2	84.0	1.00	27.8	23.6	1.18
2009	86.2	87.1	0.98	30.1	29.1	1.03

Source: Snyder and Dillow 2010.
Note: a. Male rate divided by the female rate; e.g., in 2009, 86.2 percent of males graduated from high school or more. The high school graduation rate of males was only 98 percent of the rate of females.

gap in college graduation had diminished substantially. In 1940, men were 1.45 times more likely than women to graduate from college. By 2009, that gap had narrowed to 1.03. In fact, since the 1980s, more women have attended and graduated from college than men.

In spite of these developments, men and women in the United States do not get the same educations. In 2007, for example, women earned 86 percent of the bachelor's degrees in health (mostly nursing) and 79 percent of the degrees in education, but only 18 percent of the degrees in engineering (Chronicle of Higher Education 2010). Needless to say, engineers make a lot more money than do nurses and teachers. Although American women earned more PhD degrees than American men since 2002, women earned two-thirds of the education PhDs and only one-fifth of the engineering PhDs (Wilson 2004).

These differences in fields of study and occupational distribution certainly have implications for gender differences in income. Table 5.4 shows median incomes for year-round full-time male and female workers between 1960 and 2009. Seasonal and part-time workers, most of whom are women, are excluded from these data. In 1960, women earned only 61 percent of what men earned. By 2009 the gap had narrowed considerably, so that women made 76 percent of what men made—still a substantial gap. Most of this progress occurred since 1980 and is due to the declining wages of men. According to Misha Werschkul and Jody Herman (2004, 1), "At the rate of progress achieved between 1989 and 2002, women would not achieve wage parity for more than 50 years!"

Table 5.4 Median Income of Year-Round Full-Time Workers, Fifteen Years and Older, by Sex

Year	Male	Female	F/M Ratio[a]
1960	$5,358	$3,257	0.61
1970	8,966	5,323	0.59
1980	18,612	11,197	0.60
1990	27,678	19,822	0.72
2000	37,252	27,462	0.74
2009	49,164	37,234	0.76

Source: US Census Bureau 2010b.
Note: a. Female income divided by male income; e.g., in 2009, the female median income was 76 percent of the male income.

It is also important to disaggregate these data by race/ethnicity. In Table 4.7 in the previous chapter, the data for race/gender groups were presented from 1967 to 2009 and comparisons were made between races *within* a single sex; that is, the incomes of black men were compared with the incomes of white men. Using the same raw data, we can compare the incomes of the two sexes within a given race; that is, the incomes of white women were compared with the incomes of white men. These data are presented in Table 5.5.

We can see that for whites, blacks, and Hispanics, the income gap between men and women has closed substantially. In 1967, white women made only 58 percent of the income of white men. By 2009, white women made 77 percent of the income of white men. The male/female gap among whites was still substantial, but it had closed. The same general patterns exist for male/female income differences among blacks and Hispanics. However, the data for Asians show that between 1990 and 2000 the income gap had gotten larger; by 2009 it had decreased.

Because statistical data can be somewhat sterile, another way to view the income inequality between men and women is by the concept of the "Equal Pay Day," or the date each year until which women have to work in order to earn the same annual income as a man. According to the Institute for Women's Policy Research (IWPR) and the National Committee on Pay Equity, women had to work until April 12, 2011, to earn the same income that a man would have earned between January 1 and December 31, 2010 (www.payequity.org/day .html). Furthermore,

Table 5.5 Median Income of Year-Round Full-Time Female Workers as a Percentage of Incomes of Comparable Male Workers, 1967–2009, by Race/Ethnicity

Year	White	Black	Hispanic	Asian
1967	58	67	—	—
1970	59	70	67	—
1980	59	79	71	—
1990	69	85	82	80
2000	73	83	87	75
2009	77	82	88	83

Source: Calculated from data in Table 4.7 from previous chapter.

Note: E.g., in 2009, black women made 82 percent of the income that black men made.

Hispanic women must work almost an entire extra year, until November 22, to catch up with the earnings of the average white male in the previous year. Asian American women observe Equal Pay Day slightly earlier than all women, on March 30th. Native American women would have to work until September 12 and African American women until July 19th to catch up to the average white man's earnings from the previous year. (Werschkul and Herman 2004, 7)

Once again, there's a lot of work left to be done to achieve gender equity.

Thus far, income comparisons have been made for *all* year-round full-time workers. What happens when we control for education? In Table 4.10 in the previous chapter I presented the incomes of year-round full-time workers by race/ethnicity, sex, and education and then compared race/ethnic differences in income. Using these same data, we can compare gender differences in income in Table 5.6. In all comparisons, women have lower incomes than comparable men. For example, non-Hispanic white women with a bachelor's degree earn only 71 percent of the income of comparable men. The comparable figures for women of color with bachelor's degrees are as follows: blacks, 90 percent; Asians, 85 percent; and Hispanics, 79 percent. At each level of education, the gender gap for people of color is generally lower

Table 5.6 Women's Income as a Percentage of Men's Income for Year-Round Full-Time Workers in 2009 by Education and Race/Ethnicity

Education	Non-Hispanic White	Black	Asian	Hispanic
Some high school	67	84	—	80
High school graduate	73	83	84	81
Some college	70	79	83	76
Associate degree	77	76	83	75
Bachelor's degree	71	90	85	79
Master's degree	76	91	81	76
PhD	76	—	—	—
Professional degree	70	—	—	—

Source: US Census Bureau 2010b.
Note: Data calculated using median incomes from Table 4.10 in previous chapter. E.g., black women with a bachelor's degree earn 90 percent of what black men with a bachelor's degree earn.

than it is for non-Hispanic whites. Unfortunately, the gender gap does not decrease as the level of education increases.

Some of the income differences between men and women are due to the sex-segregated labor force in which women are overrepresented in low-paying jobs. What would happen if we compared male and female incomes in the same occupations? Fortunately, a recent report by the Institute for Women's Policy Research allows us to do this (see Table 5.7).

Hegewisch et al. (2010) looks at median weekly income for workers in both male- and female-dominated jobs at different levels of skill. At low-skilled jobs, workers in female-dominated occupations make only 73.8 percent of the income of workers in male-dominated occupations. For medium- and high-skilled jobs, the comparable figures are 79.8 percent and 66.9 percent, respectively (also see Weinberg 2004).

In spite of some genuine progress that has been made, there is a long way to go to achieve economic parity for men and women.

Attitudes and Ideology

Unlike the long tradition of research into racial prejudice, social scientists have only recently begun to systematically study prejudice toward women. Although feminist social scientists have discussed

Table 5.7 Median Weekly Earnings in Occupations, 2009, by Gender Composition and Skill Level

	Gender Composition of Occupations			
Skill Level of Occupations	Male-Dominated (25% or less female)	Mixed (25.1%–74.1% female)	Female-Dominated (75% or more female)	Ratio of Female-Dominated/ Male-Dominated[a]
Low-skilled	$553	$435	$408	73.8
Medium-skilled	752	735	600	79.8
High-skilled	1,424	1,160	953	66.9

Source: Hegewisch et al. 2010.
Note: a. Earnings in female-dominated occupations divided by earnings in male-dominated occupations; e.g., in highly skilled occupations, workers in female-dominated occupations earn 66.9 percent of the income of workers in male-dominated occupations.

negative stereotypes and attitudes toward women for decades, this has largely been done outside of the discourse of the social psychology of prejudice. This is beginning to change.

One of the early attempts to measure prejudice toward women was the Attitudes Toward Women Scale (Spence, Helmreich, and Stapp 1973). This scale consists of agree-disagree statements like "Sons in a family should be given more encouragement to go to college than daughters" and "Women should worry less about their rights and more about becoming good wives and mothers." On the fifteen-item scale, scores ranged from 0 (traditional beliefs) to 45 (egalitarian beliefs). In a 1972 study of students at the University of Texas, for example, the mean score for men was 21.3 and the mean score for women was 24.3. Not surprisingly, men were somewhat more traditional in their beliefs than women. Those who scored low on the ATW Scale were not afraid to publicly articulate traditional stereotyped beliefs about gender roles.

By the mid-1990s it was becoming less fashionable to express these beliefs, and J. T. Spence and E. D. Hahn (1997) found that fewer and fewer people were scoring high on their ATW Scale. In their study of University of Texas students in 1992, for example, the mean score for men was 32.1 and the mean for women was 36.3. Although men were still more traditional in their views than were women, the men in the 1992 study had more egalitarian scores than did the women in the 1972 study! Several of the scale items were no longer useful because virtually everyone scored at the egalitarian end.

Jean Twenge (1997) showed that these same trends were found in seventy-one different studies of undergraduates across the country that used the ATW Scale. She also found that southern men and women had more traditional scores than did northern men and women. Both the women's liberation movement and structural changes in the economy had strongly influenced attitudes toward women. This doesn't mean that sexism had disappeared, only that it had changed and become more complex.

A dramatic example of how unfashionable some of these traditional beliefs have become can be seen in the negative reaction to the sexist remarks of Harvard University president Lawrence Summers. In January 2005, Summers publicly suggested that the underrepresentation of women in the sciences may be due to the fact that women are biologically less capable than men in the area of math and science. The intense criticism forced him to apologize numerous times.

Summers also said that Harvard would spend $50 million over ten years to encourage more women to enter the math and science fields (Healy and Rimer 2005).

Even though attitudes have changed quite a bit in the past fifty years, there are still substantial differences in the way women and men view gender issues. In 2008, for example, two-thirds of a national sample said that they were very or somewhat satisfied with the way women were treated in the United States: 75 percent of the men said they were satisfied, and 61 percent of the women were satisfied.

In spite of the statistics that we reviewed in the previous section, a majority of the population (57 percent) answered "yes" to the following question: "Do you feel that women in this country have equal job opportunities to men, or not?" However, whereas 71 percent of men said that women had equal job opportunities, only 45 percent of the women agreed. In other words, most men seem to think that discrimination against women is a thing of the past (Gallup 2008).

Janet K. Swim and her colleagues (1995) approached the changing nature of prejudice by developing measures of "old-fashioned" and "modern" sexism (prejudice) toward women. The Old-Fashioned Sexism Scale included traditional items of stereotyped attitudes toward women like those in the ATW Scale.

The Modern Sexism Scale, taking its cue from some of the "new prejudice" literature discussed in the previous chapter on race, included questions that tapped a more current set of negative attitudes toward women. It included statements such as

> "Women often miss out on good jobs due to sexual discrimination."
> "It is easy to understand the anger of women's groups in America."
> "Government and news media have been showing more concern about the treatment of women than is warranted by women's actual experience."

A prejudiced person would disagree with the first two items and agree with the third. These items are considered to be examples of modern sexism because "they support the maintenance of the status quo of gender inequality" (Swim and Campbell 2001, 221).

Although there is some correlation between these two measures, scoring high on the Old-Fashioned Sexism Scale didn't necessarily mean that you would score high on the Modern Sexism Scale, and vice versa. Swim and her colleagues argue that the two scales measure two different types of prejudice. The Neosexism Scale (Tougas et al. 1995), developed in Canada, is another attempt to measure this new form of prejudice.

The Ambivalent Sexism Inventory (Glick and Fiske 1996) also tries to make sense out of the changing nature of prejudice toward women. Previous attempts to measure sexism focused on attitudes with negative or hostile affect, such as "Most women interpret innocent remarks or acts as being sexist." Glick and Fiske also include a "benevolent sexism" subscale, which is "a set of interrelated attitudes toward women that are sexist in terms of viewing women stereotypically and in restricted roles, but that are subjectively positive in feeling tone" (491). Examples of benevolent sexism would be the following: "In a disaster, women ought to be rescued before men" and "A good woman should be set on a pedestal by her man" (Glick and Fiske 2001, 118). People who express benevolent sexism have positive attitudes toward women as long as women agree to stay in their place. The authors argue that these two types of sexism often coexist within the same individual.

The important point to take away from this discussion is that prejudice toward women is a complex phenomenon. A person can be prejudiced even if he or she doesn't endorse traditional gender stereotypes and even if he or she believes that a man is not complete without a woman. These beliefs also reinforce the inequality associated with patriarchy.

Discrimination

Although public opinion polls show that most Americans believe that discrimination against women is a thing of the past, the evidence shows otherwise. The income data presented earlier in this chapter clearly showed that women earn substantially less than men, even with the same education and in similar occupations. However, though these findings should raise suspicions, they do not *prove* that discrimination exists. The pay gap could be due to sex differences in amount of time out of the labor force, level of education, subspecialization within a given job, and so on. In large-scale studies, when these factors are considered, the male/female income gap generally declines but is still substantial (Weinberg 2004; General Accounting Office 2003). At least some of this unexplained income gap is certainly due to discrimination. Whether one examines discrimination at the individual, institutional, or structural level, the evidence clearly shows that discrimination is alive and well.

Individual Discrimination

Britney Brinkman and Kathryn Rickard (2009) asked 103 college students at a large western university to keep a diary for two weeks listing all the events that they observed or experienced involving gender discrimination and prejudice. The students came up with over one thousand events, for an average of 2.8 events per student each day. The most common events involved sexual objectification (being treated as if your body exists for the pleasure of others). This was followed by demeaning and derogatory comments and pressure to conform to traditional gender role stereotypes (also see Swim et al. 1995).

In a campus-related study that I helped develop (Ehrlich, Pincus, and Lacy 1997), a representative sample of undergraduates at a mid-Atlantic university were asked if they had personally experienced ethnoviolent acts (from name-calling and graffiti to physical attacks) because of their gender during the academic year on campus. More than 11 percent of the women and less than 2 percent of the men responded "yes." A quarter of the women said that they had been victims of sexual harassment on campus.

The three military academies run by the Department of Defense are also not immune from sexual misconduct. A recent study of students found that more than half of the women and 14 percent of the men said that they had been sexually assaulted while at the academies. More than two-thirds of the assaults were not reported to campus authorities, in part (according to the study respondents) because authorities were often less than sympathetic to the victims (Hirsch and Knight 2005).

Sexual assaults in the military, as a whole, have also been an increasing problem. Almost 4,400 reports of assaults by one service member against another were reported in 2009. Historically, the military has not done a vigilant job about prosecuting these cases, but there is some evidence of improvement (Bumiller 2010).

The workplace is another common place in which to experience discrimination. In 2009 the Equal Employment Opportunity Commission (2010g) received 12,696 complaints of sexual harassment on the job, 28,028 complaints of sex bias discrimination, and 6,196 complaints of pregnancy discrimination. Previous research has shown that the EEOC will find between a quarter and one-fifth of these complaints to be legally valid (Pincus 2003).

Social psychologists have also conducted studies where subjects are asked to evaluate the résumés or work experiences of anonymous people. The résumés and work experiences would be the same except that one had a female name and the other had a male name. Men are generally given higher ratings than women, even with the same résumé (see Swim and Campbell 2001 for a review). It is likely that this male bias also spills into the workplace.

Here are three examples of individual sex discrimination at the workplace where a consent decree was issued in 2010:

- A female employee of a Minnesota manufacturing and machinery company was subjected to derogatory remarks and vulgar comments and was denied routine overtime that male coworkers received. She received $35,000 from the company (EEOC 2010d).
- Two female workers at a Wisconsin sawmill received $55,000 after a male supervisor continually exposed himself over a period of several years. The company did nothing to stop this conduct (EEOC 2010e).
- Two female workers at a Boeing plant received $380,000. After complaining about gender harassment and a hostile environment, an engineer was transferred to another unit that didn't meet her skill set and was then laid off. Her harasser participated in these decisions. The company did nothing after a second worker complained about her tools being broken or hidden by co-workers (AzCentral.com 2010).

Institutional Sex Discrimination

In spite of all the laws on the books, there are still many examples of institutional sex discrimination. Although women can attend government-run military academies and can serve on combat ships and planes, the US Army still doesn't permit them to be in front-line combat units or in noncombat units that "collocate" with (i.e., serve alongside) all-male combat units. The reasons for the anticollocation policy, according to conservative columnist Cal Thomas (2004, 23A), include "unit cohesion, increases in sex harassment, rape and pregnancy, and the social revulsion most feel about seeing women wounded or killed in combat." This is institutional discrimination. Although many women have been killed and injured in the Iraq War, the chaotic circumstances there make it impossible to determine what is a combat position and what is not. Because the armed forces were running short of male soldiers in Iraq and Afghanistan, many women have been given combat roles in spite of the regulations (Cave 2009).

Institutional gender discrimination has also been found in police departments throughout the United States. In 2004, for example, the Los Angeles Police Department (LAPD) finally settled a gender bias suit that went back to the 1980s. The plaintiffs, fifteen female and two male officers, alleged that they were fondled, ridiculed, and harassed by other officers and then retaliated against when they complained. The problem was so serious that the LAPD instituted reforms in 1997—which both sides agreed had positive effects. The main issue was money. Finally, the LAPD agreed to pay $3.6 million to the plaintiffs and their lawyers (Morin and Garrison 2004).

Organized religion provides numerous examples of institutional discrimination. The Catholic Church doesn't allow women to be priests, Orthodox Jews don't allow women to be rabbis, and Islam doesn't allow women to be imams. It would be possible to write an entire book on institutional discrimination in religion, but these are some prominent examples.

When large multinational corporations display the same patterns of mistreating women, this is also institutional discrimination. Here are several examples of consent decrees involving institutional sex discrimination in 2009 and 2010:

- Pitt Ohio Express, a trucking company with terminals in four cities, was charged with not hiring women drivers and loading dock workers. The company paid out $2.3 million to settle the case (BNA Daily Labor Report 2009).
- The Outback Steakhouse chain paid out $19 million in damages after being accused of not promoting women into jobs that would lead to advancement in the company. The entire $19 million was paid by Outback's insurance company (Harrington 2009).
- The Lawry's Restaurant Chain paid out $1.25 million in damages after being accused of not hiring men as servers. It also agreed to antidiscrimination training for its employees and advertising the availability of jobs on a gender-free basis ("Lawry's Settles Men's Sex Discrimination Suit" 2009).

- Walmart paid $11.7 million to settle charges that it refused to hire women in order-filling positions in its London, Kentucky, distribution center (EEOC 2010c).

Even more significant was a 2010 federal appeals court decision to permit an even larger class-action suit against Walmart to proceed to trial. This is the largest class-action sex discrimination suit in US history; 1.6 million current and former female employees are part of the class. The case has been bouncing around in the courts since 2001.

Structural Discrimination

Much of the sex-segregated labor force described in Table 5.2 can be attributed to structural discrimination. Many male-dominated occupations have entrance standards and/or performance standards that tend to favor men. To the extent that golf and squash are important networking activities for corporate executives, women would again be disadvantaged. The camaraderie/male bonding atmosphere that is so prevalent among police officers and firefighters would also disadvantage women. These standards may not have arisen to harm women, but they have that effect. Once again, it is important to realize that structural discrimination may well exist *in addition to* more intentional individual and institutional discrimination.

The structure of family life also has impacts on the job. The long hours required in many upscale law firms make it impossible for women (or men) to have anything approaching a normal family life. Because women tend to have more responsibility for children than men, these long hours would have a disproportionate impact on them. A recent study of women scientists shows that they spend twice as much time as their male counterparts doing household chores (Laster 2010).

In another subtle example, Linda Babcock and Sara Laschever (2003) report that although new male and female hires are offered similar starting salaries, males tend to be better negotiators and so may obtain better starting salaries than women. Employers, wanting to pay *all* employees as little as possible, regardless of sex, simply accept this state of affairs. This is structural discrimination because women get unequal pay for doing the same work.

The world of education also has a great deal of structural discrimination. Competitive and individualistic pedagogical techniques in math and science classes throughout the educational system favor males over females due to differential socialization practices. There is growing evidence that women and girls learn better in more cooperative settings. The lack of female role models among the faculty in many disciplines also hurts women.

In higher education, the relatively small number of women faculty results in greater demands on their time for advising students and participation in committee work. This, in turn, reduces the amount of time women faculty have to spend on research, which is all-important for promotion and tenure decisions.

Another demonstration of the complexity of gender discrimination concerns playwrights of Broadway theatre productions. According to researcher Emily Glassberg Sands, plays written by men and women are produced at about the same overall rate (Cohen 2009). The fact that more plays produced on Broadway are written by men than women can be explained by the greater number of male playwrights (no discrimination). Plays that featured women characters, however, were less likely to be produced than plays with male characters (discrimination).

Glassberg Sands sent out identical scripts to artistic directors and literary managers except half had a female author and half had a male author. The author's gender did not influence the way in which male directors and managers evaluated the plays (no discrimination). Female directors and managers, however, favored the male authors over the female authors (discrimination). Glassberg Sands next studied 329 plays that had been produced on Broadway in the previous ten years. She found that although plays written by women were more profitable than those written by men, they didn't have longer runs on Broadway (discrimination). This indicates that patterns of discrimination are not always clear cut.

* * *

Although articles in *Time* magazine and *The Atlantic* may disagree, this chapter has shown that women are still a subordinate group in the United States. In spite of some modest progress, women still have lower incomes and lower-paying jobs than men. In addition, women are the targets of prejudice and intentional discrimination. Many attitudinal and institutional changes must still be made in order to achieve true gender equality.

6

Sexual Orientation

People have been having sexual relations with same-sex partners for centuries. The Bible and the Koran discuss this fact, although critically. Homosexual liaisons were seen as normal and acceptable behavior among the ancient Greeks. Throughout most of history, same-sex relations were usually viewed as a *behavior* in which some people participated rather than as a separate *status*. In some societies homosexual behavior was condemned; in others it was not.

It wasn't until the second half of the nineteenth century that homosexuality began to be discussed in a way that defined one's sense of being; that is, that someone is a "homosexual" if he or she engages in homosexual behavior (Katz 1995; Baird 2001). In fact, the noun forms of *homosexual* and *heterosexual* were popularized in the 1890s and probably weren't even used in the English language prior to the 1860s.

Terminology

Like the concepts surrounding class, race, and gender that we discussed earlier, there is often disagreement about the terminology surrounding **sexual orientation**, *which is determined by those to whom we are attracted sexually, physically, and emotionally.* This is preferred to the term *sexual preference* because the latter suggests that there is a choice about whether or not we are attracted to people of the same or opposite sex. Today, most researchers believe that sexual orientation is probably something that an individual is born with.

Heterosexual *refers to individuals who are sexually, physically, and emotionally attracted to people of the opposite sex.* The term **homosexual** *refers to individuals who are sexually, physically, and emotionally attracted to people of the same sex.* Homosexual males are often called **gay males**, and homosexual females are often called **lesbians**. However, **gay** is also used as an umbrella term to refer to all homosexuals, and the term **straight** refers to heterosexuals. **Bisexual** *refers to individuals who are sexually, physically, and emotionally attracted to both same- and opposite-sex partners.* In the previous chapter, we defined **transgendered** people as *those whose gender identity doesn't match their physiological sex.*

All of these different categories of people are part of the general discussion of sexual orientation. In fact, it is common to refer to non-heterosexuals as the **LGBT** population—lesbians, gays, bisexuals, and transgendered people (sometimes the acronym is reordered as **GLBT**)—because they share many common issues. I will use this terminology in the rest of the chapter.

LGBT people may or may not acknowledge their sexual orientation to themselves and others. Someone who is **in the closet** *has not revealed his or her LGBT sexual orientation to others.* The process of **coming out** means that *an individual has revealed his or her LGBT sexual orientation to others.* Coming out is usually a process rather than a discrete event because individuals may acknowledge their sexual orientation to a close friend before telling other acquaintances or their families.

The concepts of homosexual, heterosexual, and bisexual may seem to be straightforward, but there are substantial difficulties in determining who is in what category. Although the concepts are all defined in terms of whom one is attracted to, attraction is not the same thing as actually having sex with that person. **Sexual behavior** *refers to whom we have sex with.* This raises some important questions. Is it necessary to have a sexual relationship with a same-sex partner in order to be defined as homosexual, or is *attraction* to a same-sex partner sufficient to warrant the label homosexual? For example, can a Catholic priest who is attracted to other males but who remains celibate be called gay, or would he have to engage in sex with another male to earn the gay label?

Another conceptual problem is about the timing and frequency of homosexual behaviors. In the islands of Melanesia, part of the rite of passage for boys is to have fellatio with older men. Eating another man's sperm is seen as a way to gain masculinity and bond with their

male ancestors. After the initiation, most men are exclusively heterosexual until they have to initiate younger men (Heyl 2003). We may
describe this as a kind of institutionalized homosexuality, though the
Melanesians would simply see it as normal male behavior.

In our own society, is a forty-five-year-old man gay, or straight,
if his only homosexual act was an experimental one-night stand with
another boy when both were teenagers? Is a thirty-five-year-old
woman married to a man considered a lesbian if she had a six-month
lesbian relationship when she was twenty-five? What about a fifty-
year-old man who first came out in his late forties? Can we use the
same label to describe these different behaviors?

More than fifty years ago, Alfred Kinsey and his colleagues (1948,
1953) documented the variety of sexual experiences by rating people
according to the following scale:

0. exclusively heterosexual; no homosexual experiences
1. predominantly heterosexual; only incidental homosexual
   experiences
2. predominantly heterosexual; more than incidental homosexual
   experiences
3. equally heterosexual and homosexual
4. predominantly homosexual; more than incidental heterosexual
   experiences
5. predominantly homosexual; only incidental heterosexual
   experiences
6. exclusively homosexual; no heterosexual experiences

Where on this scale must someone fall to be called homosexual (or bisexual or heterosexual)? As we have seen in previous chapters, the answer to this question is philosophical and cultural, not scientific. The
concept of sexual orientation, like the concepts of class, race, and gender, is socially constructed.

Another way to express the complexity and fluidity of sexual orientation can be seen in the Klein Sexual Orientation Grid (see Table
6.1). Along the left side of the table are seven different elements that
make up an individual's sexuality. Along the top are columns asking
about these elements in the past and present and what the person's
ideal is. A person can put one of the Kinsey numbers (0–6) in each box
and then average all of the boxes to come up with a sexual orientation
score. In terms of sexual attraction, for example, a person might put

Table 6.1 Klein's Sexual Orientation Grid

Variable	Past	Present	Ideal
Sexual attraction			
Sexual behavior			
Sexual fantasies			
Emotional preference			
Social preference			
Self-identification			
Straight/gay lifestyle			

Source: Meem et al. 2010.

a 3 in the past, a 6 in the present, and a 6 in ideal. This would average out to a score of 5 for sexual attraction. Although this is a lengthy exercise, it illustrates that sexual orientation is not a simple concept (Meem et al. 2010).

The answer, however, is important in determining the prevalence of homosexuality in the general population. According to Kinsey et al., for example, about 6 percent of adult males and 3 percent of adult females were exclusively homosexual (a 6 on Kinsey's scale) in the late 1950s and early 1960s. Under a broader definition (4–6 on that scale) 10 percent of males were exclusively or predominantly homosexual. Which figure should be used?

Lee Ellis (1996) takes a similar approach in trying to determine the prevalence of homosexuality in the United States during more recent times. Using the broad criterion of ever having a same-sex fantasy or sexual desire, 25–30 percent of males and 10–20 percent of females would be defined as gay. According to the more restrictive criterion of ever having a same-sex erotic experience to orgasm, 5–10 percent of the males and 1–3 percent of the females would be gay. Using the strictest criterion, having more or less exclusive erotic preference for one's own sex, only 1–4 percent of the males and less than 1 percent of the females would qualify. Ellis also argues that these same patterns can be found in studies in other countries. Male rates are always substantially higher than female rates.

So far, we have discussed whom people are attracted to and have sex with. There is yet another issue to contend with. **Sexual identification** *is what people call themselves.* Men who are attracted to other men and who have sexual relations with other men still don't always define themselves as homosexual. Many male prisoners, for example, have sex with other male prisoners but define themselves as straight. Only the "penetrated" male prisoners tend to be defined as gay. Also, some black men, who are said to be "on the down low" because they have public heterosexual relationships with women and multiple secret relationships with other men, insist on defining themselves as straight rather than gay or bisexual (King 2004). Is it necessary for people to define themselves as gay in order to be gay?

It is extremely difficult to answer what seem to be simple questions: Who is gay? How many people are gay? The answers always have to be qualified by another question: What do you mean by gay? There is no "objective" answer because labels are always socially constructed. Despite this, we do have some estimates of how many people participate in different kinds of sexual behaviors. What difference does it make if the behavior is labeled gay or not gay?

There are two additional concepts that are important in understanding sexual orientation. **Homophobia** *refers to the fear and hatred of those who love and sexually desire people of the same sex.* This refers to an anti-gay set of attitudes and an ideology that are major problems in the United States. As we will see, homophobia can lead to hate crimes and other forms of discrimination.

Heterosexism, in contrast, *refers to a system of oppression against the LGBT population.* Prejudice and ideology are one part of oppression, but there is more. Heterosexuals have certain privileges that gays don't, like being able to have a picture of one's partner on one's desk at work without being hassled, or being able to hold hands with one's partner in public without having to worry about verbal harassment or physical assault. There also are discriminatory laws that prevent gays from marrying and that don't protect their civil rights. Hate crimes and violence are also part of heterosexism. We will explore these issues more in the following sections.

Descriptive Statistics

In previous chapters I provided statistics on income, employment, and education that were collected by various agencies of the federal government. These data all show substantial inequalities between the dominant and subordinate groups. For a variety of reasons, it is impossible to obtain comparable data for sexual orientation.

First, the federal government doesn't collect data on groups with different sexual orientations. Even if it did, many closeted gays would not acknowledge their sexual orientations on the census forms. Finally, most of the fine books on sexual orientation don't address the issue of large-scale differences in employment, occupation, income, and education.

In 1990 and 2000, the US census did provide data on gays in the Public Use Microdata Sample (PUMS), which represents 5 percent of the population. In describing the relationship of people living in households, respondents were given the option of checking off "unmarried partner." Because it also was possible to determine if these partners were of the same or opposite sex, the PUMS data shed some light on gay and lesbian couples. Although same-sex unmarried partners living in the same household are not necessarily representative of all gays and lesbians, the data are national in scope and may be the best that are available.

There are three different analyses of the 2000 census data on same-sex couples—gaydemographics.org, the Human Rights Campaign (Smith and Gates 2001), and the National Black Justice Coalition of the National Gay and Lesbian Task Force Institute (Dang and Frazier 2004). Two of the reports agree that 601,209 same-sex couples were identified in the 2000 PUMS: 304,148 male couples and 297,061 females. This represents about 1 percent of all couples who responded to the 2000 US census. Alain Dang and Somjen Frazier (2004) put the number at "nearly 600,000." Due to undercounting caused by the reluctance of many gay couples to identify themselves as unmarried partners, David Smith and Gary Gates (2001) estimate that the true number of gay couples may be over 1.5 million.

Gaydemographics.org describes the racial distribution of same-sex couples as follows: 79 percent white, 9 percent black, 12 percent Hispanic, 2 percent Asian, and 1 percent Native American. Smith and Gates put the black percentage at 14 percent. Like other couples, most of the same-sex partners (89 percent) were of the same race. However, the rate of racially mixed same-sex partners was four times greater than in the general population.

In addition to simply describing gay and lesbian couples, the PUMS data allow them to be compared with straight couples. Unfortunately, only Dang and Frazier do this in a systematic way, and their focus is on black couples. In terms of comparisons, I will stick with these data even though they are incomplete.

The distribution of household income for gay and lesbian couples is presented in Table 6.2. There is a large range of incomes, from the very poor to the well-to-do. This is clearly inconsistent with the stereotype of all gays and lesbians being upper-middle class. The mean household income is $72,122, and the median is $57,608.

Comparative income data are presented in Table 6.3. To no one's surprise, white homosexual couples earn substantially more than black homosexual couples among both males and females. Mixed-race couples having at least one black partner earned slightly less than white couples. In addition, gay men earned more than lesbians in each racial group.

Table 6.2 Distribution (percentage) of Household Income of Same-Sex Couples in 1999

Percentage	Income
16	0–$25,000
27	$25,100–$50,000
23	$50,100–$75,000
14	$75,100–$100,000
7	$100,100–$125,000
4	$125,100–$150,000
5	$150,100–$250,000
3	$250,100+
Mean	$72,122
Median	$57,608

Source: GayDemographics.org.

Table 6.3 Median Household Income in 1999 by Race, Gender, and Sexual Orientation

	Same-Sex Couples		Opposite-Sex Couples	
Race	Male	Female	Married	Cohabiting
White	$69,000	$60,000	—	—
Black	45,000	40,000	51,000	41,000
Black/other[a]	67,000	52,000	—	—

Source: Dang and Frazier 2004.
Note: a. Mixed-race couples with at least one black member.

Among black opposite-sex couples, those who are married earned more than same-sex couples. However, black cohabiting opposite-sex couples had similar incomes to same-sex couples. Similar comparisons for whites and mixed couples are not available.

Home ownership is another indicator of economic status. In Table 6.4, white same-sex couples are more likely to own homes than are comparable blacks (70 percent and 52 percent, respectively). Home ownership differences between gay male and lesbian couples were small. Although black married opposite-sex couples were substantially more likely to own their homes than black same-sex couples, black cohabiting couples were much less likely to own their own homes.

Gay and lesbian couples are also relatively well educated. According to gaydemographics.org, 18 percent of the couples had no high school diploma, 23 percent graduated from high school but didn't attend college, 21 percent had some college, 25 percent had a bachelor's degree, and 13 percent had postgraduate degrees. Dang and Frazier (2004) present comparative data only in terms of whether respondents had education beyond high school (Table 6.5). Mixed-race and white same-sex couples were much more likely to have education beyond high school than were black same-sex couples. Black opposite-sex couples were more likely to have gone beyond high school than were black same-sex couples.

The top ten occupations for people who are part of same-sex couples are first-line supervisors of retail sales workers, truck drivers, retail salespeople, secretaries and administrative assistants, elementary and middle-school teachers, nurses, miscellaneous managers, cashiers, customer service representatives, and nursing/home health aides. Not

Table 6.4 Home Ownership Rates for Couples in 1999 by Race, Gender, and Sexual Orientation (percentage)

	Same-Sex Couples			Opposite-Sex Couples	
Race	Male	Female	Total	Married	Cohabiting
White	72	71	70	—	—
Black	54	50	52	68	28

Source: Dang and Frazier 2004.
Note: As the data indicate, 72 percent of white male same-sex couples and 54 percent of black male same-sex couples owned their homes.

Table 6.5 Percentage of Couples in 1999 Who Had Education Beyond High School by Race and Sexual Orientation

Race	Same-Sex Couples	Opposite-Sex Couples	
		Married	Cohabiting
Whites	67	—	—
Black	40	50	48
Black/other	71	—	—

Source: Dang and Frazier 2004.
Note: As the table indicates, 40 percent of black same-sex couples and 50 percent of black, married opposite-sex couples had post–high school education.

surprisingly, there was a familiar gender division of labor in the occupations held by same-sex couples. Gay men made up 66 percent of the designers who were same-sex partners; the remaining 34 percent of designers were lesbians. Sixty-one percent of the auto mechanics, 60 percent of the truck drivers, and 57 percent of the janitors were gay men. Lesbians, in comparison, were 72 percent of the childcare workers, 68 percent of the counselors, 62 percent of the accountants, and 53 percent of the waitresses (gaydemographics.org). Remember, the base upon which these percentages were calculated is people in a particular occupation who were also members of a same-sex couple.

The data in these four tables clearly show that white same-sex couples are economically better off than comparable black couples and that gay male couples are more advantaged than lesbian couples. The data are not consistent with the stereotype that gays and lesbians are more affluent than heterosexuals. Black same-sex couples, on the whole, are *less* economically advantaged than black married opposite-sex couples. The comparisons between black same-sex couples and black cohabiting opposite-sex couples are inconsistent. These conclusions are tentative because there are no comparative data about nonblacks.

M. V. Badgett (2000) and Sylvia Allegreto and Michelle Arthur (2001) have completed complex analyses of 1990 census data and several other large-scale studies. After statistically controlling for factors like education, occupation, and age, they found that the incomes of gay male unmarried partners were *lower* than the incomes of heterosexual married men. Lesbian incomes, however, were the *same* as the incomes of heterosexual married women. Looking at household income, gay male unmarried partner households earned the same or less than heterosexual married couples. Lesbian unmarried couples earned less than heterosexual married couples. Badgett (2000, 24) concludes that "lesbians, gays and bisexuals are spread throughout the range of household income distribution."

Finally, Table 6.6 looks at the percentage of couples with children living in their home. Although lesbian couples are more likely than gay male couples to have children in the home, almost one-quarter of white gay male couples and 46 percent of black gay male couples have children in the home. This certainly goes against the stereotype of childless gay and lesbian couples.

Black same-sex couples, both male and female, are more likely than comparable white couples to have children in the home. They are, however, less likely than black married opposite-sex couples to have children living in the home. The rate of children in the home for black opposite-sex cohabiting couples falls between the lesbian and gay male rates.

Prejudice

Unlike the paucity of data about gays in the labor force, there is an abundance of data on attitudes toward gays and how things have changed over time. However, the interpretation of these data results in a "glass half empty or half full" dilemma. During the past 20–30 years, attitudes have been moving in the direction of more tolerance, but a great deal of homophobia still exists.

Table 6.6 Percentage of Couples with Children in the Home in 1999 by Race, Gender, and Sexual Orientation

Race	Same-Sex Couples		Opposite-Sex Couples	
	Male	Female	Married	Cohabiting
White	24	38	—	—
Black	46	61	69	51

Source: Dang and Frazier 2004.
Note: As the table indicates, 46 percent of black male same-sex couples and 61 percent of black female same-sex couples had children living in their home.

National polls show that the American population is much more accepting of gays and lesbians now than it was forty years ago (Saad 2007; Pew Research Center 2010) Table 6.7 shows that more than half of the population believes that homosexual relations between adults should be legal, that homosexuality is an acceptable lifestyle, that gays and lesbians should have equal job rights, and that gays should be able to serve openly in the military. This is the good news.

Unfortunately, there's also bad news. A plurality (48 percent) is still opposed to same-sex marriage although the approval rate is climbing rapidly. Respondents are sharply divided when it comes to dealing with their own children. A slim plurality would not hire a gay babysitter (45 percent to 43 percent) and would not permit their child to read a book that contains a same-sex couple (45 percent to 44 percent). Two-thirds would be upset if they found that their own child was gay. In terms of political power, 32 percent felt that gays had too much,

Table 6.7 Changing Attitudes Toward Homosexuality According to National Polls, 1977–2010

	Percentage of Respondents		
Question/Year	Yes	No	No Opinion
Legality of homosexual relations (Gallup)			
1977	43	43	14
2007	59	37	4
Homosexuality is acceptable lifestyle (Gallup)			
1982	34	51	15
2007	57	39	3
Equal job rights for homosexuals (Gallup)			
1977	56	33	11
2001	89	8	2
Gays serve openly in military (Pew)			
1994	52	45	3
2010	60	30	10
Accept same-sex marriage (Pew)			
1996	27	65	8
2010	42	48	10

Sources: Saad 2007; Pew Research Center 2010.
Note: As the table indicates, the percentage of respondents who believed that homosexuality was an acceptable lifestyle increased from 34 percent in 1982 to 57 percent in 2007.

32 percent said that they had the right amount, and only 20 percent said that they had too little. Fifty-five percent said that the media gave too much coverage to gay issues (Pew Research Center 2010; Bowman 2004; Pinkus and Richardson 2004).

When these data are disaggregated to see how demographic factors affect attitudes, there are some consistent findings. Men, older people, fundamentalist Christians (those who literally interpret the Bible), frequent church attendees, blacks, those with no college education, and political conservatives are the most likely to display anti-gay prejudice. Women, younger people, whites, Catholics, Jews, infrequent church attendees, college graduates, and political liberals tend to have more tolerant attitudes toward gays (Pew Research Center 2010; D'Arcy 2005).

Studies of the attitudes of college students, summarized by Donald Hinrichs and Pamela Rosenberg (2002), have found that the two most important factors predicting attitudes toward gays and lesbians are sex-role attitudes and interpersonal relations with homosexuals. Students who have liberal sex-role attitudes have more positive feelings toward gays than those with more traditional sex-role attitudes. In addition, students who have positive interpersonal relationships with at least one homosexual will have more positive feelings toward gays than those who don't know any gays or who have negative relationships.

Gregory Lewis (2003) looked further into black and white attitudes toward gays and lesbians by reviewing thirty-one studies. He found that blacks are more likely than whites to agree with the following statements:

> "Homosexual relations are always wrong."
> "AIDS is God's punishment to homosexuals."
> "Pro-gay books should be removed from the public library."
> "Gays should not be permitted to give a public talk in the community."

In terms of employment issues, Lewis found that blacks and whites had the same attitudes about employing a gay college professor, firing gay teachers, hiring gays in five different occupations, and allowing gays to serve in the military. Blacks were, however, more likely than whites to support laws preventing anti-gay discrimination.

According to Lewis, some of the anti-gay attitudes among blacks are due to their low levels of education and high levels of membership in fundamentalist Christian churches. When these and other factors are statistically controlled, the gap in black/white hostility to gays shrinks but the greater black than white support of gay employment rights grows. In other words, a blanket statement that blacks are more homophobic than whites is oversimplified.

How are we to interpret the broad findings that American public opinion is moving in a more tolerant direction? Susan Pinkus and Jill Richardson (2004), who analyzed the *Los Angeles Times* poll, are quite clear: "The poll shows that the public appears to be more accepting and more tolerant of people in this country who are gays and lesbians than they were even just a decade ago" (1). Karlyn Bowman (2004), author of the American Enterprise Institute report, concurs.

Many social psychologists who study anti-gay prejudice are not so sure that tolerance is increasing. Melanie and Todd Morrison (2002) acknowledge that scores on two major traditional (or old-fashioned) anti-gay prejudice scales have declined. Both male and female college students now score below the neutral point (i.e., on the non-prejudiced side) on the Attitudes Toward Lesbian Scale and the Attitudes Toward Gay Men Scale (together referred to as the ATLG Scale). These two scales ask respondents to indicate whether they agree or disagree with the following types of statements:

"Gay men should be avoided whenever possible."
"Gay women should not be allowed to work with children."
"Those who support the rights of gay men are probably gay themselves."

Morrison and Morrison (2002) offer several possible explanations of the declining scores on these traditional prejudice scales. Respondents may be growing more tolerant, or they may be concealing their true feelings, or the sample may be statistically biased because most studies are done on college students.

However, Morrison and Morrison prefer a different explanation: "It is possible that scales such as the ATLG examine a specific type of homonegativity; one that many college and university students no longer endorse. . . . Students may evidence low levels of homonegativity on old-fashioned measures not because they possess favorable attitudes toward gay men and lesbians, but simply because they consider old-fashioned measures to be anachronistic" (2002, 17–18).

Morrison and Morrison instead argue that this old-fashioned prejudice has been replaced by a new form of prejudice that can be measured by their Modern Homonegativity Scale (MHS). This new scale contains twelve items, including the following:

"Many gay men use their sexual orientation so that they can obtain special privileges."
"Lesbians should stop shoving their lifestyle down other people's throats."
"If gay men want to be treated like everyone else, then they need to stop making such a fuss about their sexuality/culture.

This modern anti-gay prejudice focuses on the belief that gays and lesbians make illegitimate and unnecessary demands, that discrimination against homosexuals is a thing of the past, and that homosexuals exaggerate the importance of their sexual orientation. In a series of studies on Canadian college students, Morrison and Morrison (2002) show that the patterns of responses to the MHS are distinct from the answers to the ATL/ATG scales. In other words, it may be that one type of anti-gay prejudice is simply being replaced by another that fits in with the twenty-first century. This approach to the changing nature of anti-gay prejudice is similar to the studies of race and gender prejudice that have been discussed in previous chapters.

More research needs to be carried out to confirm the existence of these two different types of homonegativity. In a recent study of more than six hundred college students at a mid-Atlantic university, for example, Ilsa Lottes and Eric Grollman (2010) found that the two measures of prejudice are highly correlated with each other. This raises doubt about whether there are two distinct types of homonegativity.

In any case, it's sobering to remember that vicious anti-gay prejudice is still alive and well, especially among conservative Christian fundamentalists (Moser 2005). On September 12, 2004, for example, conservative televangelist Jimmy Swaggart was discussing homosexuals during one of his broadcasts and said, "I've never seen a man in my life I wanted to marry. . . . I'm going to be blunt and plain. If one ever looks at me like that, I'm going to kill him and tell God he died" (*Diversity News* 2004c). The audience laughed and applauded. Swaggart later said that he was trying to be humorous and that he was only using the "killing" expression figuratively (also see Potok 2010).

The Westboro Baptist Church, led by Fred Phelps, has been picketing the funerals of soldiers who have been killed in Iraq and

Afghanistan. They believe that God has been punishing the United States for being too tolerant of homosexuals by killing US soldiers. The noisy picketers carry signs like "God hates fags" and "Thank God for dead soldiers." In March 2011, the US Supreme Court said that their picketing was a form of free speech that is protected by the constitution (Marso 2011).

Discrimination

Given the strong incentives for many LGBT people to remain in the closet as well as the lack of systematic data collection, it is difficult to be precise about the amount of discrimination based on sexual orientation that takes place. Verbal harassment is probably too frequent to even count. Among middle and high school children, for example, it is common to use terms like *fag* and *dike* to tease and harass heterosexual classmates who are not members of the "in crowd." Known LGBT classmates also are the targets of verbal harassment. Phyllis Gerstenfeld (2004) estimates that as many as 80 percent of LGBT children and adults will be verbally harassed in any given year (also see Potok 2010).

Verbal harassment is the most common form of **individual discrimination** against gays. A recent national survey by the Gay, Lesbian, and Straight Education Network (2008) showed that 84.5 percent reported being verbally harassed at school during the past year because of their sexual orientation. Physical violence is also common. The same survey showed that 44 percent had been physically harassed (i.e., shoved or pushed) and 22 percent had been physically assaulted. Sixty-one percent said that they felt unsafe at school, and 33 percent had missed at least one day of school for safety reasons.

Since the federal government began collecting data on hate crimes in 1991, more than 12,000 anti-gay hate crimes have been reported to the police. In 2008 alone, 1,297 anti-gay hate crimes were reported. This accounted for 17 percent of all reported hate crimes that year (Federal Bureau of Investigation 2008). Everyone agrees that this is only the tip of the iceberg. Gerstenfeld (2004) estimates that 20–25 percent of LGBT people are victims of a hate crime each year. Studies have shown that anti-gay victimization follows predictable patterns—men more than women, people of color more than whites, threats and physical violence more than property crime. The perpetrators of anti-gay hate crimes are most likely to be young, lone males.

Until 2009, the federal government was not able to prosecute perpetrators of anti-gay hate crimes because they were not included in federal hate crimes bills passed by Congress. The Matthew Shepard and James Byrd Jr. Hate Crimes Prevention Act changed this and permitted federal prosecutors to bring charges on the basis of both sexual orientation and gender identification. This was the first time these two categories were included in the US Code. Forty-three states now include sexual orientation in their hate crime legislation, although only twelve also include gender identity (Human Rights Campaign 2009).

In terms of individual discrimination in employment, gays are still not protected by federal civil rights laws. Consequently, data on anti-gay discrimination are not available from the Equal Employment Opportunity Commission. Thirty-six states have laws protecting gays and lesbians from employment discrimination, although only fourteen of these also include gender identity (Human Rights Campaign 2009). Surveys have shown that more than two-fifths of gays have said that they had been harassed at work, had been denied a promotion, or were forced to quit because of their sexual orientation (Edwards 2003).

Juan Battle and his colleagues (2002) conducted a survey of 2,645 black gays who attended Black Pride events in the summer of 2002. They asked respondents about their experiences with race and sexual orientation discrimination in a variety of areas. Respondents were asked to say if most of the experiences had been negative, positive, or equally negative and positive.

In terms of experiencing some type of racial discrimination in mixed-race LGBT organizations and bars, black LGBT people reported more negative than positive experiences. In terms of racial discrimination in mixed-race community events and personal relations, they reported more positive than negative experiences. Almost half of the respondents said that racism was a problem among white LGBT people.

Respondents were also asked to evaluate homophobic experiences that they had in the black community. In terms of homophobic experiences in heterosexual black organizations and with families and friends, respondents reported more positive than negative experiences. In terms of black churches and religious organizations, they reported more negative than positive experiences. Two-thirds of the respondents said that homophobia was a problem in the black community.

This study indicates the complexity of experiences with discrimination for black LGBT individuals. Aside from problems with black religious organizations, black LGBT respondents were more likely to report *racial* discrimination from white LGBT people than *anti-gay* discrimination from the black heterosexual community.

When it comes to institutional discrimination against LGBT people, the situation in the United States is still ugly. Though legal discrimination on the basis of race and gender has been declining, discrimination on the basis of sexual orientation is still common.

Prior to 1991, the military simply excluded open homosexuals. The Clinton administration "liberalized" this policy by instituting the "Don't Ask, Don't Tell" rule. This meant that gays could serve if they were discreet (i.e., not public) about their sexual orientation. Nevertheless, Defense Department data show that more than 14,000 gays and lesbians have been discharged from the military since 1993 (Mascaro and Oliphant 2010). The Palm Center puts the figures considerably higher (Jordan 2010). Gay soldiers are unlikely to file harassment suits because doing so would require them to come out, which would in turn lead to their discharge.

In addition to civil rights concerns, this anti-gay institutionalized discrimination hurts the military itself. During the first half of 2005 the various branches of the military failed to meet their recruitment quotas, in part due to the war in Iraq. At the same time, at least twenty Arab-speaking gay soldiers were discharged. The Government Accounting Office reported that it cost more than $200 million to recruit and train new soldiers to replace the gays and lesbians that were discharged (Files 2005). More than twenty countries permit gays and lesbians to serve in their military (Palm Center 2009).

In early 2010, the Obama administration announced that it would seek the repeal of "Don't Ask, Don't Tell" and permit gays to openly participate in the military. A high-level commission was appointed to determine *how* the policy could be efficiently repealed. Congress passed a law officially repealing "Don't Ask, Don't Tell" during the lame duck session late in 2010.

During the George W. Bush administration, several federal agencies engaged in explicitly anti-gay actions. Consider the controversy over the PBS-funded program *Postcards from Buster* in the winter of 2005. Buster is an animated character who interacts with live people on the show for preschoolers that is supposed to promote diversity.

During a program on maple syrup, a girl introduces Buster to her two mothers. This was too much for then Secretary of Education Margaret Spellings, who dissociated the department from supporting the show. She also suggested that the producers return any federal money that was used to make the program. As a result of the controversy, only 18 of the 349 PBS affiliates aired the program (Zurawik 2005).

Another federal agency objected to the title of a workshop, "Suicide Prevention Among Gays, Lesbians, Bisexuals, and Transgendered Individuals." The workshop was to be part of a conference sponsored by the Suicide Prevention Resource Center in 2005. Organizers were informed that the head of the Substance Abuse and Mental Health Service Administration would not attend the conference unless the reference to LGBT individuals was removed from the workshop's title. The workshop was renamed "Suicide Prevention in Vulnerable Populations," but the term *sexual orientation* couldn't even be included in the workshop description (Vanderburgh 2005).

Laws regarding marriage and civil unions are also examples of institutional discrimination. At the federal level, the Defense of Marriage Act of 1996 defined marriage as between a man and a woman, thus making same-sex partners ineligible for a wide range of federal benefits from taxes and Social Security. During the 2008 presidential campaign, Barack Obama pledged to overturn this law. In February 2011, both President Obama and Attorney General Eric Holder announced that the Justice Department would no longer enforce the law.

The majority of states also prohibit same-sex marriages. In 2010, only five states—Connecticut, Iowa, Massachusetts, New Hampshire, and Vermont—and the District of Columbia permitted same-sex marriages, and two others (New York and Maryland) recognized same-sex marriages performed in other states. In 2010, California was in legal limbo when a federal judge ruled that Proposition 8, which prevented same-sex marriage, was unconstitutional because it violated the Due Process and Equal Protection clauses of the Fourteenth Amendment. Most observers agree that this case will eventually reach the US Supreme Court and could establish an important legal precedent however it is decided.

For more than a decade, conservatives have promoted an amendment to the US Constitution that would ban gay marriages. The amendment states: "Marriage in the United States shall consist only of the union of a man and a woman. Neither this constitution nor the constitution of any state, nor state or federal law, shall be construed to require that marital status or the legal incidents thereof be conferred upon unmarried couples or groups" (Human Rights Campaign 2004). This would be the first time that a constitutional amendment would limit rights to an entire group of people.

The marriage controversy even filters down to school textbooks on health. Two major publishers—Holt, Rinehart, and Winston, and McGraw-Hill—had used terms like "married partners" and "when two people marry." Several members of the Texas Board of Education ruled that because of this wording, the books could not be used in Texas (the nation's second-largest buyer of school textbooks); the wording is contrary to a state law banning gay civil unions and marriage. After the publishers agreed to use phrases like "husband and wife" and "when a man and a woman marry," the board approved the books for use in Texas (Associated Press 2004).

Institutional discrimination can also be seen in organized religions. Both the Jewish and Christian versions of the Bible denounce homosexuality as a sin. In some religions (e.g., Latter-Day Saints and Orthodox Judaism), gays and lesbians are banished from the family and the community. In others, there is a "hate the sin, love the sinner" approach whereby homosexuals can't be officials of the church, temple, or mosque but are still accepted into the community. In 2004 the fundamentalist Southern Baptists split off from the main Baptist organization in protest of the latter's more liberal stance regarding homosexuality (Human Rights Campaign 2004). These anti-gay religious institutions are one major cause of the strong homophobic ideology that exists in the United States.

In 2005 the United Church of Christ became the first mainstream Christian denomination to support gay marriage. A few other religious communities, including Reform Judaism, Unitarians, Episcopalians, Presbyterians, and the Metropolitan Community Church, sanction same-sex unions (*New York Times* News Service 2005). Within many conservative religions, certain groups have attempted to liberalize their policies toward gays and lesbians. For example, a group of 100 Modern Orthodox rabbis, educators, and mental health professionals issued a letter saying that homosexuals should be welcomed into the religion even though their behavior is still not seen as acceptable (*Feminist News* 2010; Baird 2001; D'Arcy 2005).

It is difficult to document institutional discrimination in the world of work, although it clearly remains a serious problem. The subtitle of a *Business Week* article, for example, states, "Gays are making huge strides everywhere but in the executive suite" (Edwards 2003, 64).

Given the continuing high incidence of anti-gay individual and institutional discrimination, it becomes somewhat less important to discuss **structural discrimination** (i.e., neutral policies that have negative impacts on gays). In the race and gender chapters, I emphasized that in spite of the decline in intentional individual and institutional discrimination, structural discrimination was still important. With sexual orientation, intentional discrimination is still dominant.

One example of anti-gay structural discrimination would be elementary school assignments asking children to draw pictures of their families. In this seemingly innocuous assignment, teachers expect children to draw a man and/or a woman. The children of gay parents, however, are put in the position of "outing" their families to the entire class and bringing anti-gay harassment onto themselves. Unless the teacher is sensitive to these issues, this could cause real problems for both the child and the family (Hofmann 2005).

Of course, there is still a great deal of individual discrimination in the field of education. In one example of an outrageously insensitive teacher, a Louisiana elementary school student was punished for telling a classmate that his mother was gay. When one child asked Marcus McLaurin about his mother and father, Marcus replied that he has two mothers. During the brief discussion, Marcus said that his mothers were gay, meaning that "gay is when a girl likes another girl" (Stepp 2003, C10). The teacher overheard the conversation and criticized Marcus for using a bad word. The teacher then filled out an official "behavior report," writing, in part, "This kind of discussion is not acceptable in my room. I feel that parents should explain things of this nature to their own children in their own way" (Stepp 2003, C10).

Before leaving the topic of anti-gay discrimination, it's important to acknowledge that there is some progress in trying to combat intentional individual and institutional discrimination. The 2010 repeal of "Don't Ask, Don't Tell" is a major civil rights milestone. In 2003 the US Supreme Court overturned the antisodomy laws in Texas that had outlawed oral and anal sex. The *Lawrence v. Texas* decision also invalidated antisodomy laws in fourteen other states. According to Richard Goldstein (2003), "It's the most momentous gay rights decision in American history. Justice Anthony Kennedy's language explicitly gives homosexuals the right to have intimate relationships . . . in private between consenting adults."

Increasing numbers of large companies have important gay-friendly policies. In 2008, for example, 88 percent of Fortune 500 corporations had explicit policies preventing discrimination based on sexual orientation, 35 percent had policies opposed to gender identity discrimination, and 57 percent provided same-sex partner benefits (Human Rights Campaign 2008).

Since 1996, the Human Rights Campaign has been issuing an annual list of the best and worst companies for LGBT employees. It rates large corporations "on a scale of 0 to 100 percent on seven criteria, including: health insurance for same-sex domestic partners; recognize and support LGBT employee groups; marketing to the LGBT market; and including the words 'sexual orientation' in their primary non-discrimination policy" (Davis 2004). In the 2004 list, fifty-six corporations received perfect scores, double the number in 2003.

Sandals Resorts International is one of the many organizations that has liberalized some of its policies. In 2004, Sandals prohibited gay couples from staying at its couples-only resorts in the Caribbean. In an unapologetic explanation, Sandals stated: "While it is understandable that some might have questions about the guest policies at Sandals, we want to underscore that everyone is welcome at our ultra all-inclusive Beaches Resorts (regardless of marital/family status or sexual orientation)" (Johnson 2004). In 2010, Sandals welcomed "all adult couples" to all of its resorts.

When it comes to gay representation on television, things are also improving according to an annual survey of TV networks conducted by GLAAD, the Gay and Lesbian Alliance Against Defamation (2010). In terms of prime-time original programming (not including reruns), the networks are devoting more time to gay issues, have more gay characters, and have more race and gender diversity than ever before.

The main focus of the study was comparing different networks. MTV was the highest-rated network and was the only one to receive a grade of "excellent." More than two-fifths of its prime-time hours included a gay character or reference to a gay issue. CW was the highest-rated broadcast network and received a grade of "good." At the other end of the spectrum, four networks received failing grades: A&E, CBS, TBS, and USA. Only 5 percent or fewer hours included gay characters or issues. The remaining networks all received grades of "good" except FX which only got an "adequate." One continuing problem, according to GLAAD, is that most of the gay characters tend to be white and male, with lesbians and people of color being highly underrepresented. Stereotyping is also an issue.

The networks still have a tendency to steer clear of controversy. In December 2004, for example, CBS and NBC refused to air a thirty-second commercial by the United Church of Christ emphasizing inclusiveness. In the ad, a bouncer-type person who was standing in front of a church allowed white mixed-sex couples to enter but turned away people of color and same-sex couples. The ad ended with the words, "Jesus didn't turn away people. Neither do we." The networks' explanation was that they don't accept controversial advertisements (Hiaasen 2004).

At least twenty-five organizations now give college scholarships to LGBT individuals, including the Point Foundation, Parents and Friends of Lesbians and Gays, the League at AT&T Foundation, and the United Church of Christ (Kahn 2004). The largest source of scholarships in 2004 was the Point Foundation, which funded twenty-seven individuals.

* * *

There's no doubt that things are much better for the LGBT community than they were several decades ago. Increasing numbers of people in the straight community are becoming allies to LGBT people or at least have a "live and let live" philosophy. In spite of this progress, the United States still has a long way to go to eliminate discrimination based on sexual orientation.

7

Disability

"People with disabilities" is one of the newer groups to be in-cluded in the field of diversity studies. Of course, such individuals have been present throughout human history, but the sense of group consciousness among people with disabilities is relatively new.

People with physical and mental disabilities have been stigmatized and discriminated against for centuries. Having a physical impairment has often been seen as a religious punishment or as a sign of evil in a wide variety of religions, including Christianity and Judaism. The disabled have been kept behind closed doors in the home or placed in asylums or other institutions to be kept out of sight. In the nineteenth and early twentieth centuries, eugenicists and social Darwinists promoted forced sterilization so that disabled people couldn't have children that would weaken the gene pool. This practice was upheld by the US Supreme Court in 1927. During World War II, Nazi Germany took this one step further by murdering tens of thousands of physically and mentally disabled people in Europe, along with millions of Jews, gypsies, homosexuals, and communists.

Terminology

Like other subordinate groups that we have discussed in this book, the concept of disability is socially constructed, and there has been considerable debate over terminology. Pejorative words like *cripple*, *abnormal*, and *invalid* are no longer considered appropriate to describe people with physical disabilities. Likewise, terms like *idiot*, *moron*, and

133

crazy are no longer used to describe those with mental disabilities. In 2010, for example, President Obama signed a law that replaced *mental retardation* with *intellectual disability* in the US Code (West 2010). Most people who are activists or writers in the field of disability studies eschew terms like *handicapped, physically/mentally challenged,* and *special,* preferring *disabled* or *people with disabilities.* Those without disabilities would be called *nondisabled.*

There is not, however, agreement about the definition of *disability.* Many contemporary writers, who use the social model of disability, differentiate between *impairment* and *disability.* According to this view, **impairment** refers to *physical or mental limitations* such as the inability to see, hear, walk, or read. This is an individual-level term. **Disability**, in comparison, is a *social exclusion* or "*a disadvantage or restriction of activity caused by a contemporary social organization which takes little or no account of people who have physical impairments and thus excludes them from participation in the mainstream of social activities* (Shakespeare 2006, 198).

This is an important distinction to understand. Not being able to walk, for example, is a physical impairment. Not being able to access a building because there is no wheelchair ramp is a disability. Similarly, not being able to see is an impairment, but not being able to read a book because it is not available in braille or on audiotape is a disability. This impairment/disability distinction has certain similarities to the sex (physical/biological) and gender (cultural) distinction that we discussed in Chapter 5.

The Americans with Disabilities Act (1990), however, equates disability and impairment. According to this landmark piece of legislation,

> The term "disability" means, with respect to an individual—
>   (a) a physical or mental impairment that substantially limits
>   one or more of the major life activities of such individual;
>   (b) a record of such impairment; or
>   (c) being regarded as having such an impairment.

This, of course, is an individualistic medical and legal definition. There are certain medical categories that people either fit or don't fit. In addition, if one is legally declared to be disabled, certain payments, accommodations, and treatment options become available. If one is designated as "learning disabled," for example, he or she must be allowed to take more time to complete an exam.

Other agencies of the federal government use different definitions (Barnow 2008). In this book, I will use the impairment/disability distinction used by the social model. Whereas some of these impairments have mainly biological causes (e.g., genetic illnesses, birth defects, hormone imbalances), others have social causes. Some mental retardation is due to lead exposure in poor communities. Wars cause the loss of limbs and other traumatic injuries. Unsafe working conditions and environmental contamination cause many cancers. These are all preventable impairments that can be reduced by changes in the larger society.

Some contemporary analysts use the term **ableism** to describe the *system of oppression based on disability status.* Because the nondisabled are politically and economically powerful, they define dominant cultural standards; because of this, the disabled are stigmatized and discriminated against by the nondisabled. According to this view, the disabled must redefine themselves as a group with common interests in order to gain power vis-à-vis the dominant group (i.e., the nondisabled). Their different impairments should not keep them apart.

There is some evidence that this may be happening. The National Organization on Disability (NOD)/Harris Poll (2004) reported that in 1986, only 40 percent of people with disabilities said that they had a "somewhat strong" or "very strong" sense of common identity with other people with disabilities. By 2004, that figure had jumped to 56 percent. The more severe a person's disability, the stronger sense of common identity he or she was likely to have (also see Darling 2003).

Descriptive Statistics

I use two major sources of statistics for this section. First, the US Census Bureau collects various statistics comparing people with disabilities and the nondisabled. Second, the NOD/Harris Poll conducted a major national survey comparing the same two populations in 2004. Although the data from these two sources are not identical, a reasonably consistent picture of the disabled begins to emerge.

Exactly how large is the population of people with disabilities? The answer, of course, depends upon who is included as disabled. The Census Bureau puts the number of disabled in 2005 at 54.4 million, or 18.7 percent of the US population.

The most common types of impairments are physical in nature (see Table 7.1). Almost 12 percent of the population cannot walk or climb stairs, and 8 percent have trouble with other physical tasks like lifting, grasping, moving chairs, standing, sitting, crouching, and

Table 7.1 Prevalence of Impediments Among Individuals Fifteen Years and Older by Specific Measures of Disability, 2005

Type of Disability	Number (millions)	Percent
Walk/use stairs	27.3	11.9
Selected physical tasks[a]	19.0	8.2
Mental[b]	16.1	7.0
Seeing/hearing/speaking	14.7	6.4
Instrumental activities of daily living[c]	13.7	5.0
Need for personal assistance	10.8	4.7
Activities of daily living[d]	8.5	3.7
Work at job (ages 16–64)	24.1	12.6
Work around house	18.9	8.4

Source: US Census Bureau 2008.

Notes: a. Lift, grasp, move chair, stand, sit, crouch, reach.

b. Learning disability, retardation, Alzheimer's/dementia, depressed/anxious, trouble getting along with others, trouble concentrating, trouble coping with stress.

c. Go out, manage money, prepare meals, do housework, take prescriptions, use phone.

d. Get around, get into bed, take bath, dress, eat, toileting.

As the table indicates, 27.3 million Americans can't walk or use the stairs. This represents 11.9 percent of all Americans fifteen years of age or older.

reaching. Seven percent have mental impairments, and 6.4 percent have trouble with vision, hearing, or speech. Together with the remaining categories shown in the table, the numbers add up to more than the total number of disabled people because an individual can have multiple impairments.

Age is an important factor in the prevalence of disability. To no one's surprise, disability increases with age. According to the Census Bureau, 8.8 percent of the under-fifteen-year-old population has a disability, compared with 51.8 percent of the sixty-five-year-old and older population. Seventy-one percent of the population of individuals aged eighty or more years consists of people with disabilities.

However, it may be surprising to learn that most people acquire their disabilities after childhood (Table 7.2). In 2004, for example, only 30 percent of the disabled acquired their disability before the age of twenty whereas 47 percent acquired it after the age of forty. The data also show that the age of acquisition seems to be declining. In 1986 the median age of acquisition was 43.3 years old; this declined to 35.7 years old in 2004. It is possible that some of this decline is due to better identification of disabilities.

Table 7.2 Percentage Distribution of Age of Onset of Disability in 1986 and 2004

Age of Onset	1986	2004
Birth to 19 years	20%	30%
20–39	25	24
40–55	23	27
56 years and older	31	20
Median age	43.3	35.7

Source: National Organization for Disability/Harris Poll 2004.
Notes: In 2004, for example, 30 percent of the disabled had their disability before they were twenty years of age.

The most complete race/gender breakdown of people with disabilities is provided by the Census Bureau and its Survey of Income and Program Participation (SIPP). As Table 7.3 shows, the 2005 SIPP data includes people fifteen years of age and older, and the 2000 census data includes people five years of age and older. The two data sets use slightly different definitions of disability.

Two important patterns can be observed in the data. First, women have higher rates of disability than men—20.1 percent for women versus 17.3 percent for men. This is true in all race/ethnic groups. Second, blacks and American Indians have the highest disability rates in both the SIPP and the census data, whereas Asians have the lowest. White non-Hispanics and Hispanics fall in between these two extremes, although the two data sets are not consistent in terms of their order.

It is also important to examine data on the employment status of people with disabilities. Table 7.4 indicates whether people are employed full-time, part-time, or are not employed. The "not employed" category includes those who are unemployed (i.e., actively looking for work) as well as those who are not in the labor force. People with disabilities are less than half as likely to be employed full-time and more than three times as likely to not be employed as people without disabilities. Among those with severe disabilities, 15.6 percent are employed full-time and 69.6 percent are not employed.

Interestingly, employment rates for the disabled have gone *down* since the Americans with Disabilities Act was signed into law. There are several possible explanations for this. It may be that increased transfer payments to the disabled have stipulations that prevent people from

Table 7.3 People with Disabilities by Race and Gender in Two Different Federal Government Studies

Race/Gender	2005 Survey of Income and Program Participation (15 years and older)		2000 Census (5 years and older)
	Number (millions)	Percent	Percent
All Races	54.4	18.7	19.3
Males	24.6	17.3	—
Females	29.8	20.1	—
White, non-Hispanic	38.4	19.7	18.3
Males	17.3	18.1	—
Females	21.1	21.2	—
Black	7.5	20.5	24.3
Males	3.3	19.3	—
Females	4.2	21.4	—
Hispanic	5.5	13.1	20.9
Males	2.6	12.0	—
Female	2.9	14.2	—
Asian	1.2	12.4	16.6
Males	0.5	10.4	—
Females	0.7	14.3	—
American Indian	—	—	24.3

Source: US Census Bureau 2008.
Note: As the table indicates, e.g., 17.3 million white, non-Hispanic males have disabilities; this accounts for 18.1 percent of the white non-Hispanic male population.

Table 7.4 Employment Status by Disability Status for Individuals 21–64 Years, 2005

Disability Status	Employment Status (percentage)			
	Full-Time	Part-Time	Not Employed[a]	Total
With no disability	62.9	20.6	16.5	100
With disability	26.5	19.1	54.4	100
With nonsevere disability	48.1	27.1	24.8	100
With severe disability	15.6	15.1	69.6	100

Source: US Census Bureau 2008.
Notes: a. Includes unemployed and people not in labor force; e.g., 62.9 percent of those with no disability are employed full-time, compared with 26.5 percent of those with a disability.
As the table indicates, 15.6 percent of those with severe disabilities were working full-time.

working. Or, the increased cost of compliance with accommodations may make disabled employees more expensive and less likely to be hired.

People with disabilities are also less educated than those without disabilities (see Table 7.5). The disabled are twice as likely to have failed to finish high school and half as likely to have graduated from college as the nondisabled. These educational differences might help to explain the employment differences in the previous table.

Not surprisingly, people with disabilities have lower incomes than the nondisabled. Table 7.6 provides data from the US Census Bureau on individual monthly income. In 2005, individuals with severe disabilities had a median income of only $909 per month (about $10,900 per year if the person worked year-round full-time). This includes any government disability payments that the person received. In 2005, those with nonsevere disabilities earned $2,000 per month, and the nondisabled earned $2,538 per month. The household incomes of people with disabilities are also substantially lower than the household incomes of the nondisabled.

Because of these low incomes, people with disabilities are more likely than the nondisabled to live in poverty. More than one-quarter of people with severe disabilities live in poverty, as do 12 percent of the nonseverely disabled and 9.1 percent of the nondisabled.

There are also important differences in wealth as measured by ownership of assets. People with disabilities are less likely than the

Table 7.5 Highest Grade in School Completed by Disability Status, 2004 (percentage)

Highest Grade in School Completed	Disability Status	
	Disabled	Nondisabled
Less than high school graduate	21	11
High school graduate	39	36
Some college	26	27
College graduate	14	25
Total	100	100

Source: National Organization for Disability/Harris Poll 2004.

Note: As the table indicates, e.g., 14 percent of people with disabilities and 25 percent of people without disabilities graduated from college.

Table 7.6 Median Monthly Income and Poverty Status of Individuals 25–64 Years Old in 2005 by Disability Status

	Disability Status		
Income/Poverty Status	Severe Disability	Nonsevere Disability	Not Disabled
Individual income	$909	$2,000	$2,538
Household income	$2,623	$4,231	$5,143
Percentage in poverty	27.1	12.0	9.1

Source: US Census Bureau 2008.
Note: As the table indicates, the median individual monthly income of those with severe disabilities was $909.

nondisabled to have checking accounts (69 percent versus 76 percent), bank savings accounts (46 percent/65 percent), government savings bonds (15 percent/21.5 percent), or corporate and municipal stocks and bonds (21 percent/34 percent). However, home ownership rates are fairly comparable, with 58 percent of the disabled and 61 percent of the nondisabled owning their own homes (NOD/Harris, 2004).

As a consequence of the differences in income and wealth, people with disabilities have a smaller financial cushion to use during hard times. When asked if they had adequate financial assets to "support yourself for three months with no earned income or gifts from others," 58 percent of people with disabilities said "no" compared to only 36 percent of those with no disabilities.

Prejudice and Ideology

Discussing prejudice toward people with disabilities is more complex than other types of prejudice. Some years ago, Erving Goffman (1963) wrote about how people with physical deformities were often stigmatized by the rest of society. However, negative attitudes toward people with disabilities have not been conceptualized as prejudice until relatively recently. In addition, there are multiple ways to measure attitudes toward people with disabilities. Reviewing literature that was available on the subject, Richard Antonak and Hanoch Livneh (2000) identified twenty-four different methods of measurement, including prejudice scales, stereotype check lists, and experimental manipulations.

In addition, the multiple types of disabilities (physical, sensory, intellectual, emotional) present a challenge to investigators. Some studies ask about attitudes toward the disabled, in general, whereas others inquire about attitudes toward people who are deaf, blind, quadriplegic, and so on. The results can vary depending upon the object of the question. In addition, several scholars talk about a *hierarchy of disabilities* wherein some are viewed more negatively than others. Brigida Hernandez, Christopher Keys, and Fabricio Balcazar (2000), for example, show that employers view intellectual and emotional disabilities more negatively than physical and sensory disabilities. They argue that this hierarchy has been stable over time. In contrast, Mark Deal (2003) reviews a number of studies of students, practitioners, and the general public that show inconsistent hierarchies that change over time.

Most scholars who write about prejudice argue that although negative attitudes toward the disabled still exist, the degree of prejudice that exists now is much less than existed in the past. They point to the passage of major legislation protecting the rights of the disabled as proof of the declining nature of prejudice as well as the greater integration of individuals with disabilities into everyday life.

Although it is difficult to find recent public opinion polls that show the decline in prejudice, the Kaiser Public Opinion Spotlight (2004) has gathered some data that addresses the relatively positive attitudes toward people with disabilities. For example, 60 percent of a national sample believed that people with disabilities have too little influence in society, and 65 percent said that they faced "a lot" or "some" discrimination. Over half believe that the government does too little to protect people with disabilities, and two-thirds strongly support health reforms for the disabled including government funding for long-term care, volunteer organizations, and tax breaks for care takers. These are much more positive attitudes than one might find toward people of color and toward the LGBT population.

Some scholars are skeptical of this "declining prejudice" view and argue that these relatively positive attitudes are partly due to social desirability pressures that make people want to show themselves as nonprejudiced. These scholars use the traditional/new prejudice model that was discussed in previous chapters and argue that contemporary prejudice toward people with disabilities is often more subtle and indirect. Deal (2007), for example, argues that many people still have feelings of ambivalence, discomfort, uneasiness, disgust, and fear toward the disabled, which he refers to as "aversive disablism." This contemporary prejudice would cause people to want to avoid contact with the disabled.

> Support for well-meaning social policies that reduce the possibility of meaningful interactions between disabled people and others are therefore likely to be supported by aversive disablists, for instance: supporting segregated schooling due to the belief that it can offer a higher quality education to disabled children, rather than mainstream education with appropriate backing within the school; the continuation of Day Centers, rather than providing the same services and support within an integrated environment; [and] the use of residential care homes rather than community-based housing schemes. (Deal 2007, 96)

MayLynn Castaneto and Eleanor Willemsen (2006a, 2006b) use an experimental design to demonstrate what they call "modern prejudice." Subjects were asked to evaluate the personality of a disabled person they saw in a video in two different ways. They would fill out the evaluation first according to their own personal beliefs and, second, in terms of how they believed others would evaluate the same person. A physically disabled person also administered the evaluation. Subjects' own ratings were more positive than the ratings that they attributed to others. Because the disabled person would see the ratings, the experimenter argued that the subject indirectly expressed prejudice through the "other" rating.

The nature and extent of prejudice toward people with disabilities is still a lively topic for researchers. Most scholars usually end their articles with a phrase like "more empirical research is needed."

Discrimination

Discrimination on the basis of disability was not part of the public discourse until the last third of the twentieth century. Discrimination regularly occurred, of course, but there was no label for it and it was not usually illegal.

The first major federal law on the topic was Section 504 of the Rehabilitation Act of 1973, which made employment discrimination by federal contractors illegal. Although President Richard Nixon signed the act, his administration did little to enforce it.

In 1990 Congress passed the Americans with Disability Act, which banned discrimination in employment, public accommodations, commercial facilities, public transportation, and many other areas of life. This was extended to include information technology in 2001. A variety of Supreme Court decisions clarified the meaning of these laws, sometimes expanding them but often restricting their scope.

Although laws are valuable tools to fight against discrimination, unequal treatment still exists. The NOD/Harris Poll (2004) asked a national sample of employed individuals with disabilities if they had encountered discrimination on the job because of their disability. Twenty-two percent said "yes." When asked what kind of discrimination they had encountered, the top three responses were that they were refused a job (31 percent), refused a job interview (27 percent), and denied a workplace accommodation (21 percent). Of course, alleging discrimination is not the same thing as actually being discriminated against.

The Equal Employment Opportunity Commission (EEOC 2010a) recorded disability discrimination complaints filed with the organization between 1997 and 2009. During this thirteen-year period, 294,000 complaints were filed with the EEOC, with more than 21,000 filed in 2009 alone—the highest on record. After completing an investigation of each complaint, the EEOC concluded that 19 percent of them (almost 56,000) had enough evidence to warrant an administrative penalty and/or trial.

Pamela Robert and Sharon Harlan (2006) conducted a study of disabled workers employed by an unnamed state government. Most of the workers reported being "marginalized"—that is, being ignored, excluded, and/or stared at. This made them feel like outsiders in their own workplace. They also reported being "fictionalized" in that other workers saw them in inaccurate ways. The two biggest fictionalizations were being seen as incompetent and helpless. A third large problem was "harassment," whereby disabled workers were the recipients of jokes, name-calling, insensitive remarks, needling, and sabotage. This created what is commonly known as a "hostile work environment."

The important part of the Robert and Harlan study was that these actions by individual workers (individual discrimination) often were translated into corporate policy (institutional discrimination).

Marginalization led to the creation of a "backroom" or "dumping ground" where many disabled workers were placed. In other words, they were physically segregated from nondisabled workers. Fictionalization led disabled workers to be placed in lower level jobs that required fewer skills and provided more limited career ladders.

Robert and Harlan found that harassment was the result of workplace tensions. When employers were told to improve their performance or that layoffs might occur, for example, disabled workers became the scapegoats. There was also resentment about disabled workers receiving accommodations so that they could do their jobs effectively. Supervisors in the Robert and Harlan study tolerated this hostile environment and often did nothing to change it. Because this was a study of a single state government, it would be helpful to undertake additional studies to see if these findings could be generalized.

Discrimination against the disabled continues to occur in the United States. Recent legal decisions about disability discrimination involve employment issues, often in well-known multinational corporations and government agencies.

For example, in 2009 the package delivery company UPS agreed to an out-of-court settlement with a group of deaf drivers. The company had required drivers to meet the national hearing standard for the drivers of vehicles in excess of 10,000 pounds even though the UPS trucks were significantly lighter. UPS agreed to a new hearing protocol and training for employees who couldn't meet the national standards. Drivers' hearing would also be monitored (Disability Rights Advocates 2009).

In another case, Walmart was sued by a prospective employee with cerebral palsy. The company refused to hire the man out of concern that his crutches and wheel chair would be a safety risk to customers. In 2008 Walmart paid the man $300,000 and initiated a supervisor training process at the local store (Diversity Insight 2008).

Other recent cases concerned issues of accessibility, not employment. In 2009, Walmart agreed to change its policy of banning service animals (e.g., seeing eye dogs) from entering its stores. The company paid $150,000 to resolve outstanding complaints and an additional $100,000 to help fund a public service campaign (Disability Rights Online News 2009).

Target, one of Walmart's competitors, was named in a class-action suit by the National Federation of the Blind for having an inaccessible website. Blind people can purchase software to vocalize a visual website, but the website must contain the appropriate enabling software. Target initially refused to alter its website but in 2008 agreed to install the necessary software and pay the plaintiffs $6 million—about $3,500 each (Walker 2008).

State government agencies have also been the targets of disability lawsuits. The University of Michigan began a significant expansion of its football stadium but only planned to add a small number of seats for the disabled, claiming it was doing "repairs" rather than a "renovation." The Michigan Paralyzed Veterans of America sued and, in 2008, the university agreed to add additional seats and to take other steps to improve accessibility (Disability Rights Online News 2008).

* * *

Scholarship, lawsuits, and political activism around the issue of disability are certain to continue in the coming years. Since the public seems to be more sympathetic toward people with disabilities than with those who occupy other subordinate master statuses, it is likely that prejudice and discrimination will continue to decline.

8

Social Change
and Social Movements

How can we achieve greater equality when it comes to issues of race, class, gender, sexual orientation, and disability? The answer: more of us must participate in social change activities. According to a slogan popularized in the 1960s, "If you are not part of the solution, you are part of the problem."

Beverly Tatum (2003) uses the analogy of a pedestrian conveyor belt at an airport. Being on the conveyor belt gives you an advantage over those walking beside it, whether you are taking steps or standing still. You must get off the belt or stop the belt to get rid of the unfair advantage. Similarly, members of dominant groups must take action to create more equality for subordinate groups. Doing nothing simply perpetuates the privilege of the dominant groups.

The next logical question is, What is to be done? There should be no surprise when I tell you that neither social scientists nor activists agree on the answer to this important question. Throughout this book I have emphasized the need to look at issues from different levels of analysis. This is also true of change.

Action for Social Change

Levels of Action

There are at least three different levels of action with regard to change. The lowest level is to *change yourself*. To the extent that you hold prejudiced attitudes or buy into the dominant ideology, try to

147

ask yourself whether this is what you really want to believe. One of my aims with this book was to make you aware of various forms of oppression and how you, if you are a member of the dominant group, may be perpetuating them. You may have already begun to examine some of your beliefs and to question others. You can also change your behavior if that is warranted. If you sometimes make racist remarks, you don't have to keep doing this. If you are a male who tends to treat women as sex objects, you can change. I hope that none of you participate in hate crimes, but if you do, stop! We all have the ability to change what we believe and how we act.

Although self-change is a good thing, it is not nearly enough. We live in a world with other people who have their own attitudes and behaviors. More important, we exist within a set of social, cultural, and economic institutions that are all part of the oppressions that we have been discussing. True change must go beyond changing oneself.

The other end of the levels-of-action spectrum is *collective social action*, which refers to joining together with others to seek institutional change. This could mean joining and becoming active in an informal group or a formal organization that is committed to change. The action could involve letter writing, lobbying, and voter registration. It could also involve protest marches, demonstrations, and rallies. Minimally, you could participate in some of these activities. Those more committed would help to organize these activities. This takes more time and effort than self-change activities.

Another form of collective social action is to become part of a social movement. According to Jo Freeman and Victoria Johnson (1999, 3), a social movement refers to "the mobilization and organization of large numbers of people to pursue a common cause. It is also used for the community of believers that is created by that mobilization." Social movements usually contain many organizations that are willing to act on the same issue. A single organization that influences only its own members is not usually thought of as a social movement.

The goals of collective social actions are (1) to attract new members, (2) to educate those who are participating for the first time, and (3) to let decisionmakers know that there will be consequences for not doing what the activists advocate. The consequences could include being voted out of office, being faced with political disruptions around the country, being confronted by consumer boycotts, and being forced to spend more funds on security. In some cases, social movements can result in genuine revolutions where the nature of political and economic power is fundamentally changed. Strong, broad-based social movements are much more likely to result in institutional change than any kind of individual actions. "Research shows that social movements can affect government policy, as well as how it is made. And movement influence extends further. Activism often profoundly changes the activists, and through them, the organizations in which they participate, as well as the broader culture" (Meyer 2003, 31).

One of the most dramatic contemporary example of collective social action is the political upheaval that took place in a number of Arab countries in early 2011. Spontaneous and largely nonviolent street demonstrations in Egypt and Tunisia led to the downfall of authoritarian leaders in those countries. When hundreds of thousands of people protest, even brutal leaders can be forced out. Whether the new regimes are more egalitarian than the ones they replaced still remains to be seen.

One of the most visible recent examples of domestic collective social action is the Tea Party, a network of conservative groups that had a substantial impact on the 2010 election. Unfortunately, Tea Party members have shown little interest in promoting the type of diversity that we have been discussing in this book. This predominantly white group is more interested in protecting its own privileges.

Somewhere in the space between individual change and collective social action approaches to change lies a third approach: *the micropolitics of subtle transformation.* According to this approach,

> We are doing important social justice work when we stop someone at a party from telling a racist joke, when we build ways for people to express themselves in classrooms, [and] when we find ways to get institutions to serve the interests of members of groups that have been excluded. These sorts of actions can change social institutions when many people are doing them at the same time. They operate as subtle but persistent internal pressure. (Kaufman 2003, 296–297)

In this way, micropolitics can result in discussions and actions at the individual level as well as lawsuits against individual employers, schools, and local governments. Cynthia Kaufman cautions that simply being nice to people isn't enough: "A kindness that stays within the boundaries of the social structures that continually reproduce themselves doesn't make much of a difference except to the people it touches.

But when our small-scale challenges interrupt the reproduction of a system of oppression, then something more is happening" (Kaufman 2003, 298).

If one were interested in promoting gay rights, for example, the individual change approach would suggest that you understand and try to overcome whatever homophobia you have internalized over the years. The micropolitics approach would suggest that you object to homophobic remarks among your friends and coworkers. The collective social action approach would suggest that you help to organize and attend local and national gay rights demonstrations to promote gay marriage or to protest against violence against gays.

Political Philosophy

Change also depends on one's political and philosophic perspectives about how society is supposed to work. Although people often identify themselves as conservatives, liberals, or radicals, it is becoming more and more difficult to give concise descriptions of these terms (see Chapter 2).

Traditional conservatives tend to put their faith in the market forces of capitalism and favor limited government programs and regulations, especially at the federal level. In terms of race and gender discrimination, conservatives now reluctantly acknowledge that the federal government has a limited role to play by punishing individual perpetrators and compensating individual victims.

Traditional liberals are also procapitalist in that they believe in market forces, but they understand that an unrestrained economy can get itself into difficulty. Liberals, therefore, believe that some limited regulation of the economy by the federal government is a necessity, as are programs for the dispossessed. They also believe that the federal government has a legitimate role in passing laws and programs to improve equal opportunities for women and people of color.

Radicals tend to be anticapitalist in that they see a market-oriented economy as part of the problem. They argue that liberals and conservatives simply have different ways of maintaining American capitalism and the race, class, gender, sexual orientation, and disability inequalities that go along with it. They are likely to promote social movements for change. Unfortunately, radicals don't agree about what to replace capitalism with. Some argue for a centrally planned, democratically controlled, government-owned economy called socialism. Others believe that there should be a more mixed economy where publicly and privately owned institutions coexist. Some radicals emphasize race whereas others emphasize class, gender, disability, or sexual orientation.

One way to look at how these different political perspectives might deal with a social problem is to consider the Great Recession that began in late 2007. Conservatives tend to believe that economic growth comes from reductions in social spending by the federal government, tax cuts (especially for the wealthy), and deregulation of industry. In this way, the argument goes, both business leaders and workers would be motivated to work hard and increase profitability. Although this may increase economic inequality in the short run, conservative argue that everyone will benefit in the long run. The benefits of the rich getting richer will "trickle down" to everyone else in the form of jobs and improved lifestyles.

This is generally the strategy that was pursued during the administration of former President George W. Bush between 2000 and 2008. The deregulation of the banking and financial system, which was begun during the Democratic administration of former President Bill Clinton, helped to fuel speculation, bad decisions regarding home mortgages, and outright fraud. When the housing bubble burst in late 2007, the economy entered a sharp downturn and the Great Recession began.

Many conservatives continued to argue for more tax cuts and sharp reductions in social spending. Former President Bush, however, saw that capitalism was threatened because some corporations were "too big to fail," and he began to promote the Targeted Asset Relief Program (TARP), which would help prop up failing banks and insurance companies. He acknowledged that this policy was inconsistent with his conservative beliefs but that limited government intervention was necessary to "save capitalism." Although the Great Recession seems to prove that conservative policies were wrongheaded, many Republicans accused President Bush of rejecting conservative principles.

Liberals, in comparison, always believed that some government intervention was necessary to regulate the excesses of capitalism. President Barack Obama continued with TARP and added additional government spending to help stimulate the economy. He supported new, modest regulations to control financial institutions from some of the excesses that contributed to the recession in the first place. The argument was that this would help to provide more jobs and to keep people in their homes by preventing foreclosures. Although the Obama policies also tended to favor the wealthy, some of them also helped the working and middle classes. Both conservatives and some centrist democrats opposed these "big government" policies. By the end of 2010, some of the worst aspects of the recession had subsided somewhat, but even President Obama said that the country was "not out of the woods."

Radicals tended to see the recession as caused by contradictions in the capitalist system itself. Although not part of the national political discourse, radicals argued that capitalism has a tendency toward overproduction (i.e., producing more than can be sold) and growing economic inequality. When capitalism could no longer sell enough manufactured products, capitalists began to make profits from banks, insurance companies, and other financial institutions. This "financialization of capitalism," in turn, led to speculation in home mortgages, derivatives, and other risky financial transactions. Deregulation by the Clinton and Bush administrations only encouraged this speculation—and the bubble began to burst in late 2007 (Foster and Holleman 2010).

According to radicals, neither liberals nor conservatives can solve the country's economic problems because they don't deal with the financialization of capitalism. President Obama's stimulus policies are seen as too weak and too oriented toward the wealthy, say radicals. According to one observer, it is "as if a town's fire chief dealt with a conflagration by protecting the biggest office buildings but leaving smaller fires simmering all over town: housing foreclosures, job losses, lower earnings, less economic security, soaring pay on Wall Street and in executive suites" (Reich 2010). An alternative to capitalism in the form of democratic socialism is needed.

Electoral Politics

In the United States, when most people think of political activism, they probably think of elections. I always vote, and I usually find myself voting for the Democratic Party candidate for the simple reason that he or she is the lesser of two evils. There has rarely been a major party candidate that I enthusiastically supported.

During the 2008 presidential election, I voted for Barack Obama and was thrilled when he became the first black US president. Although I believed that he was too moderate for what the country needed, he was better than Republican candidate John McCain and former President Bush. When conservatives called Obama "radical" or "socialist," I laughed and thought to myself: "I wish it were true."

Unfortunately, my low expectations turned out to be true. During the health care debate of 2009, Obama refused to even put the single-payer option on the table. His economic stimulus programs still favor big business and the wealthy. He escalated the war in Afghanistan and plans to leave 50,000 troops in Iraq even after "withdrawing combat troops." He's better than Bush, but not by much.

Some radical supporters of Obama say that he should be supported because he is trying to be politically "realistic" and has good intentions (Newby 2010). The problem with the two-party political system in the United States is that both parties tend to move to the center and ignore those to the left and right. Third parties have an almost impossible chance to succeed. This curtails the political discourse that takes place.

The parliamentary systems that exist in European capitalist democracies are a more democratic alternative. Even small parties have representation in parliament and can make their voices heard on the national stage.

Although this is not the place to debate the efficacy of electoral politics, I have not included mainstream electoral groups in the list of activist organizations in the next section. In some cases, elections can be part of a program of collective social action. When Jesse Jackson ran for president in 1984 and 1988, his campaign was part of an attempt to build the Rainbow Coalition, which was to be an independent organization that would survive the election. The 1980 election of Harold Washington as mayor of Chicago was another example of genuine grassroots mobilization.

Although many young people were excited about the Obama election, it was a typical top-down political campaign that relied on donations from wealthy and powerful forces. After the emotional celebrations after the election and the inauguration, no independent organization was left to pursue the lofty principles that were articulated during the campaign. Fundamental social change requires political action that goes above and beyond electoral politics (Zinn 2003).

Single Versus Multiple-Category Approaches

Some individuals and organizations focus on change in single categories—race *or* class *or* gender *or* sexual orientation *or* disability. They may focus on only one of these issues without dealing with any of the others. Women might focus on gender issues exclusively, or Asians might focus only on racial issues. Other groups may focus on more than one category, but they may see one category as the most fundamental and the others being of lesser importance. Marxists, for example, have traditionally viewed class as the main axis of oppression, with race and gender being less important.

Intersectionality theorists argue that all these categories are so interconnected that change in one requires changes in the others. Domestic violence, for example, is often seen mainly as a gender issue, but scholars such as Natalie Sokoloff (2008) argue that class and race are also involved because the highest rate of domestic violence is among poor blacks. Immigrant status also figures in the mix, as immigrant women may not report domestic violence to the authorities because of fear of deportation and/or fear of ostracism in their own communities. Any attempt to develop anti–domestic violence policy is likely to fail without considering all these factors.

This multiple-category approach can be confusing if proponents don't accurately connect the dots to explain how one type of oppression is connected with another. In addition, this approach can create tensions when not everyone accepts the connection. Gay males and lesbians, for example, say that laws that prevent them from marrying are a civil rights issue, not unlike the laws that discriminated against blacks during the Jim Crow era. Many blacks, especially those involved with Christian fundamentalist churches, strongly object to this attempt to equate the two types of oppression on moral grounds. Other black leaders, such as Julian Bond (former chair of the board of the NAACP) and US Representative John Lewis (D-Ga.), support gay marriage as a civil rights issue (Bean 2004).

My experience tells me that the majority of students feel most comfortable with liberal, single-category approaches to individual change and micropolitics. My own approach is to emphasize radical, multiple-category, collective social action. Because I have found that most students don't know very much about the important impact that collective social action, especially social movements, has had in the United States, I will spend the rest of the chapter discussing this. First, I will provide a brief history of social movements dealing with class, race, gender, sexual orientation, and disability. Then I will discuss contemporary collective social action possibilities in the twenty-first century.

The History of Collective Social Action

The United States has had a long history of collective social action in the fight for class, race, and gender equality.[1] Sometimes the action is carried out by individual organizations and their members. Other times the action rises to the level of being a social movement. Unfortunately, many history books do not emphasize the role of collective social action in achieving progressive change.

Before the Civil War

During the first half of the nineteenth century, a strong biracial antislavery movement developed. White abolitionists (e.g., William Lloyd Garrison, Elizabeth Cady Stanton, and John Brown) and black abolitionists (e.g., David Walker, Frederick Douglass, and Martin Delany) traveled the country calling for the end of slavery. Harriet Tubman and others helped thousands of slaves to escape through the Underground Railroad. In addition, more than 200 documented slave revolts occurred, the most famous of which was led by Nat Turner.

There were important contradictions within the abolitionist movement, however. Many abolitionists believed in genuine racial equality. Others believed that blacks were inferior to whites but disagreed with slavery as an institution. White and black women were an important part of the abolitionist movement, but they were also promoting women's rights. In her famous "Ain't I a Woman" speech in 1851, Sojourner Truth made the argument that black women were also women even though they didn't have the privileges that white women had. In the end, male abolitionists decided to put women's rights on the back burner until slavery was abolished.

The first convention to promote women's rights, including the right to vote, was held in Seneca Falls, New York, in 1848. Elizabeth Cady Stanton and Lucretia Mott were the main organizers. It took seventy-two more years for the suffragist movement to win the right for women to vote; the states finally approved the Nineteenth Amendment to the Constitution in 1920. This came to be known as the "first wave" of the women's movement.

Civil War–World War I

After the post–Civil War period of Reconstruction came to an end, legal segregation was reimposed in the South in the 1880s and 1890s. The US Supreme Court put its stamp of approval on legal segregation in the *Plessy v. Ferguson* decision in 1896. The Court declared that policies of "separate but equal" (which were actually separate and unequal) were consistent with the US Constitution.

The black community was politically mobilized to fight for equality in the late nineteenth and early twentieth centuries. W. E. B. DuBois and Booker T. Washington had a running debate during this period over the issue of Jim Crow (legal) segregation in the South. Washington argued, on the one hand, that blacks should try to make the best of a bad situation by acquiring business skills and technical education but not challenging segregation. DuBois, on the other hand, argued for high quality, integrated education and the end of segregation. He helped to found the Niagara Movement in 1909, which evolved into the National Association for the Advancement of Colored People (NAACP). Using the courts, the NAACP led a decades-long struggle against lynching, school segregation, and the lack of voting rights.

Workers began to organize trade unions in the late nineteenth century to combat the growing power of the owners of large corporations, including J. P. Morgan, John D. Rockefeller, Andrew Carnegie, James Mellon, Cornelius Vanderbilt, and Leland Stanford. These men were often referred to as "robber barons." Because workers didn't have the right to organize at that time, they had to fight against the private armies of the robber barons. This was class struggle in its most literal sense—strikes often involved violent actions on both sides. Gradually, some employers were forced to recognize unions, wages in some industries increased, and the length of the workday was reduced somewhat. Workers did not get the right to collective bargaining until 1935.

The labor movement had a mixed record when it came to dealing with black and women workers. The American Federation of Labor (AFL, founded in 1881) consisted mostly of white male skilled workers. At various times the AFL excluded blacks, women, and immigrants from Mexico, Japan, and China. The more radical International Workers of the World (founded in 1905) included everyone in its "One Big Union." The Congress of Industrial Organizations (CIO), which formed in 1935, also organized all workers. In some industries, blacks and women formed their own unions, including the Brotherhood of Sleeping Car Porters and the International Ladies Garment Workers Union.

Founded in 1901, the American Socialist Party had 100,000 members at the height of its influence. In 1911 there were more than 1,200 elected socialist officials in 340 municipalities. Eugene Debs ran for president of the United States on the Socialist Party ticket five times. In 1912 in the election eventually won by Woodrow Wilson, Debs received 900,000 votes, about 6 percent of the total vote. Although the Socialist Party included some blacks in its membership, it "did not go much out of its way to act on the race question" (Zinn 2003, 347).

World War I–1940s

The Communist Party split off from the Socialist Party after World War I and was active during the Great Depression in an attempt to mobilize working people. The Communist Party fought for stronger unions and more government services for the unemployed and fought against evictions when people couldn't afford to pay rent. It also actively recruited blacks and other people of color and campaigned against segregation and lynchings. The black author Richard Wright was a member for a period of time, and W. E. B. DuBois and Paul Robeson were publicly sympathetic to the party.

The Wagner Act, passed in 1935, finally gave workers the right to collective bargaining. The National Labor Relations Board was established to enforce worker rights. However, the act didn't cover domestic workers and agricultural workers, most of whom were people of color and/or women.

The federal government, including the military, remained segregated even under liberal president Franklin Delano Roosevelt. In 1941, A. Phillip Randolph, the head of the Brotherhood of Sleeping Car Porters, threatened to organize a march on Washington to protest discrimination, especially in defense industries. Faced with the possibility of 100,000 angry blacks in Washington, President Roosevelt signed Executive Order 8822, which created the Equal Employment Practices Committee and abolished race discrimination in the federal government and in defense industries. During World War II, blacks, who were still treated as second-class citizens, and Japanese Americans, who were interned in US concentration camps, still enlisted in the armed forces. However, they fought in segregated units led by white officers. After the end of World War II, in 1948, President Harry Truman issued an executive order that banned race discrimination in the armed forces.

Brown Decision–1970s

After many years of political struggle and legal battles, the US Supreme Court outlawed legal segregation in public education in the 1954 *Brown v. Board of Education* decision. This overturned the "separate but equal" doctrine of *Plessy v. Ferguson.* Although *Brown* established an important legal precedent, many southern politicians refused to implement it, so the rule of Jim Crow remained throughout much of the South until a powerful grassroots social movement challenged racism.

The modern civil rights movement is usually said to have begun in 1955 with the boycott of public buses in Montgomery, Alabama. Buses then had a movable partition that blacks had to sit behind. When all the white seats were filled the driver would move the partition, and blacks would have to give their seats to whites. Rosa Parks, an NAACP activist, refused to move one day and was arrested. The black community boycotted the buses for 381 days, at which point a federal court declared the Montgomery law unconstitutional. The Southern Christian Leadership Conference (SCLC) grew out of this boycott, and the young Martin Luther King Jr. came into national prominence.

The civil rights movement was largely based on a combination of Christian faith and the principles of nonviolence articulated by Mahatma Gandhi during the anti-British revolution in India. Through boycotts, sit-ins, freedom rides, marches, demonstrations, and various other kinds of civil disobedience, King hoped to embarrass the South before the rest of the country in order to promote federal civil rights legislation. Because of southern intransigence and the growing strength and militancy of the civil rights movement, Presidents Dwight D. Eisenhower and John F. Kennedy were forced to use federal troops to enforce the *Brown* decision on school desegregation throughout the South.

Because the civil rights activists were largely integrationists in that they wanted black people to be accepted into the mainstream of American life as equals, they tried to project an image of middle-class respectability. Demonstrators often marched and went to jail dressed in their Sunday best. They were encouraged to be disciplined and nonviolent and to control their anger at the police, who often abused them. White allies, especially liberals and labor union members, were welcomed in civil rights protests and organizations.

By 1960, however, a parallel movement for black liberation began to develop. Increasing numbers of young black activists began to articulate the ideology of Black Power. Organizations like the Student Nonviolent Coordinating Committee (SNCC) and the Congress of Racial Equality (CORE) talked about black political and economic power as well as cultural pride in their African heritage. Blacks, they demanded, must be accepted and negotiated with as a group and on their own terms. Nonviolence was downgraded from a religious principle to a political tactic that was appropriate in some situations and not in others. Whites who were interested in civil rights were told to do their political work in the white community and in white organizations, not in the black community. In some cases, the tactics of the Black Power movement conflicted with those of the civil rights movement. Malcolm X, Stokely Carmichael, and H. Rap Brown were some of the major Black Power leaders.

The famous March on Washington, wherein Martin Luther King gave his "I Have a Dream" speech, was held in 1963 to convince President Kennedy and the Congress to pass a federal civil rights act that was stalled in Congress. Two hundred thousand people attended the nonviolent demonstration. It took the assassination of President Kennedy to get the Civil Rights Act of 1964 passed by Congress and signed by President Lyndon Johnson, a southern Democrat. The following year, the Voting Rights Act was passed by Congress. A few days later, the predominantly black Watts section of Los Angeles exploded in violence. This was the first of many riots and urban insurrections that were to plague the country for the rest of the decade, especially after the assassination of King in 1968. American cities were literally going up in flames. According to Howard Zinn (2003), the year 1967 saw eight major riots, thirty-three serious riots, and 125 minor incidents.

The Black Panther Party and the League of Revolutionary Black Workers were both black Marxist organizations that were explicitly anticapitalist. The league did most of its organizing work in the automobile factories of Detroit and other Midwestern cities, seeing its enemies as both the big three automobile corporations and the United Auto Workers Union. The Panthers, in comparison, tried to organize poor black communities in cities outside of the South. Both groups worked in coalition with predominantly white anticapitalist groups.

The civil rights movement inspired Mexican and Filipino migrant farm workers in California to form the United Farm Workers Union (UFW) under the leadership of Cesar Chavez, who was sometimes called the Mexican Martin Luther King. Because farm workers were not covered under the National Labor Relations Act, they had to fight to get growers to recognize their union with no help from federal officials. The strike began in the grape fields in 1965 and later spread to the lettuce fields. Not having enough power to confront the growers at the local level, the UFW launched a national grape boycott in 1967, asking ordinary citizens throughout the country not to buy grapes grown in California. After three years, the growers finally gave in and negotiated contracts with the UFW. This organizing campaign would not have been successful without broad-based support for the grape boycott.

The civil rights and Black Power movements spawned several other important social movements in the early 1960s. Students for a Democratic Society (SDS), a predominantly white and middle-class group, fought for student rights and racial and economic equality on and off college campuses. SDS became more Marxist and anticapitalist by the end of the 1960s and was an important force among young people. The Weather Underground split off from SDS and believed it was necessary to engage in armed struggle to achieve change. As students became older and graduated or became young faculty members, many joined the New University Conference (NUC), which was known as the "adult SDS."

The movement against the war in Vietnam was also a major force in the 1960s, especially after 1964. Because young men were being drafted into the armed forces, the war had a personal effect on many families. In addition to groups like SDS and NUC, there were several large coalitions that organized major demonstrations each year in Washington, New York, San Francisco, and/or Los Angeles. More than half a million people gathered at some demonstrations to protest the war. Most of the time the demonstrations were peaceful, but other times demonstrators destroyed property that was symbolically linked to the war (e.g., a recruiting station) or to the capitalist class (e.g., a bank). SDS was one of the main organizers of the militant demonstrations and the resulting police riot at the Democratic National Convention in Chicago in 1968. The antiwar movement had become so strong that national leaders had to consider the potentially militant reaction by demonstrators when they talked about escalating the war in Vietnam.

Government officials were so concerned with the rising level of militancy, especially in the black community, that the Federal Bureau of Investigation launched a counterintelligence program in the late 1960s called COINTELPRO. The FBI spied on activist groups, tried to disrupt the planning of demonstrations, and worked to discredit movement leaders (e.g., tapping the phone of Martin Luther King).

Local police departments organized "red squads," which did the same thing on the local level. Due to violent attacks by the police and political repression by the courts, the Black Panthers were eliminated as an effective organization by the early 1970s.

The late 1960s also saw the early developments of the second wave of the women's liberation movement. In 1963, the President's Commission on the Status of Women issued a widely publicized report documenting the second-class status of women in and out of the labor force. That same year, Betty Friedan's *Feminine Mystique* (1963) raised a number of issues, including educated, middle-class women being unhappily confined in isolated nuclear families. In 1964 the word *sex* was inserted into the Civil Rights Act, thereby banning discrimination against working women. The EEOC, however, didn't enforce the sex provision and said that an NAACP-like organization for women was needed.

As a result, the National Organization for Women (NOW) was founded in 1966. A predominantly white, middle-class organization, NOW began to raise issues such as childcare, sex-role socialization, reproductive rights, equal pay for equal work, women entering predominantly male jobs, and electing more women to political office. It unsuccessfully tried to gain passage of an Equal Rights Amendment to the US Constitution in the 1970s. This simple amendment stated, "Equality of rights under the law shall not be denied or abridged by the United States or by any State on account of sex" (Eisler and Hixson 2001, 424). The amendment was passed by Congress in 1972 but fell three states short of ratification.

Women around the country began meeting in small "consciousness-raising groups" to discuss what was going on in their family, work, and political lives. By learning that what appeared to be personal, private problems were also shared by other women, thousands of women grew to understand the nature of patriarchy. One important slogan became "The personal is political." Whereas NOW represented mostly liberal feminists, these smaller groups fed into the radical feminist and socialist feminist wings of the women's movement.

The gay liberation movement came to national prominence in 1969 when gay males fought back after police raided the Stonewall bar in New York's Greenwich Village. However, two early gay rights organizations, the Mattachine Society and the Daughters of Bilitis, had been founded in the 1950s. After Stonewall, gay men and lesbians began coming out of the closet in large numbers and demanding their rights in the workplace, schools, and cultural institutions as well as freedom from police harassment (Esterberg 1996).

The disability rights movement became active in the 1970s. Prior to this, a number of organizations had been lobbying on behalf of people with specific disabilities. This resulted in the passage of the Vocational Rehabilitation Act of 1973, a landmark law that prevented discrimination against people with disabilities. Because the regulations to enforce this law were slow in coming, a group called the American Coalition of People with Disabilities organized sit-ins in the offices of the Department of Health, Education, and Welfare in 1977 in San Francisco, Washington, and several other cities. This eventually led to the signing of Section 504 of the Vocational Rehabilitation Act.

Also in the 1970s, centers for independent living began to emerge in Berkeley, California, and other cities. These centers were run by the disabled and promoted living in the community rather than in institutions. Mental patients also began to mobilize to protest against the abuses that existed in many mental hospitals around the country.

These movements had an impact on social change. The antiwar movement put restraints on how much military force could be used in Vietnam, and this contributed to the US withdrawal in 1973. The civil rights and Black Power movements, along with the urban rebellions, forced policymakers to think about how to address the issues in America's inner cities. The women's movement helped to produce a sea change in the relations between men and women as well as changes in the labor market. Unfortunately, many contemporary young women believe that a women's movement is no longer necessary.

One of the slogans that came out of the 1960s was "The people, united, can never be defeated." Although the different social movements were not always united with each other, they show that groups of people, acting together, can achieve meaningful institutional change. This lesson should not be lost in the twenty-first century.

Contemporary Issues and Activism

Because a complete history of social activism in the United States is beyond the scope of this book, I'd like to fast-forward to the first decades of the twenty-first century. In spite of the increasingly conservative nature of the political times, there are still a variety of issues that are of interest to college-age young people, and there are a variety of organizations that address themselves to these issues. Toward the end of the semester, a handful of students usually ask me that big question: What can I do? In the last part of this chapter, I'd like to answer that question by discussing some of the main activist organizations that are working on the issues that have been discussed in previous chapters.

I've tried to limit this discussion to national organizations that have regional or local affiliates that readers can join and be active in. I have omitted many excellent organizations that only exist in one or two cities. Due to space limitations, I have also omitted organizations that provide excellent educational resources but that do not participate in activism themselves. Finally, most of the organizations have a liberal or radical political orientation. This reflects the reality that most conservatives are just not interested in promoting the rights of workers, people of color, women, and gays as separate groups either through activism or other means.

Workers' Rights

US workers face difficult times in the early twenty-first century. During the four years of the first George W. Bush administration (2000–2004), there was a net loss of more than 1 million jobs from the United States, part of which has been caused by multinational corporations outsourcing some jobs and moving entire factories overseas because of cheaper labor. Computers and other labor-saving devices have also reduced jobs. Benefits and retirement pensions have been reduced, as have government transfer payments. The percentage of workers in labor unions has been declining for several decades, and, as a result, workers have less decision-making power than they did in the past. Since the beginning of the Great Recession in late 2007, unemployment jumped to 9.6 percent in 2009 due to the contracting economy.

Some unions are beginning to understand "that organizing and growth are linked to mobilizing outsiders in the new labor markets, including new-economy workers, people of color, women, and immigrant workers" (Ness 2003, 56). The Hotel Employees and Restaurant Employees Union (HERE) has been increasingly successful in organizing hotel workers around the country, especially in Las Vegas, Nevada. The Service Employees International Union (SEIU) has successfully organized custodians and other building service workers. The United Needletrades, Industrial, and Textile Employees Union (UNITE) has organized industrial laundries. In order to increase their bargaining power, UNITE merged with HERE in 2004 to form UNITE HERE.

SEIU and UNITE HERE have been critical of the AFL-CIO leadership for spending too much time supporting Democratic Party political candidates and not enough resources increasing the number of workers that are in unions. In September 2005 these two unions, along with five others, broke away from the AFL-CIO and formed another national labor organization, called Change to Win.

College students can support workers' rights in several ways. If workers on your campus are trying to organize a union, support them. They could be janitors, clerical workers, or teaching assistants. Join their picket lines and help pressure the administration to recognize the union and increase wages and benefits. Because many campus workers are people of color, immigrants, and women, union struggles involve more than just class issues.

United Students Against Sweatshops (USAS, www.USAS.org) often supports these struggles. It also focuses on increasing funding for higher education and making sure that the licensed equipment sold by universities is not made in sweatshops either here or abroad. The term *sweatshop* usually refers to workplaces with long hours, low pay, and unsafe and/or unhealthy working conditions. With chapters at over 150 college campuses around the country, USAS has gotten many universities to adopt campus codes of conduct, which include public disclosure of factory sites, independent monitoring of factory conditions, and guaranteed living wages for workers that produce the licensed equipment (Kelly and Lefkowitz 2003). In 2009, after numerous demonstrations, USAS forced Russell Athletic to rehire 1,200 Honduran workers who had lost their jobs during the course of a union organizing campaign (Greenhouse 2009).

Jobs With Justice (JWJ, www.jwj.org) is a somewhat broader organization that "connect[s] labor, faith-based community, and student organizations to work together on workplace and community social justice campaigns." According to its website, JWJ has coalitions in forty cities throughout the country. Its Student Labor Action Project is geared specifically to high school and college students.

Some students may want to get training to become a union organizer. The Union Summer Program (www.unionsummer.aflcio.org), begun by the AFL-CIO in 1996, has trained over 3,000 activists. It is a ten-week, paid educational internship that includes a week-long orientation and placement in various parts of the country.

Another summer experience is the Strategic Corporate Research Summer School (www.campaignforlaborrights.org/index/apr03/announce5_school.htm) at the Cornell University School of Industrial and Labor Relations. Graduate students and advanced undergraduates are exposed to a one-week course emphasizing "understanding and researching corporate ownership structure, corporate finance, and the sources of corporate power." The goal is to provide students with research skills that can be helpful during union-organizing drives.

The AFL-CIO also has an Organizing Institute (www.organize.aflcio.org) that offers two programs. The 3–Day Training Program teaches the basic tactics and strategy used by the labor movement; housing and food are provided. The Field Training Program includes a two-week orientation and three months of field training wherein students work in an actual organizing campaign. The weekly stipend was $500 in 2010 plus housing, transportation, and health insurance. Successful trainees will be hired as union organizers.

The Asian-Pacific American Labor Alliance (www.aplanet.org), affiliated with the AFL-CIO, is a membership organization of Asian Pacific Union members. It sponsored the 2003 Immigrant Workers Freedom Ride, which toured the country to raise consciousness about the problems of immigrant workers. The "freedom ride" designation, of course, was taken from the freedom rides of the 1960s that protested segregated public transportation.

Finally, those interested in the concerns of women in the labor force should check out 9 to 5, National Association of Working Women (www.9to5.org). Founded in 1974, 9 to 5 is committed to improving the position of women in the paid labor force. It lobbies for legislation at the federal, state, and local levels to win family-friendly policies for low-wage women, including welfare reform and equal rights on the job. It also has a Job Survival Hotline to handle individual complaints.

Race Rights

There are many organizations involved in protecting and enhancing the civil rights of specific race and ethnic groups. This includes issues concerning education, voting rights, employment, and government programs providing help for the disadvantaged. Typically, these groups are politically liberal and tend to focus on a specific race and/or ethnic category.

The oldest of the organizations is the 100-year-old NAACP—the National Association for the Advancement of Colored People (www.naacp.org). Although it gained a somewhat "stodgy" reputation during the turbulent 1960s and 1970s, the NAACP has begun to recruit more young people in recent years and is one of the most well-known of the civil rights organizations in the black community. The National Urban League (www.nul.org) is another traditional civil rights organization.

Other race and ethnic groups also have this type of civil rights organization. The National Council of La Raza (www.nclr.org) is the umbrella group for the Hispanic community. The Asian community has the Organization of Chinese Americans (www.ocanational.org), which advocates for all Asian-Pacific Americans; the Organization of Japanese Americans (www.janet.org), and the Japanese American Citizens League (www.jacl.org). American Indians don't have a national organization that individuals can join at the local level; the closest to that would be the National Congress of American Indians (www.ncai.org), a tribal membership organization. The National Network for Immigrant and Refugee Rights (www.nnirr.org) handles issues regarding immigrants of all races.

The civil rights organizations of Arab Americans and Muslims have become especially important since the terrorist attacks of September 11, 2001. They include the Arab-American Anti-Discrimination Committee (www.adc.org) and the Council on American-Islamic Relations (www.CAIR-net.org). The Tikkun Community (www.tikkun.org) is a predominantly Jewish group that supports Arab and Muslim rights in both the United States and the Middle East.

In addition to these civil rights organizations, there are other race-related groups that go beyond civil rights. Right to the City (www.righttothecity.org) is a national alliance of local organizations of poor people who fight for urban justice, human rights, and democracy. It is possible to join as an individual member in support of the general goals of the organization.

The Black Radical Congress (www.blackradicalcongress.org) is a more left-leaning group that calls for large-scale social change. As its website states, "Recognizing the contributions from diverse tendencies within Black Radicalism—including socialism, revolutionary nationalism and feminism—we are united in opposition to all forms of oppression, including class exploitation, racism, patriarchy, homophobia, anti-immigration prejudice and imperialism." This is a relatively new group that formed in 1998.

Critical Resistance (www.criticalresistance.org), another left-leaning group, focuses on prisons where there is a huge overrepresentation of blacks and Hispanics. According to its website, "Critical Resistance seeks to build an international movement to end the Prison Industrial Complex by challenging the belief that caging and controlling people makes us safe. . . . As such, our work is part of global struggles against inequality and powerlessness."

The Anti-Defamation League (www.adl.org) is a more mainstream group that does excellent work monitoring a broad range of right-wing hate groups like the Aryan Nation and the various formations of the Ku Klux Klan. In addition to being explicitly racist, these predominantly white hate groups promote a vicious form of anti-Semitism.

Finally, the Color of Change (www.colorofchange.org) is an Internet-based group that deals with a variety of issues affecting people of color. Although there are no local chapters, it is possible to sign petitions and contact power brokers about the issues followed on the website.

Gender Rights

There are a wide variety of national women's organizations with local chapters. The largest is the National Organization for Women (NOW), which was founded in 1966 (www.now.org). NOW claims 500,000 contributing members and 550 chapters in all fifty states and Washington, D.C. The organization is involved in a large variety of issues, including employment discrimination, reproductive rights, education, childcare, health, politics, and peace. The Feminist Majority (www.feminist.org) is another multi-issue organization, and it has an affiliated student organization called Feminist Campus (www.feministcampus.org).

Several women's organizations focus primarily on reproductive rights. Planned Parenthood (www.plannedparenthood.org) is primarily a service provider where women can get birth control counseling, gynecological exams, and abortions. NARAL Pro-Choice (www.naral.org) is an activist organization that fights for reproductive rights in terms of national and state legislation and court decisions. All four of these organizations were among the many cosponsors of the large national reproductive rights demonstrations that have been held since 2000.

The Women of Color Network (www.womenofcolornetwork .org) is a national coalition of organizations and individuals that opposes violence against women and families in communities of color. INCITE! Women of Color Against Violence (www.incite-national .org), one of the member organizations of the network, works against all forms of violence against women. As stated on its website, the organization's goal is to "advance a national movement to nurture the health and well-being of communities of color." The National Organization for Men Against Sexism (www.nomas.org) is also dedicated to stopping violence against women and to promoting gender equality.

Finally, there are a number of women's organizations whose mission is to achieve peace and justice around the world and in the United States. The Women's International League for Peace and Freedom (www.wilpf.org) was founded in 1915 by Jane Addams of Hull House fame. Women's Actions for New Directions (www.wand .org) was founded in 1982 as Women's Action for Nuclear Disarmament. Women in Black (www.womeninblack.org) is an international organization that was founded in 1988 by Israeli women who called for a just peace between Israelis and Palestinians. Women in Black still focuses on the Middle East but is now also involved in other international issues. Code Pink: Women for Peace (www.codepink.org) is a much newer organization that was founded in 2002 as part of the movement against the war in Iraq. All of these organizations have participated in the various demonstrations against the war in Iraq.

Gay Rights

As discussed in the previous chapter, a lot of work remains to be done in order to achieve equality for the LGBT population. There are civil rights and legal issues with regard to employment, housing, education, health care, marriage, and domestic partnerships. In addition, AIDS prevention and treatment is a major issue, especially for gay men and for heterosexual women of color.

There are two national civil rights organizations with local chapters for the LGBT community. The Human Rights Campaign (HRC, www.hrc.org) website describes it as "a bipartisan organization that works to advance equality based on sexual orientation and gender expression and identity, to ensure that gay, lesbian, bisexual and transgender Americans can be open, honest and safe at home, at work and in the community." The HRC lobbies Congress, provides campaign support for gay-friendly candidates, and conducts public education campaigns. It has recently established Partnerships for Equality, which provides funds to state advocacy organizations to promote gay-friendly legislation.

The National Gay and Lesbian Task Force (NGLTF, www.the taskforce.org) has a similar mission with a somewhat more activist orientation. According to its website, "We're building a social justice movement that unites ideas with action. We organize activists. We train leaders. We equip organizers. We mobilize voters. We build coalitions. We teach-and-learn from today's vibrant GLBT youth movement. We're proud of our commitment to the linkages between oppressions based on race, class, gender and sexual orientation." The NGLTF also has a think tank (The Policy Institute), tracks state legislation, and promotes local organizing through the Federation of Statewide Lesbian, Gay, Bisexual, and Transgender Political Organizations. Soulforce (www.soulforce.org) is another gay activist organization.

The only national activist organization with local chapters that deals with AIDS is ACT UP (www.actupny.org). ACT UP is really a loose network of groups that began in New York City and has spread to a dozen other cities. According to the website of the New York ACT UP chapter, "ACT UP is a diverse, non-partisan group of individuals united in anger and committed to direct action to end the AIDS crisis. We advise and inform. We demonstrate. WE ARE NOT SILENT." Tactically, ACT UP is more militant than most other groups in that it advocates direct action and civil disobedience to get its point across. Members have disrupted professional conferences and political meetings, and civil disobedience manuals are offered on the ACT UP website. In one of its early actions in 1993, ACT UP members dumped the ashes of friends and loved ones who died of AIDS on the steps of the California state capitol to protest cuts in health-care spending (Shepard 2003). A twentieth-anniversary march in 2006 ended at Wall Street in New York with the ears of the famous bull being adorned by condoms.

According to ACT UP activist Vito Russo, "After we kick the shit out of this disease, I intend to be able to kick the shit out of this system, so that this never happens again" (Shepard 2003, 153). Russo was referring to the fact that "fighting the AIDS pandemic [means] fighting institutional racism, sexism [and] the class system as well as homophobia" (Shepard 2003, 153).

Straight people who want to be supportive of LGBT friends and relatives can join Parents, Families, and Friends of Lesbians and Gays

(PFLAG, www.pflag.org). With more than 500 affiliates throughout the country, PFLAG engages in a number of activities, including "education, to enlighten an ill-informed public; and advocacy, to end discrimination and to secure equal civil rights." It also provides opportunities to "dialogue" about a variety of issues around sexual orientation. The Gay, Lesbian, and Straight Education Network (www .glsen.org) focuses on safety in the schools for gay students.

Finally, Freedom to Marry (www.freedomtomarry.org) focuses on the issue of gay marriage. Log Cabin Republicans (online.logcabin.org) is a conservative organization that supports gay marriage and a variety of other gay issues.

Disability Rights

Although there are many national organizations that promote the rights of people with disabilities, most represent a single type of disability (e.g., blindness or a particular illness) and tend to use conventional methods of lobbying, education, service, or advocacy.

ADAPT (www.adapt.org) is one of the few groups that has local chapters that participate in direct action. Its April 2010 action "Defending Our Freedom" featured five days of marching, lobbying, and Internet protests in Washington, D.C. Its members demanded that President Obama fully implement the American With Disabilities Act as well as other legislation. They encouraged people with disabilities to file complaints of discrimination with the Office of Civil Rights and the Department of Justice, and they encouraged members to learn from each other about local successes and failures to fight state budget cuts.

Peace and Justice

A number of organizations focus on war and militarism. The current focus is on the US wars against Afghanistan, which began in October 2001, and against Iraq, which began in March 2003. In addition to questions concerning the immorality of war and the critique of American militarism, wars have implications for some of the issues discussed in previous chapters. The huge expense of war makes it more difficult to fund a wide variety of social programs geared toward poor and working people, both whites and people of color. By the middle of 2010 the wars in Afghanistan and Iraq had cost more than \$1 trillion

($1,000,000,000,000). Until 2010, more money was spent on occupying Iraq than Afghanistan. Now, the reverse is true. This huge amount of money means that there is less to spend on other more important projects.

The National Priorities Project (2010) looked at what else could be funded if the $170.5 billion that was proposed for the wars in FY2010 were spent on other domestic programs. This money could have funded 22.4 million Head Start slots for poor children, the salaries of 2.6 million elementary school teachers or 3 million fire fighters, or 30.7 million Pell grants (at $5,500 each) for college students. When politicians claim that there isn't enough money to spend on these and other programs, the money that goes to war is one of the main reasons why.

The movement to oppose the war in Iraq began before the invasion. There was a national demonstration on October 26, 2002, and international demonstrations followed on January 18, 2003. After the invasion, the protests continued. Over 100,000 people protested the war on October 25, 2003. Between 400,000 and 500,000 people marched outside the Republican National Convention on August 29, 2004.

Two national groups organize these large-scale national demonstrations and are active in local communities: International A.N.S.W.E.R. Coalition (Act Now to Stop War and End Racism; www.internationalANSWER.org) and United for Peace and Justice (www.unitedforpeace.org). In addition to opposing the war, coalition members support the rights of women and people of color in the United States. The websites of both groups list hundreds of local activist organizations. The American Friends Service Committee (www.afsc.org) and the War Resisters League (www.warresistersleague.org), two pacifist organizations, and Not in Our Name (www.notinourname.net) also participate in antiwar activities and have local offices throughout the country. Amnesty International (www.amnestyusa.org) focuses on human rights around the world.

Although it was formed in 1998, MoveOn (www.moveon.org) really took off in 2002 with online petitions and calls for activism. In 2004, MoveOn organized a serious of house parties in concert with the opening of Michael Moore's film *Fahrenheit 911*. After typing in your zip code on the MoveOn website, you would click on a home near you to reserve a seat. People then gathered in small groups to discuss the film and participate in a national conference call with

Moore. A few months later, this same process was repeated with the showing of *Outfoxed*, a blistering critique of the conservative bias of the Fox News Network. These house parties have a huge potential to mobilize people at the local level.

Left-Wing Political Formations

Several organizations are working to build a socialist, rather than a capitalist, society. The Democratic Socialists of America (DSA, www.dsausa.org) is explicitly anticapitalist but does not want to repeat the authoritarian errors of countries like the former Soviet Union. The DSA is calling for a democratic form of socialism wherein the government would own a greater portion of the economy and ordinary people would have a much larger say in political decisions than they now have. The Committees of Correspondence for Democracy and Socialism (www.cc-ds.org) is also working for a socialist transformation. Neither of these groups runs candidates for political office; the DSA sees itself as trying to push the Democratic Party to the left.

The Green Party of the United States (www.gp.org), in contrast, does field candidates and sees itself as a third political party. Focusing on "environmentalism, non-violence, social justice, and grassroots organizing," Green Party candidates have participated in federal, state, and local political races since 1996. In the 2008 election, Green Party presidential candidate Cynthia McKinney received less than 1 percent of the popular vote. In November 2010, 136 Green Party members held elected office in 23 states and the District of Columbia.

Other Activist Groups

Independent Media Centers (www.indymedia.org) describes itself as "a network of collectively run media outlets for the creation of radical, accurate, and passionate tellings of the truth." The web-based organization arose in 1999 in conjunction with the Seattle, Washington, antiglobalization protests by broadcasting real-time coverage of the demonstrations. Local outlets generally invite articles from radical writers on a variety of topics and have calendars of local events and demonstrations. This is one of the few media sources where one can learn what happened at local demonstrations; mainstream media frequently ignore these protests.

Another outlet for people who are interested in writing and research that can lead to activism is the US Public Interest Research Group (USPIRG, uspirg.org). Its mission is to "deliver persistent, result-oriented public interest activism that protects our environment, encourages a fair sustainable economy, and fosters responsive democratic government." USPIRG projects involve corporate reform, student aid, right-to-know rules, and a variety of environmental concerns, including Arctic drilling, clean air and water, and power plants.

Avaaz (www.avaaz.org) operates via its website to address poverty and inequality around the world. Although there are no national chapters to join, it is possible to engage in on-line activism through this group.

* * *

As this chapter shows, there are numerous ways to become an activist to achieve a more just world. Many of these national organizations have chapters or affiliates in your city, possibly even on your campus. There are also thousands of local organizations that are working on the issues raised in these pages. Get involved! Remember, if you are not part of the solution, you are probably part of the problem.

Note

1. This section was compiled from a number of sources, especially Takaki (1993) and Zinn (2003).

Key Terms

Ableism is the system of oppression based on disability status.

Bisexual refers to individuals who are sexually, physically, and emotionally attracted to both same- and opposite-sex partners.

Coming out refers to someone who has revealed his or her LGBT sexual orientation to others.

Conflict diversity refers to understanding how different groups exist in a hierarchy of inequality in terms of power, privilege, and wealth.

Counting diversity refers to empirically enumerating differences within a given population.

Culture diversity refers to the importance of understanding and appreciating the cultural differences between groups.

Disability is a social exclusion, disadvantage, or restriction of activity caused by a contemporary social organization that takes little or no account of people who have physical impairments and thus excludes them from participation in the mainstream of social activities.

Discrimination refers to actions that deny equal treatment to persons perceived to be members of some social category or group.

A **dominant group** is a social group that controls the political, economic, and cultural institutions in a society.

The **essentialist** perspective argues that reality exists independent of our perception of it; that is, that there are real and important (essential) differences among categories of people.

An **ethnic group** is a social group that has certain cultural characteristics that set it off from other groups and whose members see themselves as having a common past.

175

Ethnoviolence refers to acts motivated by prejudice intending to do physical or psychological harm because of the victims' group membership.

Exploitation means that the dominant group uses the subordinate group for its own ends, including economic profit and higher position in the social hierarchy.

Feminism is a movement to end sexist oppression.

Gay usually refers to homosexual males, although it is also used as an umbrella term for homosexuals in general.

Gender refers to the behavior that is culturally defined as appropriate and inappropriate for males and females.

GLBT stands for gay, lesbian, bisexual, and/or transgender. *See also* LGBT.

Good-for-business diversity refers to the argument that businesses will be more profitable, and government agencies and not-for-profit corporations will be more efficient, with diverse labor forces.

Hegemonic ideologies are those ideas that are so influential that they dominate all other ideologies.

Heterosexism refers to a system of oppression against the LGBT population.

Heterosexual refers to persons who are sexually, physically, and emotionally attracted to people of the opposite sex.

Homophobia refers to the fear and hatred of those who love and sexually desire people of the same sex.

Homosexual refers to persons who are sexually, physically, and emotionally attracted to people of the same sex.

Ideology is a body of ideas reflecting the social needs and aspirations of an individual group, class, or culture.

Impairment refers to physical or mental limitations.

Income is the amount of money that a family earns from wages and salaries, interest, dividends, rent, gifts, and transfer payments.

Individual discrimination refers to the behavior of individual members of one group/category that is intended to have a differential and/or harmful effect on members of another group/category.

Institutional discrimination refers to the policies of dominant group institutions, and the behavior of individuals who implement these policies and control these institutions, that are intended to have a differential and/or harmful effect on subordinate groups.

Intergenerational mobility is a child's class position relative to the child's parents.

In the closet refers to someone who has not revealed his or her LGBT sexual orientation to others.

Intersexed refers to a person having physical attributes of both males and females.

Intragenerational mobility is the degree to which a young worker who enters the labor force can improve his or her class position within a single lifetime.

Lesbian refers to homosexual females.

LGBT stands for lesbian, gay, bisexual, and transgendered people. It is used interchangeably with GLBT.

A **master status** is one that has a profound effect on one's life and that dominates or overwhelms the other statuses one occupies.

Meritocracy is a stratified society wherein the most skilled people have the better jobs and the least skilled people have the lowest-paying jobs, regardless of race, gender, age, and so on.

Occupational sex segregation refers to the differential distribution of men and women into sex-appropriate occupations in the labor force.

Oppression is a dynamic process by which one segment of society achieves power and privilege through the control and exploitation of other groups, which are burdened and pushed down into the lower levels of the social order.

The other is viewed as being unlike the dominant group in profoundly different, usually negative ways.

Passing refers to a subordinate-group member who successfully pretends to be a dominant-group member.

Patriarchy is a hierarchical system that promotes male supremacy.

Politics refers to any collective action that is intended to support, influence, or change social policy or social structures.

Prejudice refers to negative attitudes toward a specific group of people.

Privilege means that some groups have something of value that is denied to others simply because of the groups they belong to; these unearned advantages give some groups a head start in seeking a better life.

A **racial group** is a social group that is socially defined as having certain biological characteristics that set it apart from other groups, often in invidious ways.

Racial ideology is the racially based framework used by actors to explain and justify (dominant race) or challenge (subordinate race or races) the racial status quo.

Racism is a system of oppression based on race.

Role specifies expected behavior that goes along with a specific status.

Sex refers to the physical and biological differences between the categories of male and female.

Sexism is a system of oppression based on gender.

Sexual behavior refers to whom we have sex with.

Sexual identification refers to what people call themselves.

Sexual orientation is determined by to whom we are attracted sexually, physically, and emotionally.

The **social constructionist** perspective argues that reality cannot be separated from the way a culture makes sense of it—that meaning is "constructed" through social, political, legal, scientific, and other processes.

Social mobility refers to individuals moving up or down in terms of their class level.

Status refers to a position that one holds or a category that one occupies in a society.

Stereotypes are cultural beliefs about a particular group that are usually highly exaggerated and distorted, even though they may have a grain of truth.

Stigma is an attribute for which someone is considered bad, unworthy, or deeply discredited because of the category that he or she belongs to.

Straight refers to heterosexual people.

Stratification refers to the way in which societies are marked by inequality, by differences among people that are regarded as being higher or lower.

Structural discrimination refers to policies of dominant-group institutions, and the behavior of the individuals who implement these policies and control these institutions, that are neutral in intent—in terms of race, class, gender, and sexuality—but that have a differential or harmful effect on subordinate groups.

A **subordinate group** is a social group that lacks control of the political, economic, and cultural institutions in a society.

Transgendered people feel that their gender identity doesn't match their physiological body.

Transsexuals are people who have had sex change operations.

Transvestites are people who like to cross-dress, that is, wear clothes that are culturally appropriate to the opposite sex.

Wealth refers to the assets that people own and is often expressed in terms of net worth.

Bibliography

Adams, J. Q., and Pearlie Strother-Adams. 2001. *Dealing with Diversity*. Dubuque, IA: Kendall-Hunt.

Adams, Maurianne, Warren J. Blumenfeld, Rosie Castaneda, Heather W. Hackman, Madeline L. Peters, and Ximena Zuniga, eds. 2000. *Readings for Diversity and Social Justice: An Anthology on Racism, Antisemitism, Sexism, Heterosexism, Ableism, and Classism*. New York: Routledge.

Akom, A. A. 2000. "The House That Race Built: Some Observations on the Use of the Word *Nigga*, Popular Culture, and Urban Adolescent Behavior." In Lois Weis and Michelle Fine (eds.), *Construction Sites: Excavating Race, Class, and Gender Among Urban Youth*. New York: Teachers College Press.

Albert, Judith Clavira, and Steward Edward Albert. 1984. *The Sixties Papers: Documents of a Rebellious Decade*. New York: Praeger.

Allegretto, Sylvia, and Michelle M. Arthur. 2001. "An Empirical Analysis of Homosexual/Heterosexual Male Earnings Differentials: Unmarried and Unequal?" *Industrial and Labor Relations Review* 54, no. 3 (April): 631–646.

Allport, Gordon W. 1954. *The Nature of Prejudice*. Cambridge, MA: Addison Wesley.

Alonso-Zaldivar, Ricardo, and Jennifer Oldham. 2002. "New Airport Screener Jobs Going Mostly to Whites." *Los Angeles Times*, September 25. www.latimes.com.

Altemeyer, Bob. 2001. "Changes in Attitudes Toward Homosexuals." *Journal of Homosexuality* 42, no. 2: 63–75.

American-Arab Anti-Discrimination Committee. 2002. "Facts About Arabs and the Arab World." www.adc.org/index.php?id=248.

American Association of Retired People. 2004. "Civil Rights and Race Relations." www.aarp.org/research/reference/publicopinions/aresearchimport-854.html.

Americans with Disabilities Act. 1990. Public Law No.101-336, 42 U.S.C. 12101-213.

Anderson, Margaret L. 2003. *Thinking About Women: Sociological Perspectives on Sex and Gender.* Boston: Allyn and Bacon.

Anderson, Margaret L., and Patricia Hill Collins, eds. 2004. *Race, Class, and Gender: An Anthology,* 5th ed. Belmont, CA: Wadsworth.

Anderson, Sarah, John Cavanagh, Chuck Collins, Sam Pizzigati, and Mike Lapham. 2008. *Executive Excess 2008.* Washington, DC: Institute for Policy Studies and United for a Fair Economy.

Antonak, Richard F., and Hanoch Livneh. 2000. "Measurement of Attitudes Towards Persons with Disabilities." *Disability and Rehabilitation* 22, no. 5: 211–224.

Armstrong, David, and Peter Newcomb. 2004. "The Forbes 400." *Forbes* 174, no. 7 (October 11): 103–278.

Associated Press. 2004. "Texas Texts Won't Have 'Married Partners.'" *Baltimore Sun,* November 6: 5A.

———. 2003. "DeShawn Might Be Less Employable Than Cody, Research Shows." *Baltimore Sun,* September 28: 4A.

Azcentral.com. 2010. "Boeing Settles Discrimination Lawsuits at Mesa Plant." February 1. www.azcentral.com.

Babcock, Linda, and Sara Laschever. 2003. *Women Don't Ask: Negotiation and the Gender Divide.* Princeton, NJ: Princeton University Press.

Badgett, M. V. Lee. 2000. "The Myth of Gay and Lesbian Affluence." *Gay and Lesbian Review Worldwide* 7, no. 2 (Spring): 22–26.

Baird, Venessa. 2001. *The No-Nonsense Guide to Sexual Diversity.* London: Verso.

Baker, Al. 2010. "Judge Finds 'Intentional Discrimination' Against Blacks in Fire Dept. Hiring." *New York Times,* January 14: A27.

Baltimore Sun. 2004. "Military Discharged 770 in '03 for Homosexuality." *Baltimore Sun,* June 21: 6A.

Banks, James A. 1994. *An Introduction to Multicultural Education.* Boston: Allyn and Bacon.

Barnow, B. S. 2008. "The Employment Rate of People with Disabilities." *Monthly Labor Review,* November: 44–50.

Battle, Juan, Natalie Bennett, and Todd C. Shaw. 2004. "From the Closet to a Place at the Table: Past, Present, and Future Assessments of Social Science Research on African American Gay, Bisexual, and Transgender Populations." *African American Research Perspectives* 10 (Spring/Summer): 9–26.

Battle, Juan, Cathy J. Cohen, Dorian Warren, Gerard Fergerson, and Suzette Audam. 2002. *Say It Loud, I'm Black and I'm Proud: Black Pride Survey 2000.* New York: Policy Institute of the National Gay and Lesbian Task Force.

Bean, Linda. 2004. "Are Civil-Rights Leaders Afraid of Same-Sex Marriage?" *DiversityInc*, February 6. www.diversityinc.com.

Beeghley, Leonard. 2005. *The Structure of Social Stratification in the United States*, 4th ed. Boston: Allyn and Bacon.

Bendick, Marc, Jr., Charles W. Jackson, and Victor A. Reinoso. 1994. "Measuring Employment Discrimination Through Controlled Experiment." *Review of Black Political Economy* (Summer): 24–48.

Berg, John C., ed. 2003. *Teamsters and Turtles? US Progressive Political Movements in the Twenty-First Century*. Lanham, MD: Rowman and Littlefield.

Bilefsky, Dan. 2008. "Old Custom Fades in Albania: Woman as Man of Family." *New York Times*, June 25: A1, A12.

Blauner, Bob. 2001. *Still the Big News: Racial Oppression in America*. Philadelphia: Temple University Press.

———. 1992. "Talking Past Each Other: Black and White Languages of Race." *American Prospect* 10 (Spring): 55–64.

Blauner, Robert. 1972. *Racial Oppression in America*. New York: Harper and Row.

Blumenfeld, Warren J., and Diane Raymond. 2000. "Prejudice and Discrimination." In Maurianne Adams et al. (eds.), *Readings for Diversity and Social Justice*. New York: Routledge.

BNA Daily Labor Report. 2009. "$2.4 Million Penalty in Sex Discrimination Case." Teamsters for a Democratic Union, January 26. www.tdu .org.

Bonilla-Silva, Eduardo. 2003. *Racism Without Racists: Color-Blind Racism and the Persistence of Racial Inequality in the United States*. Lanham, MD: Rowman and Littlefield.

———. 2001. *White Supremacy and Racism in the Post–Civil Rights Era*. Boulder, CO: Lynne Rienner.

Boudreaux, Richard, Louise Roug, Doug Smith, and P. J. Huffstutter. 2005. "2000th Death Spotlights Insurgents' Persistence, Lethal Roadside Bombs." *Baltimore Sun*, August 26: 1A, 11A.

Bowman, Karlyn H. 2004. "Attitudes About Homosexuality and Gay Marriage." *American Enterprise Institute Studies in Public Opinion*. www.aei.org.

Boylan, Jennifer Finney. 2003. *She's Not There: A Life in Two Genders*. New York: Broadway.

Brinkman, Britney G., and Kathryn M. Rickard. 2009. "College Students' Descriptions of Everyday Gender Prejudice." *Sex Roles* 61: 461–475.

Browning, Lynnley. 2003. "US Income Gap Widening, Study Says." *New York Times*, September 23. www.nytimes.com/2003/09/25/business/25 POOR.html.

Bumiller, Elisabeth. 2010. "Sex Assault Reports Rise in Military." *New York Times*, March 17: A14.

———. 2002. "Displaced Workers Summary." US Department of Labor. http://stats.bls.gov/news.release/disp.nr0.htm.

California Employment Lawyers Blog. 2010. "California Hotel Pays $500,000 in Racial and Sexual Harassment Lawsuit Settlements." February 4. www.califoniaemployomentlawyersblog.com.

Campbell, Bernadette, E. Glenn Schellenberg, and Charlene Y. Senn. 1997. "Evaluating Measures of Contemporary Sexism." *Psychology of Women Quarterly* 21: 89–102.

Carr-Ruffino, Norma. 2003. *Managing Diversity: People Skills for a Multicultural Workplace*, 6th ed. Boston: Pearson.

Carroll, Joseph. 2007. "Most Americans Approve of Interracial Marriage." Gallup News Service, August 16. www.gallup.com.

Castaneto, MayLynn V., and Eleanor W. Willemsen. 2006a. "Social Perception of the Personality of the Disabled." *Social Behavior and Personality* 34, no. 10: 1217–1232.

———. 2006b. "Social Perception of the Development of Disabled Children." *Childcare, Health, and Development* 33, no. 3: 308–318.

Cave, Damien. 2009. "A Combat Role, and Anguish, Too." *New York Times*, November 1. www.nytimes.com.

Chronicle of Higher Education. 2010. *The Almanac Issue 2010–2011* (August 27).

———. 2004. "Educational Attainment of the US Population by Racial and Ethnic Group, 2003." *CHE Almanac Issue 2004–2005* 51, no. 1 (August 27): 18.

Cohen, Patricia. 2009. "Rethinking Gender Bias in Theater." *New York Times*, June 24: C1.

Cole, Yoji. 2004. "For $50M + Diversity Plan, Abercrombie and Fitch Makes Racism Suit Go Away." *DiversityInc*, October 17. www.diversityinc.com/members/10331print.cfm.

Cyrus, Virginia. 2000. *Experiencing Race, Class, and Gender in the United States*, 3rd ed. Mountain View, CA: Mayfield.

Dang, Alain, and Somjen Frazier. 2004. "Black and Same-Sex Households in the United States: A Report from the 2000 Census." New York: National Gay and Lesbian Task Force Policy Institute and the National Black Justice Coalition. www.thetaskforce.org.

D'Arcy, Janice. 2005. "Religious Houses Stand Divided on Gay Marriage Debate." *Baltimore Sun*, January 30: 1A, 6A.

Darling, Rosalyn Benjamin. 2003. "Toward a Model of Changing Disability Identities." *Disability and Society* 18, no. 7: 881–895.

Davis, Riccardo A. 2004. "Rating Best and Worst Companies for GLBT Workers—New HRC Data." *DiversityInc*, September 29. www.diversityinc.com.

Deal, Mark. 2007. "Aversive Disablism: Subtle Prejudice Toward Disabled People." *Disability and Society* 22, no. 1: 93–107.

———. 2003. "Disabled People's Attitudes Toward Other Impairment Groups." *Disability and Society* 18, no. 7: 897–910.

DeCarlo, Scott. 2010. "What the Boss Makes." Forbes.com, April 28.

Detroit Free Press. 2001. "100 Questions and Answers About Arab Americans: A Journalist's Guide." www.freep.com/jobspage/arabs/arab1.html.

Dill, Bonnie Thornton, and Maxine Baca Zinn, eds. 1994. *Women of Color in US Society*. Philadelphia: Temple University Press.

Disability Rights Advocates. 2009. "Deaf and Hearing Impaired Employees Settle Class Action Lawsuit with UPS." Press release, June 16. www.dralegal.org.

Disability Rights Online News. 2009. "Walmart to Improve Access for People with Disabilities Nationwide." April. www.ada.gov/disabilitynews.htm.

———. 2008. "University of Michigan Agrees to Improve Accessibility at Football Stadium." April. www.ada.gov/disabilitynews.htm.

DiversityInc. 2004. "DiversityInc's Top 50 Companies for Diversity 2004." *DiversityInc* 13 (June/July): 46–114.

DiversityInc Staff and Associated Press. 2004. "Cracker Barrel Racial-Bias Case Settled: Company OKs Training, Undercover Probes." *DiversityInc*, May 12. www.diversityinc.com/members/6806print.cfm.

Diversity Insight. 2008. "Walmart Agrees to Pay $300,000 to Rejected Applicant to Settle Disability Discrimination Lawsuit." July 21. www.employomentlawpost.com.

Diversity News. 2004a. "Ex–Merrill Lynch Broker Wins $2.2M in Gender Bias Lawsuit." *DiversityInc*, April 21. www.diversityinc.com/public/6730print.cfm.

———. 2004b. "Gay Discrimination Policy Decision Chided." *DiversityInc*, May 12. www.diversityinc.com/public/6641.cfm.

———. 2004c. "Evangelist Apologizes for Anti-Gay Remark." *DiversityInc*, September 24. www.diversityinc.com/public/8737_2.cfm.

———. 2004d. "Printing Giant Ends Race-Bias Lawsuit with $15 Million." *DiversityInc*, October 25. www.diversityinc.com/public/9816print.cfm.

———. 2004e. "Third Airline Settles Discrimination Charges." *DiversityInc*, May 12. www.diversityinc.com/public/6655print.cfm.

D'Souza, Dinesh. 1999. "The Billionaire Next Door." *Forbes*. www.forbes.com/Forbes/99/1011/6409050a.htm.

DuBois, W. E. B. 1990. *The Souls of Black Folk*. New York: Vintage.

Economic Policy Institute. 2003. "Racial Discrimination Continues to Play a Part in Hiring Decisions." www.epinet.org/content.cfm/webfeatures_snapshots.

Economist. 2004. "Ever Higher Society, Ever Harder to Ascend." www.economist.com/world/na/PrinterFriendly.cfm?Story_ID.

Edwards, Cliff. 2003. "Coming Out in Corporate America: Gays Are Making Huge Strides Everywhere but in the Executive Suite." *Business Week*, December 15: 64–72.

EEOC (Equal Employment Opportunity Commission). 2010a. "Americans with Disabilities Act of 1990 Charges (includes concurrent charges with

Title VII, ADEA, and EPA), FY1997–FY2009. www.eeoc.gov/stats/
ada-charges.html.

———. 2010b. "Early Agreement on Decree Ends EEOC Race Case Against
Medical Device Supplier." January 20. www1.eeoc.gov.

———. 2010c. "Walmart to Pay More Than $11.7 Million to Settle EEOC
Sex Discrimination Suit." Press release, March 1. www1.eeoc.gov.

———. 2010d. "$35,000 Consent Decree Resolves EEOC Sex Discrimina-
tion Lawsuit Against Former Milwaukee Machine Tool Company."
Press release, March 19. www1.eeoc.gov.

———. 2010e. "Federal Court Enters Consent Decree Resolving EEOC
Sex Harassment Suit Against Biewer Sawmill." Press release, June 15.
www1.eeoc.gov.

———. 2010f. "Race-Based Charges, FY1997–FY 2009." www.eeoc.gov.

———. 2010g. "Sex-Based Charges, FY1997–FY 2009." www.eeoc.gov.

———. 2004. "Sexual Harassment Charges." wysiwyg:http://www.eeoc.gov/
stats/harass.html.

Ehrenreich, Barbara. 2001. *Nickel and Dimed: On (Not) Getting By in America.* New York: Metropolitan.

Ehrlich, Howard J. 1999. "Campus Ethnoviolence." In Fred L. Pincus and
Howard J. Ehrlich (eds.), *Race and Ethnic Conflict: Contending Views on
Prejudice, Discrimination, and Ethnoviolence.* Boulder, CO: Westview.

Ehrlich, Howard J., Fred L. Pincus, and Deborah Lacy. 1997. *Intergroup Relations on Campus: UMBC, the Second Study.* Baltimore: Prejudice Institute.

Eisenstein, Zillah. 2004. "Sexual Humiliation, Gender Confusion, and the
Horrors at Abu Ghraib." www.portside.edu.

Eisler, Riane, and Allie C. Hixson. 2001. "The Equal Rights Amendment:
What Is It, Why Do We Need It, and Why Don't We Have It Yet?" In
Shelia Ruth (ed.), *Issues in Feminism: An Introduction to Women's Studies.*
Mountain View, CA: Mayfield.

Ellis, Lee. 1996. "Theories of Homosexuality." In Ritch C. Savin-Williams
and Kenneth M. Cohen (eds.), *The Lives of Lesbians, Gays, and Bisexuals:
Children to Adults.* Fort Worth, TX: Harcourt Brace.

Espiritu, Yen Le. 1992. *Asian-American Panethnicity: Bridging Institutions and
Identities.* Philadelphia: Temple University Press.

Esterberg, Kristin Gay. 1996. "Gay Cultures, Gay Communities: The Social
Organization of Lesbians, Gay Men, and Bisexuals." In Ritch C. Savin-
Williams and Kenneth M. Cohen (eds.), *The Lives of Lesbians, Gays, and
Bisexuals: Children to Adults.* Fort Worth, TX: Harcourt Brace.

Fausto-Sterling, Anne. 2000. "The Five Sexes Revisited." *Sciences* 40, no. 4
(July/August): 18–24.

———. 1993. "The Five Sexes: Why Male and Female Are Not Enough."
Sciences 33, no. 2 (March/April): 20–26.

Feagin, Joe R. 2010. *Racist America: Roots, Current Realities, and Future Reparations,* 2nd ed. New York: Routledge.

————. 2000. *Racist America: Roots, Current Realities, and Future Reparations.* New York: Routledge.

————. 1991. "The Continuing Significance of Race: Anti-Black Discrimination in Public Places." *American Sociological Review* 56 (February): 101–116.

Federal Bureau of Investigation. 2009. "Hate Crime Statistics, 2008." *Uniform Crime Report.* November.

————. 2008. "Hate Crime Statistics: Incidents and Offenses." www.fbi.gov.

Feminist News. 2010. "Orthodox Rabbis Issue Statement Supporting Gays and Lesbians." August 3. www.feminist.org/news.

Fields, Reginald. 2004a. "City Fire Department Recruits 1st All-White Class in 50 Years." *Baltimore Sun,* April 20: 1A, 9A.

————. 2004b. "Fire Department Alters Hiring Policy." *Baltimore Sun,* April 23: 1B, 5B.

Files, John. 2005. "Ruling on Gays Exacts a Cost in Recruiting, a Study Finds." *New York Times,* February 24: A16.

Forbes. 2010. "Forbes 400 Richest Americans." www.forbes.com.

————. 2003. "Forbes Executive Pay." www.forbes.com/lists.

Forsythe, Jason. 2004. "Winning with Diversity." *New York Times Magazine,* September 19: 95–132.

————. 2003. "Diversity Works." *New York Times Magazine,* September 14: 75–100.

Fortune. 2010. "Annual Ranking of America's Largest Corporations." www.fortune.com.

Foster, John Bellamy, and Hannah Holleman. 2010. "The Financial Power Elite." *Monthly Review* 62, no. 1 (May): 1–19.

Frankel, Barbara, and Yoji Cole. 2004. "DiversityInc's Top 50 Companies for Diversity." www.diversityinc.com/members/6719print.cfm.

Freeman, Jo, and Victoria Johnson, eds. 1999. *Waves of Protest: Social Movements Since the Sixties.* Lanham, MD: Rowman and Littlefield.

Frye, Marilyn. 1983. *The Politics of Reality: Essays in Feminist Theory.* Freedom, CA: Crossing.

Gallup. 2008. "Race Relations." www.gallup.com/poll/1687/race-relations.aspx.

Gay and Lesbian Alliance Against Defamation. 2010. "Network Responsibility Index 2009–2010." www.glaad.org.

GayDemographics.org. N.d. "PUMS Information, Same-Sex Couples." www.gaydemographics.org/USA/PUMS/nationalintro.htm.

Gay, Lesbian, and Straight Education Network. 2008. "The 2007 National School Climate Survey." www.glsen.org.

General Accounting Office. 2003. "Women's Earnings: Work Patterns Partially Explain Difference Between Men's and Women's Earnings." GAO-04-35, October. Washington, DC: General Accounting Office.

Gerstenfeld, Phyllis B. 2004. *Hate Crimes: Causes, Controls, and Controversies.* Thousand Oaks, CA: Sage.

Gibbs, Nancy. 2009. "What Women Want Now: A *Time* Special Report." *Time* 174, no. 16 (October 26): 24–35.

Gibson, Gail. 2004. "Women Workers in US Have Bias in Common." *Baltimore Sun*, July 16: 1A, 11A.

Gilbert, Dennis. 2008. *The American Class Structure: In an Age of Growing Inequality*, 7th ed. Belmont, CA: Wadsworth.

Glenn, David. 2003. "The *Economist* as Affable Provocateur." *Chronicle of Higher Education*, December 5: A10–11.

Glick, P., and S. T. Fiske. 2001. "An Ambivalent Alliance: Hostile and Benevolent Sexism as Contemporary Justifications for Gender Inequality." *American Psychologist* 56, no. 2: 109–118.

———. 1996. "The Ambivalent Sexism Inventory: Differentiating Hostile and Benevolent Sexism." *Journal of Personality and Social Psychology* 70: 491–512.

Goffman, Erving. 1963. *Stigma: Notes on the Management of Spoiled Identity.* Englewood Cliffs, NJ: Prentice-Hall.

Goldstein, Richard. 2003. "What the Sodomy Ruling Has Changed—and What It Hasn't." *Village Voice* online, July 2–8. www.villagevoice.com/issues/0327/goldstein.php.

Granados, Christine. 2000. "Hispanic vs. Latino: A New Poll Finds that the Term 'Hispanic' Is Preferred." *Hispanic Magazine*, December. www.latinostories.com.

Green Party. 2004. "Green Party Election Results." www.gp.org/2004 election/pr_11_04.html.

Greenhouse, Steven. 2009. "Labor Fight Ends in Win for Students." *New York Times*, November 17.

Haniffa, Aziz. 2004. "Asian Groups Dispute FBI Report on Hate Crimes." *India Abroad*, December 10. Posted on www.portside.org.

Harrington, Jeff. 2009. "Outback Steakhouse Settles Class-Action Sex Discrimination Case for $19M." *St. Petersburg Times*, December 29.

Harrison, Lawrence E. 1992. *Who Prospers? How Cultural Values Shape Economic and Political Success.* New York: Basic.

Harvey, William B., and Eugene L. Anderson. 2005. *Minorities in Higher Education: Twenty-First Annual Status Report, 2003–2004.* Washington, DC: American Council on Education.

Haskins, Ron. 2008. "Wealth and Economic Mobility." In Ron Hankins, Julia B. Issacs, and Isabel V. Sawhill, *Getting Ahead or Losing Ground: Economic Mobility in America.* Washington, DC: Brookings Institution. www.brookings.edu.

Healy, Patrick D., and Sara Rimer. 2005. "Furor Lingers as Harvard Chief Gives Details of Talk on Women." *New York Times*, February 18: A1, A16.

Hecker, Daniel E. 2004. "Occupational Employment Projections to 2012." *Monthly Labor Review*, February: 80–105.

Hegewisch, Ariane, Hannah Liepmann, Jeffrey Hayes, and Heidi Hartmann. 2010. "Separate and Not Equal? Gender Segregation in the Labor Market and the Gender Wage Gap." Institute for Women's Policy Research Briefing Paper C377.

Helwig, Ryan. 2004. "Worker Displacement in 1999–2000." *Monthly Labor Review*, June: 54–68.

Hernandez, Brigida, Christopher Keys, and Fabricio Balcazar. 2000. "Employer Attitudes Toward Workers with Disabilities and Their ADA Employment Rights: A Literature Review." *Journal of Rehabilitation* (October–December): 4–16.

Heyl, Barbara Sherman. 2003. "Homosexuality: A Social Phenomenon." In Karen E. Rosenblum and Toni-Michelle C. Travis (eds.), *The Meaning of Difference: American Constructions of Race, Sex, and Gender, Social Class, and Sexual Orientation*, 3rd ed. Boston: McGraw-Hill.

Hiaasen, Rob. 2004. "One House, Many Voices." *Baltimore Sun*, December 11: 1D, 8D.

Hinrichs, Donald W., and Pamela J. Rosenberg. 2002. "Attitudes Toward Gay, Lesbian, and Bisexual Persons Among Heterosexual Liberal Arts College Students." *Journal of Homosexuality* 43, no. 1: 61–84.

Hirsch, Arthur, and Molly Knight. 2005. "Assaults Underreported at the Military Academies." *Baltimore Sun*, March 19: 1A, 4A.

Hofmann, Sudie. 2005. "Framing the Family Tree: How Teachers Can Be Sensitive to Students' Family Situations." *Rethinking Schools* 19 (Spring): 20–22.

hooks, bell. 2000. "Feminism: A Movement to End Sexist Oppression." In Maurianne Adams, et al. (eds.), *Readings for Diversity and Social Justice: An Anthology on Racism, Antisemitism, Sexism, Heterosexism, Ableism, and Classism*. New York: Routledge.

Hossfeld, Karen J. 1999. "Hiring Immigrant Women: Silicon Valley's 'Simple Formula.'" In Fred L. Pincus and Howard J. Ehrlich (eds.), *Race and Ethnic Conflict: Contending Views on Prejudice, Discrimination, and Ethnoviolence*. Boulder, CO: Westview.

Human Rights Campaign. 2009. "Equality from State to State 2009." www.hrc.org.

———. 2008. "The State of the Workplace for Lesbian, Gay, Bisexual and Transgender Americans 2007–2008." www.hrc.org.

———. 2004. "Equality in the States: Gay, Lesbian, Bisexual, Transgender Americans and State Laws and Legislation in 2004." www.hrc.org.

Humphreys, Debra. 2000. "National Survey Finds Diversity Requirements Common Around the Country." *Diversity Digest*. www.diversityweb.org/Digest/F00/survey.html.

Hurst, Charles E. 2004. *Social Inequality: Forms, Causes, and Consequences*, 5th ed. Boston: Allyn and Bacon.

Infoplease. 2004. "Preference for Racial or Ethnic Terminology." www.info please.com/ipa/A0762158.html.

Institute for Policy Studies. 2005. "The Iraq Quagmire: The Mounting Costs of the Iraq War." www.ips-dc.org/iraq/quagmire/cow.pdf.

Jezebel. 2008. "Sarah Palin on Feminism, and How Homosexuality Is a 'Choice.'" Jezebel.com.

Johnson, Allan. 2001. *Privilege, Power, and Difference*. Mountain View, CA: Mayfield.

Johnson, Angela D. 2004. "No Gay Honeymooners Welcome at This Resort." *DiversityInc*, March 9. www.diversityinc.com/members/6495print .cfm.

Jones, James M. 1997. *Prejudice and Racism*, 2nd ed. Hightstown, NJ: McGraw-Hill.

Jordan, Bryant. 2010. "Booted Gays Consider Life After DADT." Palm-center.org.

Kahn, Robert. 2004. "Scholarships Reach Out to Gays in College." *Baltimore Sun*, October 5: 1C, 5C.

Kaiser Public Opinion Spotlight. 2004. "American Views of Disability." June. ww.kff.org/spotlight.

Kansas City Infozine 2010. "Spencer Reed Group to Settle EEOC Race and Age Discrimination Lawsuit." June 13. www.infozine.com.

Katz, Jonathan Ned. 1995. *The Invention of Heterosexuality*. New York: Dutton/Penguin.

Kaufman, Cynthia. 2003. *Ideas for Action: Relevant Theory of Radical Change*. Cambridge, MA: South End.

Keister, Lisa A. 2005. *Getting Rich: America's New Rich and How They Got That Way*. New York: Cambridge University Press.

Kelly, Christine, and Joel Lefkowitz. 2003. "Radical and Pragmatic: United Students Against Sweatshops." In John C. Berg (ed.), *Teamsters and Turtles? US Progressive Political Movements in the Twenty-first Century*. Lanham, MD: Rowman and Littlefield.

Kendall, Diana, ed. 1997. *Race, Class, and Gender in a Diverse Society: A Text-Reader*. Boston: Allyn and Bacon.

Kerbo, Harold R. 2009. *Social Stratification and Inequality: Class Conflict in Historical, Comparative, and Global Perspective*, 7th ed. Boston: McGraw-Hill.

Kettani, Houssain. 2010. "2020 World Muslim Population." Proceedings of the Eighth Hawaii International Conference on Arts and Humanities, Honolulu, January 13–16.

Kimmel, Michael S. 2004. "Inequality and Difference." In Lisa Heldke and Peg O'Connor (eds.), *Oppression, Privilege, and Resistance: Theoretical Perspectives on Racism, Sexism, and Heterosexism*. Boston: McGraw-Hill.

King, J. L. 2004. *Living on the Down Low: A Journey into the Lives of "Straight" Black Men Who Sleep with Men.* New York: Broadway.

Kinsey, Alfred C., Wardell B. Pomeroy, Clyde E. Martin, and Paul H Gebhard. 1953. *Sexual Behavior in the Human Female.* Philadelphia: W. B. Saunders.

———. 1948. *Sexual Behavior in the Human Male.* Philadelphia: W. B. Saunders.

Kochhar, Rakesh. 2004. *The Wealth of Hispanic Households: 1996 to 2002.* Washington, DC: Pew Hispanic Center.

Lacey, T. Alan, and Benjamin Wright. 2009. "Occupational Employment Projections to 2018." *Monthly Labor Review* 132 (November): 82–123.

Ladd, Everett Carll, and Karlyn H. Bowman. 1998. *Attitudes Toward Economic Inequality.* Washington, DC: American Enterprise Institute for Public Policy Research.

Langfitt, Frank. 2004. "Violence, Bias Against Muslims up Nearly 70 Percent." *Baltimore Sun,* May 4: 9A.

Laster, Jill. 2010. "Unlike Men, Female Scientists Have a Second Shift: Housework." *Chronicle of Higher Education,* January 20: A10.

"Lawry's Settles Men's Sex Discrimination Suit." 2009. KLAS-TV Channel 8 News (Las Vegas, NV), November 2. www.8newsnow.com.

LeDuff, Charlie. 2000. "At a Slaughterhouse, Some Things Never Die." *New York Times,* June 16. www.nytimes.com.

Lewis, Gregory B. 2003. "Black-White Differences in Attitudes Toward Homosexuality and Gay Rights." *Public Opinion Quarterly* 67: 59–78.

Lorber, Judith. 1998. *Gender Equality: Feminist Theory and Politics.* Los Angeles: Roxbury.

Lottes, Ilsa, and Eric Grollman. 2010. "Conceptualization and Assessment of Homonegativity." *International Journal of Sexual Health* 22: 219–233.

Marger, Martin N. 2011. *Social Inequality: Patterns and Processes,* 5th ed. New York: McGraw-Hill.

Marso, Andy. 2011. "Funeral Protesters Vow to Fight Picketing Curbs." *Baltimore Sun,* March 5: 7.

Mascaro, Lisa, and James Oliphant. 2010. "Senate Votes to Repeal 'Don't Ask, Don't Tell.'" *Los Angeles Times,* December 18.

Masser, Barbara, and Dominic Abrams. 1999. "Contemporary Sexism: The Relationships Among Hostility, Benevolence, and Neosexism." *Psychology of Women Quarterly* 23: 503–517.

McCullough, Brian. 2010. "Vanguard Settles Race Discrimination Suit." *Daily Local News* (Charlotte, NC), January 6, www.dailylocalnews.com.

McGeehan, Patrick. 2004a. "Discrimination on Wall St.? Run the Numbers and Weep." *New York Times,* July 14: C1, C7.

———. 2004b. "Morgan Stanley Settles Bias Suit with $54 Million." *New York Times,* July 13: A1, C9.

Medina, Jennifer. 2010. "Head of City's Arabic-Language Public School Leaves." *New York Times*, March 17: A20, A23.

Meem, Deborah T., Michelle A. Gibson, and Jonathan F. Alexander. 2010. *Finding Out: An Introduction to GLBT Studies*. Thousand Oaks, CA: Sage Publications.

Meyer, David S. 2003. "How Social Movements Matter." *Contexts* 2, no. 4 (Fall): 30–35.

Millman, Jennifer. 2010. "Largest Discrimination Case in History: Walmart's Appeal Denied." www.diversityinc.com.

Mishel, Lawrence, Jared Bernstein, and Sylvia Allegretto. 2005. *The State of Working America, 2004/2005*. Ithaca, NY: ILR Press.

Mishel, Lawrence, Jared Bernstein, and Heidi Shierholz. 2009. *The State of Working America: 2008–2009*. Ithaca, NY: Cornell University Press.

Morin, Monte, and Jessica Garrison. 2004. "City Settles Decade-Old Suits over Gender Bias." *Los Angeles Times*, December 16: B3.

Morrison, Melanie, and Todd G. Morrison. 2002. "Development and Validation of a Scale Measuring Modern Prejudice Toward Gay Men and Lesbian Women." *Journal of Homosexuality* 43, no. 2: 15–37.

Moser, Bob. 2005. "The Religious Crusade Against Gays Has Been Building for 30 Years—Now the Movement Is Reaching Truly Biblical Proportions." *Intelligence Report* 117 (Spring): 9–21.

National Opinion Research Center. 2006. General Social Survey. www.norc.org/homepage.htm.

National Organization for Disability/Harris Poll. 2004. "The NOD/Harris 2004 Survey of Americans with Disabilities." New York: Harris Interactive.

National Priorities Project. 2010. www.nationalpriorities.org.

Navarro, Vicente. 2007. "The Worldwide Class Struggle." In Michael D. Yates (ed.), *More Unequal: Aspects of Class in the United States*. New York: Monthly Review Press.

Ness, Immanuel. 2003. "Unions and American Workers: Whither the Labor Movement?" In John C. Berg (ed.), *Teamsters and Turtles? US Progressive Political Movements in the Twenty-first Century*. Lanham, MD: Rowman and Littlefield.

Newby, Robert. 2010. "The 'New Majority' Defeats White Nationalism? Assessing Issues of Race and Class in the Obama Presidency." *Critical Sociology*, 36, no. 3: 371–386.

Newport, Frank 2007. "Black or African American?" Gallup News Service, June 17.

New York Times/CBS News. 2010. "Poll: National Survey of Tea Party Supporters." www.nytimes.com.

———. 2005. "Class Project" poll. www.nytimes.com.

———. 2004. "Target Corp. Contractor Settles Labor Law Violations." *Baltimore Sun*, August 26: 1D, 10D.

New York Times News Service. 2005. "United Church of Christ Endorses Gay Marriage." *Baltimore Sun*, July 5: 3A.

O'Brien, Eileen. 2001. *Whites Confront Racism: Anti Racists and Their Paths to Activism*. New York: Rowman and Littlefield.

Ollenberger, Jane C., and Helen A. Moore. 1998. *A Sociology of Women: The Intersection of Patriarchy, Capitalism, and Colonization*, 2nd ed. Upper Saddle River, NJ: Prentice Hall.

Ore, Tracy E., ed. 2003. *The Social Construction of Difference and Inequality*, 2nd ed. Boston: McGraw-Hill.

Orfield, Gary. 2001. *Diversity Challenged: Evidence on the Impact of Affirmative Action*. Cambridge, MA: Civil Rights Project, Harvard Publishing Group.

Ortiz, Peter. 2004a. "Another Huge Gender-Bias Settlement: Boeing to Pay up to $72.5 Million." *DiversityInc*, July 17. www.diversityinc.com/members/7678print.cfm.

———. 2004b. "Women of Color Are on a Buying Spree." *DiversityInc*. www.diversityinc.com/members/7495print.cfm.

"Outsourcing Is Breaking Out of the Back Office." 2007. *New York Times*. www.nytimes.com.

Pager, Devah. 2003. "The Mark of a Criminal Record." *American Journal of Sociology* 108 (March): 937–975.

Palm Center. 2009. "Countries That Allow Military Service by Openly Gay People." Palmcenter.org.

Pew Research Center. 2010. "Gay Marriage Gains More Acceptance." PewResearch.org.

———. 2008. "Inside the Middle Class: Bad Times Hit the Good Life." PewResearch.org.

Pincus, Fred L. 2003. *Reverse Discrimination: Dismantling the Myth*. Boulder, CO: Lynne Rienner.

Pincus, Fred L., and Howard J. Ehrlich, eds. 1999. *Race and Ethnic Conflict: Contending Views on Prejudice, Discrimination, and Ethnoviolence*. Boulder, CO: Westview.

Pinkus, Susan, and Jill Darling Richardson. 2004. "Americans Oppose Same-Sex Marriage but Acceptance of Gays in Society Grows." *Los Angeles Times* Poll/Gay Issues Survey, Study #501. www.latimes.com.

Potok, Mark. 2010. "Gays Remain Minority Most Targeted by Hate Crimes." *Intelligence Report* 140 (Winter). www.splcenter.org.

Price, Barbara Raffel, and Natalie J. Sokoloff, eds. 2004. *The Criminal Justice System and Women: Offenders, Prisoners, Victims, and Workers*, 3rd ed. Boston: McGraw-Hill.

Rai, Saritha. 2004. "An Outsourcing Giant Fights Back." *New York Times*, March 21: A1, A10.

Rainey, Susan Smith. 2011. *Love, Sex, and Disability: The Pleasures of Care*. Boulder, CO: Lynne Rienner.

Reich, Robert. 2010. "Unjust Spoils." *The Nation,* June 30.

Renzetti, Claire M., and Daniel J. Curran. 1999. *Women, Men, and Society,* 4th ed. Boston: Allyn and Bacon.

Robert, Pamela M., and Sharon L. Harlan. 2006. "Mechanisms of Disability in Large Bureaucratic Organizations." *Sociological Quarterly* 47: 599–630.

Rosenblum, Karen E., and Toni-Michelle C. Travis, eds. 2003. *The Meaning of Difference: American Constructions of Race, Sex, and Gender, Social Class, and Sexual Orientation,* 3rd ed. Boston: McGraw-Hill.

Rosin, Hanna. 2010. "End of Men." *The Atlantic,* July/August. www.the atlantic.com.

Roth, Byron. 1994. "Racism and Traditional American Values." *Studies in Social Philosophy and Policy* 18: 119–140.

Rothenberg, Paula S., ed. 2004. *Race, Class, and Gender in the United States,* 6th ed. New York: Worth.

Saad, Lydia. 2007. "Tolerance for Gay Rights at High-Water Mark." Gallup News Service, www.gallup.com.

Sachdev, Ameet. 2004. "Accountants Next Target for Underdog and Underdog." *Baltimore Sun,* May 3. www.baltimoresun.com.

Salz, Arthur, and Julius Trubowitz. 1999. "It Was All of Us Working Together: Resolving Racial and Ethnic Tension on College Campuses." In Fred L. Pincus and Howard J. Ehrlich (eds.), *Race and Ethnic Conflict: Contending Views on Prejudice, Discrimination, and Ethnoviolence.* Boulder, CO: Westview.

Savage, David G. 2010. "Ruling Favors Blacks in Chicago Firefighter Case." *Baltimore Sun,* May 25: 8.

Savin-Williams, Ritch C., and Kenneth M. Cohen. 1996. *The Lives of Lesbians, Gays, and Bisexuals: Children to Adults.* Fort Worth, TX: Harcourt Brace.

Sawhill, Isabel V. 2008. "Trends in Intergenerational Mobility." In Ron Hankins, Julia B. Issacs, and Isabel V. Sawhill, *Getting Ahead or Losing Ground: Economic Mobility in America.* Washington, DC: Brookings Institution. www.brookings.edu.

Scarborough, Rowan. 2004. "Report Leans Toward Women in Combat." *Washington Times,* December 1. www.washtimes.com.

Seid, Judith. 2001. *Good Optional Judaism.* New York: Citadel Press.

Shakespeare, T. 2006. "The Social Model of Disability." In Leonard J. Davis (ed.), *The Disability Studies Reader,* 2nd ed. New York: Routledge.

Shapiro, Thomas M., Tatjana Meschede, and Laura Sullivan. 2010. "The Racial Wealth Gap Increases Fourfold." Research and Policy Brief, Institute on Assets and Social Policy.

Shepard, Benjamin. 2003. "The AIDS Coalition to Unleash Power: A Brief Reconsideration." In John C. Berg (ed.), *Teamsters and Turtles? US Progressive Political Movements in the Twenty-first Century.* Lanham, MD: Rowman and Littlefield.

Shin, Annys. 2005. "$80 Million Settles Race-Bias Case." *Washington Post,* April 28: A1.

Sincavage, Jessica R., Carl Haub, and O. P. Sharma. 2010. "Labor Costs in India's Organized Manufacturing Sector." *Monthly Labor Review* 132 (May): 3–22.

Small, Mario Luis, David J. Harding, and Michele Lamont. 2010. "Reconsidering Culture and Poverty." *Annals of the American Academy of Political and Social Science* 629 (May): 6–29.

Smith, David M., and Gary J. Gates. 2001. "Gay and Lesbian Families in the United States: Same-Sex Unmarried Partner Households." Human Rights Campaign, www.hrc.org.

Sneiderman, Paul M., and Edward G. Carmines. 1997. *Reaching Beyond Race.* Cambridge, MA: Harvard University Press.

Snyder, Thomas D., and Sally A. Dillow. 2010. *Digest of Education Statistics, 2010.* Washington, DC: National Center for Education Statistics.

Sokoloff, Natalie J. 2008. "Expanding the Intersectional Paradigm to Better Understand Domestic Violence in Immigrant Communities." *Critical Criminology* 16: 229–255.

Southall, Ashley. 2010. "Senate Approves Payment of Black Farmers' Claims." *New York Times,* November 20: A11.

Southern Poverty Law Center. 2004. "Center Responds to Hate and Bias on Campuses." *SPLC Report* 34 (March): 1, 5.

Spence, J. T., and E. D. Hahn. 1997. "The Attitudes Toward Women Scale and Attitude Change in College Students." *Psychology of Women Quarterly* 21: 17–34.

Spence, J. T., R. Helmreich, and J. Stapp. 1973. "A Short Version of the Attitudes Toward Women Scale (AWS)." *Psychology of Women Quarterly* 2: 219–220.

Spencer, Rainier. *Reproducing Race: The Paradox of Generation Mix.* Boulder, CO: Lynne Rienner.

Spiro, Leah Nathans. 1996. "Smith Barney's Woman Problem." *Business Week,* June 3. www.businessweek.com/1996.

Stepp, Laura Sessions. 2003. "In La. School, Son of Lesbian Learns 'Gay' Is a 'Bad Wurd.'" *Washington Post,* December 3: C1, C10.

Swain, John, and Sally French. 2000. "Towards an Affirmation Model of Disability." *Disability and Society* 15, no. 4: 569–582.

Swarns, Rachel L. 2004. "Hispanics Debate Racial Grouping by Census." *New York Times,* October 24: A1, A18.

Swim, Janet K., Kathryn J. Aikin, Wayne S. Hall, and Barbara A. Hunter. 1995. "Sexism and Racism: Old-Fashioned and Modern Prejudices." *Journal of Personality and Social Psychology* 68, no. 2: 199–214.

Swim, Janet K., and Bernadette Campbell. 2001. "Sexism: Attitudes, Beliefs, and Behaviors." *Blackwell Handbook of Social Psychology: Intergroup Processes.* Malden, MA: Blackwell.

Swim, Janet K., and Laurie L. Cohen. 1997. "Overt, Covert, and Subtle Sexism." *Psychology of Women Quarterly* 21: 103–118.

Takaki, Ronald. 1993. *A Different Mirror: A History of Multicultural America.* Boston: Back Bay Books.

Tatum, Beverly Daniel. 2003. *"Why Are All the Black Kids Sitting Together in the Cafeteria? And Other Conversations About Race.* New York: Basic.

Thomas, Cal. 2004. "A Rear-Guard Effort to Put Women in Combat." *Baltimore Sun,* December 22: 23A.

Timmons, Heather. 2010. "Outsourcing to India Draws Western Lawyers." *New York Times.* August 4.

Torlina, Jeff. *Working Class: Challenging Myths About Blue-Collar Labor.* Boulder, CO: Lynne Rienner.

Tougas, F., R. Brown, A. M. Beaton, and S. Joly. 1995. "Neosexism: *Plus ca change, plus c'est pareil."* *Psychology of Women Quarterly* 21: 842–849.

Turner, Jonathan H., Royce Singleton Jr., and David Musick. 1997. "Born on Third Base: The Sources of Wealth of the 1997 Forbes 400." www.fair economy.org/press/archive/Pre_1999/forbes_400_study_1997.html.

———. 1984. *Oppression: A Socio-History of Black-White Relations in America.* Chicago: Nelson Hall. www.ufenet.org/research/CEO_Pay_charts.html.

Twenge, Jean M. 1997. "Attitudes Toward Women, 1970–1995: A Meta-Analysis." *Psychology of Women Quarterly* 21, no.1 (March): 35–51.

US Bureau of Labor Statistics. 2010. "Current Employment Statistics: Highlights, February 2010." Press release, March 5. www.bls.gov.

———. 2004. Table 11. "Employed Persons by Detailed Occupation, Sex, Race, and Hispanic or Latino Ethnicity." www.bls.gov.

US Census Bureau. 2011. "Overview of Race and Hispanic Origin, 2010." March. www.census.gov.

———. 2010a. "Annual Estimates of the Resident Population by Sex, Race, and Hispanic Origin for the United States: April 1, 2000 to July 1, 2009." www.censusbureau.gov.

———. 2010b. "Income." http://www.census.gov/hhes/www/income/income .html.

———. 2009. "Income in the United States: 2009." Washington, DC: US Department of Commerce, 2009. www.census.gov.

———. 2008. "Americans with Disabilities 2005." Washington, DC: US Department of Commerce.

———. 2004a. "Census Bureau Projects Tripling of Hispanic and Asian Populations in 50 Years; Non-Hispanic Whites May Drop to Half of Total Population." Press release, March 18. Washington, DC: US Department of Commerce. www.census.gov/popest/national/asrh/NC-EST 2003-srj.html.

———. 2004b. *Statistical Abstract of the United States.* www.census.gov/statab/ www/.

———. 2003a. "Income in the United States: 2002." Washington, DC: US Department of Commerce. www.census.gov.

————. 2003b. *Net Worth and Asset Ownership of Households: 1998 and 2000.* Washington, DC: US Department of Commerce. www.census.gov.

————. 2003c. *Poverty in the United States: 2002.* Washington, DC: US Department of Commerce. www.census.gov.

————. 1995. *Household Wealth and Asset Ownership: 1993.* Washington, DC: US Department of Commerce. www.census.gov/prod/1/pop/p70-47.pdf.

US Department of Justice. 2010. "Justice Department Settles Lawsuit Alleging Racial Discrimination by the Township of Green Brook, New Jersey." June 14. www.justice.gov.

Vandenburgh, Reid. 2005. Personal communication.

Walker, Andrea K. 2008. "Target Settles Lawsuit with Advocates for Blind." *Baltimore Sun*, August 28: 20.

————. 2004. "Giants of Retail." *Baltimore Sun*, March 21: 1D, 2D.

Walmart, 2010. "Corporate Facts: Walmart by the Numbers." March. Walmartstores.com.

Watanabe, Teresa, and Nancy Wride. 2004. "Stark Contrasts Found Among Asian Americans." *Los Angeles Times*, December 16: A1, A33.

Weeden, Kim A. 2004. "Profiles of Change: Sex Segregation in the United States, 1910–2000." In Maria Charles and David B. Grusky (eds.), *Occupational Ghettos: The Worldwide Segregation of Women and Men.* Stanford, CA: Stanford University Press.

Weinberg, Daniel. 2004. "Evidence from Census 2000 About Earnings by Detailed Occupation for Men and Women." CENSR-15, May. www.census.gov/newonsite.

Weinberg, Rick. 2002. "Smith Barney Wins Arbitration Order in 'Boom Boom' Case." *Registered Rep.* http://registeredrep.com.

Weinraub, Bernard, and Jim Rutenberg. 2003. "Gay-Themed TV Gains a Wider Audience." July 29. www.nytimes.com.

Welch, Ed. 2004. "TV's Disappearing Gays." www.365gay.com.

Werschkul, Misha, and Jody Herman. 2004. "New IWPR Report Addresses Women's Employment Equity and Earnings: How Many More Years Until Equality?" *Institute for Women's Policy Research Quarterly Newsletter* (Winter/Spring): 1, 7.

West, Paul. 2010. "A New Law to Protect the Disabled." *New York Times*, October 9: A1, A12.

Williams, Susan L., and Michelle Bemiller. 2010. *Women at Work: Tupperware, Passion Parties, and Beyond.* Boulder, CO: Lynne Rienner.

Wilson, Robin. 2004. "Where the Elite Teach, It's Still a Man's World." *Chronicle of Higher Education* 51, no. 15 (December 3): 8–14.

Wire Services. 2005. "Wal-Mart Agrees to Pay $11 Million to Settle Illegal-Immigrant Case." *Baltimore Sun*, March 19: 13C–14C.

Wise, Tim. 2002. "Honkey Wanna Cracker?" Z-Net Daily Commentary. June 10.

Wood, Peter. 2003. *Diversity: The Invention of a Concept.* San Francisco: Encounter.

Wright, Erik Olin. 1997. *Class Counts: Student Edition*. New York: Cambridge University Press.

Yates, Michael D. 2005. "A Statistical Portrait of the US Working Class." *Monthly Review* 56 (April): 12–31.

Zack, Naomi, Laurie Shrage, and Crispin Sartwell. 1998. *Race, Class, Gender, and Sexuality: The Big Questions*. Malden, MA: Blackwell.

Zinn, Howard. 2003. *A People's History of the United States: 1492–Present*. New York: Perennial Classics.

Zurawik, David. 2005. "Despite Denunciation, 'Buster' Episode to Air." *Baltimore Sun*, February 1: 1A, 6A.

Zweig, Michael. 2000. *The Working Class Majority: America's Best Kept Secret*. Ithaca, NY: Cornell University Press.

Index

About the Book

Accessible and practical, yet theoretically rich, *Understanding Diversity* has been carefully designed for classroom use. This new edition has been thoroughly updated and expanded. The emphasis of the text, however, continues to be on introducing and demystifying the concepts of class, race, gender, sexual orientation, and now, disability.

Fred L. Pincus is professor of sociology at the University of Maryland Baltimore County. He is author of *Reverse Discrimination: Dismantling the Myth* and coeditor of *Race and Ethnic Conflict: Contending Views on Prejudice, Discrimination, and Ethnoviolence.*